JOY RAINEY

FAST LADY

JOY RAINEY

FAST LADY

My Life in Motorsport

Foreword by **Alan Jones** MBE

Haynes Publishing

First published in October 2004

A catalogue record for this book is
available from the British Library

ISBN 1 84425 038 5

Library of Congress control no 2004106166

Published by Haynes Publishing, Sparkford,
Yeovil, Somerset BA22 7JJ, UK.
Tel: 01963 442030 Fax: 01963 440001
Int.tel: +44 1963 442030 Int.fax: +44 1963 440001
E-mail: sales@haynes.co.uk
Website: www.haynes.co.uk

Haynes North America Inc.,
861 Lawrence Drive, Newbury Park,
California 91320, USA.

Designed and typeset by G&M,
Raunds, Wellingborough, Northamptonshire
Printed and bound in Britain by
J. H. Haynes & Co. Ltd., Sparkford

Contents

DEDICATION

I dedicate this book to my father Murray, for his life-long support, my mother Norma, who is always there to assist, and to Trevor, my dearest friend.

FOREWORD

by Alan Jones, 1980 Formula 1 World Champion

I first met Joy Rainey in the 1950s in the paddock area at race meetings and hill climbs in Australia when we were young kids. My father, Stan Jones, drove at many of the same events as Joy's father, Murray. As children we had plenty of time to fill in and probably both of us had aspirations to drive in competition when we were old enough.

My own motor racing career started in the sixties in a go-kart. When my kart suffered a serious breakdown just weeks before the Victorian Go-Kart Championships I felt devastated, but then my father's secretary, Elsie Pretty, came to the rescue. One of the top lady go-karters in Victoria, she agreed to lend me her go-kart – a Rainey Kart. I took a couple of races to get the hang of the superior handling of my new mount, but then we won the championship – my first major success in motorsport.

Joy and I have continued to cross paths over the years. Before I won the Formula 1 World Championship in 1980 we occasionally met in the UK and Australia, then we lost contact for about twenty years. We saw each other again at the 2003 Goodwood Festival of Speed where we were both competitors, she in a 1936 Alfa Romeo, me driving the Williams in which I won the F1 title.

I am delighted to have been asked to write the foreword for this book. Joy is a remarkable lady and, as the title suggests, an extremely fast driver. She has competed in an unusually wide range of cars and events, culminating in the 2004 London to Sydney Marathon, and that, like every event she has ever campaigned, was undertaken with a characteristic seriousness of purpose. Joy may be a social animal off the track – but put her behind the wheel of a racing car and she's a fighter. That's why she's beaten so many records at hill climbs like Shelsley Walsh.

This is a great book. It is full of interesting detail about motorsport and motor racing characters, and gives a privileged insight into the life and times of one extremely Fast Lady.

PUBLISHER'S FOREWORD

by John Haynes OBE, Chairman of Haynes Publishing

At Silverstone in 1992 I was told of Joy Rainey, who was running the recently formed Hillclimb & Sprint Association Disabled Drivers Championship, that she had initiated. I passed this information to my son Marc who met her at Curborough the following year, taking part in his inaugural sprint driving a Nissan Silvia Turbo. Marc went on to become the first paraplegic to get a full competition licence for circuit racing, and has been much encouraged by Joy throughout his motorsport endeavours.

Joy comes from a family steeped in grassroots motor racing and historic cars, her father, Murray Rainey, being highly regarded in their native Australia. Despite her physical restrictions, Joy achieved admirable goals in various forms of motorsport, including holding the ladies hill climb record at Shelsley Walsh from 1979 to 2002, except for 1992. She also proved her literary capabilities, writing articles in the *Telegraph* motoring section about rebuilding her Pilbeam single-seater for the 100th anniversary of the Midland Automobile Club, which runs Shelsley.

Joy then accepted the challenge of taking part in the London to Sydney Marathon in a 1970 Morris Minor, which she and her partner Trevor Hulks modified to make into a reliable long-distance rally car. This latest adventure was itself an act of considerable courage, determination and sheer 'brio'.

We therefore had not the slightest hesitation in offering to publish her autobiography, not only about the Marathon, but also featuring her previous motorsport successes and entire fascinating life. It is a thrilling book.

INTRODUCTION

While visiting the Motor Show in October 2002 I happened to meet up with John Haynes, Chairman of Haynes Publishing. At that stage I was hoping to enter the 2004 London to Sydney Marathon – that is, if sponsorship could be found. I also wanted to write a book about the event. Although this would be my first attempt as an author, I had been writing motoring articles for the *Daily Telegraph* for a couple of years. Plucking up a bit of courage, I told John about my plans and asked him if he might be interested in publishing my book. He told me to send a synopsis and I did so, about four months later, after acquiring sponsorship from Autobytel. The upshot was that my partner and co-driver Trevor Hulks and I attended a meeting at Haynes.

I was rather flabbergasted when John wanted me to write an autobiography, with just the final section about the marathon. I knew that writing about my life would be a major task and over the next year there was already much to do in preparing the car for the marathon. But now it was my time to surprise. As it happened I had already completed half my autobiography. Two years before, during an extremely black period, I started to write about my early life – I'm not sure why or if I hoped to have it published. However, after the meeting at Haynes I completed the work, did the marathon, and here is the upshot of it all, a chronicle of my life from nought to now. It is not entirely about motoring, but also includes the magical time when I studied in Italy and memories of roaming round Europe and Morocco in a

Morris Minor with Pat, Inge and Dodie, three Australian girls I met in the UK.

Writing about my life was not easy, particularly revisiting some painful periods that I would rather not think about again, but some of the lowest ebbs also provided a turning point so had to be mentioned. Also, I'm not accustomed to writing about emotional stuff – I'm probably a bit of a show-off behind the wheel of a powerful car but take me away from that and there might be a shy person in the background.

Remembering old friends has been a lot of fun. I still giggle about Ian, my frisky neighbour in Geelong, south east Australia, who regularly lowered his mother's white washing onto the ground. The poor woman would chase him up and down the lane, which my friend Heather and I found hilarious. Ian loved an audience and found a most admiring one with us. We were all aged five.

When my father competed his Cooper in Europe, I remember the excitement of meeting such famous racing drivers as Bruce McLaren, Jack Brabham and Stirling Moss – and can you imagine the thrill I felt when Jean Behra lifted me into his bright red Ferrari at Reims in 1959!

Later on, when I came to live in England in the seventies and joined the Brooklands Society, I was privileged to meet many of the pioneers of motor racing. I had fascinating conversations with Captain George Eyston, Kenneth Neve, Whitney Straight and Kaye Don and formed an unlikely friendship with 80-year-old Sammy Davis, one of the Bentley Boys and winner of the 1927 Le Mans 24-hour race. And I still chuckle at some of the risqué jokes related to me by Bob Dicker, motorcycle record holder at Brooklands.

Then there is my own life in motorsport. I entered my first hill climb at Shelsley Walsh in an E-type Jaguar that was my road car at the time. Entering was a secret from my father, Murray Rainey, three-times Australian Formula 3 Champion, in case I made a fool of myself and shamed the family name. I did OK, however, and thus started an addiction which led on to a sports racer and single seater. There were records and wins and of course many disappointments but motor racing to me is a way of life. I don't mind working extremely hard as long as I am able to compete. My greatest pleasures in life have all come from this.

Then, to complete the story, my latest adventure with Trevor – the London to Sydney Marathon, in the summer of 2004. It was an emotional moment as the chequered flag dropped at the finish, just by the Sydney Opera House. Throughout the gruelling 30-day rally we had been given heart-warming support by local people in the countries we crossed, and also by Morris Minor enthusiasts, many of whom had travelled very long distances to give us their backing. It was all pretty emotional. And you can imagine my delight at seeing familiar faces in the crowd of spectators waiting to cheer the finishers. Friends I had met while motor racing in England were there – also Pat. Just three days before this, at the night stop at Noosa Heads in Queensland, Jeanette, a friend from teenage days, came to welcome us; so did a long-lost first cousin. At the start in London, Sally and John had appeared, a couple I had not met for more than thirty years. It made me realise how important motorsport – and friendship – has been to me.

I have been fortunate to have met so many wonderful people through my father's involvement in motor racing when I was a kid and then, later on, with my own participation.

I hope you enjoy joining me in this trip down memory lane.

Chapter 1

First taste of speed

The bike, the XK120 and racing the Holden

Wheels have played an important part in my life since I was five years old. I had been born with a genetic condition resulting in short stature but this in itself was never an issue – my father, also a short person, led a full and vigorous life and I had great expectations about the opportunities that lay ahead for me too.

The problem was that when I was four the orthopaedic surgeons decided that my legs needed straightening. This meant I had to wear clumsy leg-irons, initially for two years but actually for twelve. My pretty feminine shoes were replaced by heavy masculine boots. The leg-irons – slotted into a steel ferrule placed in the heel of the boot – were secured to my legs by wide felt-lined leather straps placed at the ankle, knee and just below the crutch. To enable me to stand in an upright position each leg-iron was joined by a strap that went right across the lower end of my back. They prevented any knee movement so I had to learn a new style of walking, swinging each leg from the hip. The situation was quite traumatic for a four-year-old, and as an inquisitive child I found my nature curtailed overnight. I felt self-conscious at kindergarten and rather excluded from childhood games – even from things like hide and seek.

Then at five years old my life changed again, and very much for the better. Dad purchased my first set of wheels, a brand-new British-made tricycle fitted with pneumatic tyres. When I got home from school each day my leg-irons were quickly disposed of and I was placed on the 'bike'. I soon learnt to manoeuvre this well, building up the muscles that had not been used for some time. The bike was to become my freedom right into adolescence.

There was not one part of Geelong, my home town in south-east Australia that the bike and I did not explore – including almost every shop and department store. I worried about misjudging things and knocking over display shelves so, when it came to judging space efficiently, the fear of an irate shopkeeper yelling about his broken china contributed to a quick learning process.

We lived not far from the centre of the town. The front entrance of our house was situated on a busy road with trams running up the middle. A lane ran down the hill at the back of the house and this was where much of my childhood activity took place. At age five I was not permitted to cross the busy road at the end of the lane, so I spent many hours sitting on my bike at the corner, watching the other kids play on the opposite vacant block with their bikes, racing around a makeshift track.

Ian Andrews was my friend and next-door neighbour. Like me, he was an only child and a late arrival for his mother at age 45. He was also known by other parents as 'a little bugger' because his behaviour could become quite energetic, particularly when his mother was in earshot. He liked to show off. Heather, my friend and neighbour from the corner at the bottom of the lane, and I used to collapse with laughter as Ian let down his mother's white weekly wash onto the ground, then she would take off after him at great speed up and down the lane. I never saw Mrs Andrews catch Ian and the constant exercise must have been beneficial for both as Ian grew up to become an international baseball player and Mrs Andrews lived well into her nineties. As a teenager Ian spent many a school day, without his mother's knowledge, frequenting the local snooker hall and with all that early training he also became a well-known snooker player.

But to me, as a five-year-old, Ian's greatest achievement was to stop the trams in front of his house for a whole three quarters of an hour. After the usual curfew and bed at 7pm Ian must have decided that he was not tired and escaped outside without being seen, to sit in the middle of the tram lines, dressed in his pyjamas. As the first tram approached, the tram-driver dinging loudly on the warning system, Ian refused to budge. The driver was forced to stop the tram and try to coax him to go home. Trams began queuing up from both sides and when anyone approached Ian he would throw a convincing tantrum. Nearly an hour passed before Mrs Andrews became aware of her son's disruptive actions and set out with a big stick to chase him home. That was the beginning of Ian's fame as he made the front page of the local newspaper.

I rebelled rather more quietly. My mother and grandmother bought me dolls and other toys that girls are meant to play with. One doll even had a cane bassinet that rocked back and forth. At Christmas I was given quite a tall (and, I suspect, expensive) walking doll, with a collection of clothes that had been specially made. There was a school uniform, a pretty evening frock, a smocked nightdress and several pairs of shoes, and my grandfather, an amateur carpenter, built a miniature revolving wardrobe. Unfortunately, no-one seemed to have noticed that this little girl was not even mildly interested in dolls. I thought it much more fun to be out riding the bike and watching Ian and his friends playing cricket in the lane. At times, before the leg-irons were removed, I was allowed to join the game. I would bat and Ian did the runs for me.

Playing cowboys and Indians was also popular with the boys and after I'd pestered my mother to buy me a Hopalong Cassidy outfit she eventually conceded. It felt good strutting down the lane, dressed in my black jeans, fringed tartan shirt and cowboy hat, with two six shooters strapped round my waist. Most likely I managed to get shot more often than not, as I couldn't get out of the way if still wearing leg-irons, but I sure could pursue hard when riding the bike. Not many baddies escaped my fire then.

My introduction to motorsport came at an early age. Geelong had its own grass circuit. Race meetings were held regularly and every category of motorcar competed, from family saloons to sports cars and single-seater racing cars. My father, Murray Rainey, had been interested in fast cars since boyhood. While studying architecture he spent many hours in the engineering department at the Institute of Technology and built a special Fiat 501 by turning the chassis upside-down and creating a low sports car. Offered a job in the drawing office at the Ford Motor Company, he soon forgot about architecture and began designing vehicles. Later he drove a taxi. After the war Dad, a determined character, purchased a disused building in the main street of Geelong, installed sophisticated machinery and started an engine reconditioning works, employing eight skilled tradesmen. My mother Norma, who he had met during the time he worked at Ford, ran the office and before long work was coming in from garages throughout the region. They also purchased a fleet of nine taxis and formed an association with several other cab owners. Their taxis were the first in the Southern Hemisphere to install two-way radio. The association was called Radio Cabs.

At Geelong my father competed with a Wylie Car, a typical dirt track single-seater, fitted with a modified Model B Ford engine and supercharged. I spent many hours sitting behind the steering wheel counting the years before I would be allowed to drive. Our road car, a 1938 two-door Chevrolet, had none of the excitement of the racing car: it just seemed to me big, high, really uninteresting and difficult to get into. There were photographs on the mantelpiece of Dad sitting in his Brooklands Riley, which he had sold before he was married, and the SS1, the car he owned when I was too young to remember. How I wished we owned such low, aesthetically pleasing motorcars now.

One day my father arrived home to collect some paperwork before returning to his work. When he came back out of the house to get into the Chev it had disappeared. As he looked down the lane, there it was, being stolen. Dad rushed after the car. The thief had reversed into a culvert and was having difficulty getting free. Seeing my father he got out of the car but Dad caught hold of his tie (robbers had class in those days), hauled him into the back and took off to drive to the police station. The thief tried to hit my father on the head, but Dad noticed him in the rear view mirror and slammed on the brakes, catapulting him into the front seat, where he managed to open the door and escape. Hot in pursuit Dad followed him down a cul-de-sac, pinning him against the wall with the bonnet of the Chev. Unfortunately, the man extricated himself and vanished over a fence, not to be caught again.

The Chev was sold not long after that episode and for the first time we had a brand-new car, a Riley RME. We were all so excited at the luxury: the leather seats, the wood trimming and the gleaming paint finish. The excitement soon turned to disappointment however. Every time we ventured out in the Riley my father would complain bitterly. He loathed the car. The engine pinked in every gear. Petrol in those days had quite a low octane level but when mixed with benzole the characteristics improved. However, the damage was done. Dad just could not learn to like the Riley and it was soon disposed of, much to my sorrow.

This grief was short-lived. When the replacement for the Riley arrived I could not believe my eyes. In the lane stood the most beautiful car imaginable – a Jaguar XK120. I kept walking round and round the car, then sat behind the steering wheel, enraptured. The Riley was forgotten.

We travelled great distances. At last Dad had a car he found enjoyable to drive. The XK120 was a two-seater sports car and I perched between the seats on a cushion. For a fidgety child this arrangement was not very comfortable. My father could not resist demonstrating the power of the XK. As we left friends' houses he would take off in a spectacular fashion, squealing the tyres and leaving a trail of smoke and rubber on the road. Travelling at speeds of over 100mph soon appeared to me quite normal. Every 'green light grand prix' was won by us. Local drivers contested these with great vigour. No Australian likes to be beaten at the traffic lights.

The sight of the little XK120 had a strange effect. Australians had a penchant for big American type cars at that time and, when we overtook, many a driver would accelerate, determined to demonstrate his superior horsepower, but father just extended his right foot a bit more, leaving the 'yank tanks' behind as we sped into the distance.

My own inclination for speed was fulfilled on the bike. As I raced down the lane and round the corner I was oblivious to any pedestrian who might be venturing along the footpath. There were a few close calls, such as when Ian dared Heather to stand on the back of my bike for a ride to the bottom of the hill. Heather climbed onto the frame and leaned over me, gripping the handlebars. As we flew down, I went to use the handbrake – the bike had no foot brake – but Heather's hand was in the way. I screamed at her to move it but she was frozen with fear and could not respond. Fortunately, two neighbours walking up the lane heard the screams and stepped into our path, grabbing the handlebars. We fell off but it saved us from careering into the busy road and perhaps ending up as mincemeat.

Geelong is a hilly city. Bicycling up steep gradients was difficult, but so was going down – because the bike had a fixed wheel, the pedals rotated at huge speed. The transformation came when Dad fitted a three-speed Sturmey Archer gearbox. What a change! Tackling the steepest hill required less effort now, but going down the other side created a new challenge. I was now able to free wheel and the speeds got even higher. Sometimes, misjudging the corners and ending up in the gutter, the bike resting on its handlebars, I would eventually arrive home with elbows and knees painfully grazed.

Every Easter holiday we spent camping in the Grampians. A tow bar was fitted to the XK120, which pulled our caravan very effectively. Three leather straps were mounted to the front of the caravan and each wheel of the bike was secured, so my transport came too. The caravan was parked under the tall eucalyptus trees at the town of Halls Gap and each day we set off in the XK to explore the surrounding areas. The Grampians rise abruptly from the Wimmera and Western Plains of Victoria and form the south-western extremity of the Great Dividing Range, covering an area of about 60 miles long and 30 miles wide. The area is renowned for its magnificent scenery – spectacular rock formations, waterfalls, mountains and plains that provide a most beautiful habitat for native Australian vegetation, animals and birds. Many different kinds of flora are unique to this area, and it was exciting for a kid brought up in a city to watch the wildlife and to hear the screeching of the cockatoos, the melodic bellbirds and the laughing call of the kookaburras.

During the fifties there were few roads for public use but a network of gravel forestry roads and tracks provided access to the remote places. For several years Dad started and organised the Grampians Car Rally on behalf of his local Western District Car Club. Much of the holidays would be spent travelling up and down forestry roads, mapping the route of the forthcoming event. The XK proved its versatility and endurance by traversing rough tracks, creek beds and every type of terrain imaginable without any problems. One day we came across several emus. They ran beside the car and Dad accelerated to 60mph before we began to edge in front. At night the kangaroos came into the camp and I liked to watch them through the caravan window, fossicking for any food left out.

My father spent part of his childhood in Minyip, a small town in the wheat-growing district of the Wimmera, where his father was the local policeman in charge. Minyip supported a population of about 1,000 and serviced the surrounding area of wheat farms. As Minyip was only 50 miles from the Grampians, Dad liked to make a day trip to catch up with old friends. One of his best friends was Jack Rowan, whose family ran the only general store. This was the hub of the town and sold everything from groceries, drapery and clothing to farming supplies. It was the place where everyone exchanged gossip and news. There did not seem much else to do in Minyip, apart from the fortnightly movie show in the town hall and the inevitable two pubs, frequented only by the male population.

The first time we visited Minyip in the XK and parked in front of Rowan's Store, everybody came running out to look. Most of the farmers' vehicles were utes (utilitarian pick-ups) or large Australian or American saloons. People seemed amused at our little car.

Dad offered to take Jack for a spin. He revved the Jaguar, let out the clutch and did the most spectacular racing take-off that Minyip has ever seen. As the XK roared off up the Main Street, people hurried out of the pubs to see what was happening. When they returned Jack's face was a very pale shade of white. He had never been over 50mph in his life and Dad had driven at twice the speed. That drive became a big talking point in Minyip. Fifteen years later Jack told me he could still see the rubber marks on the road. After 45 years he is still talking about it.

At Christmas we headed off in an easterly direction to Gippsland and camped on the edge of the lake at Metung. Often when we stopped for petrol or supplies, people laughed at the small sports car towing a caravan. Little did they realise that, even with its load, the XK could still probably outstrip their own transport.

After a year it became obvious that the XK120 was likely to stay in the family for some time. Dad decided to fit a hardtop and wind-up windows, and make a small seat in the back for the dog and me. A new Morris Minor hardtop was purchased from the local dealer and thus began a complicated project. Using the services of two local panel beaters, Bob Pohlman and Jim Duff, Dad set about creating a 2+2 hardtop XK120, long before the Jaguar factory in England introduced the two-seater hardtop. A 14ins length was cut out of the roof of the Minor to shorten the length from back to front, and then welded on to the top of the Jaguar. He also cut into the boot area to make room for the small seat. New doors were manufactured to house the mechanism for winding the windows up and down, and safety glass was cut to the new specification.

The project took six months to complete, but the wait was worthwhile. Out of the garage emerged the most elegant car of all time, to my eyes anyway. It looked magnificent, all finished and painted red. When I sat on the new matching rear leather seat, this felt comfortable, just the right height for all-round vision. The XK became a truly versatile workhorse, towing the Wylie Car to hill climb events at Rob Roy and Templestowe, just outside Melbourne, and circuit races at Ballarat and Altona. My father competed the XK in the sports car class and then drove it home towing the racing car.

The Wylie Car stayed in the family for two years, but the handling was not to my father's liking. I often heard the car described as 'a bitch of a thing to drive' and even after experimentation and improvements Dad decided it was time to move on to a more competitive class. When a Formula 3 Cooper Mk 4, fitted with a JAP motorcycle engine, became available he snapped it up. Compared to the high Wylie Car, the Cooper was low and streamlined. I soon discovered that it was easy for a kid to hop in and out of – much more user-friendly.

The Cooper was campaigned with great enthusiasm, although the results did not always match the excitement. At a race meeting at Altona my father was dicing with another driver for the lead, and we were all jumping up and down cheering him on, when suddenly Ron Barker, the English mechanic, yelled that he did not know why Dad was trying so hard as he had forgotten to fill the tank up with petrol. Sure enough, half a lap later we saw the Cooper slow down and stop. What a disappointment! Ron was never able to live down that memory loss – I didn't allow him to.

The first time Dad competed interstate was at a hill climb at Collingrove, South Australia. Before setting out on the 500-mile trip, the team talked excitedly as preparations were finalised. I was devastated to find I was not included: instead I was packed off to my grandparents ... complete with dolls. My poor grandmother coped well to put up with a sulking child who would not even pretend that she was interested in girlie play. But we survived, and were excited to hear that Dad had won his class driving the XK120.

When I was ten years old my parents decided to move to another area about two miles from where we lived. The house and garden were bigger, but more importantly there was ample space to build a garage and workshop to house the XK and Cooper. Dad desired to become more involved in motorsport and it was easier to work on the car at home rather than at his workplace, particularly if all-night sessions were needed before an event.

He was also anxious to park the car in a safer place than the lane. Ian's father owned a plastering business and each night parked his V8 truck at the rear of the XK120, sometimes so close that Dad was unable to get the car out. During the fifties in Victoria, pubs closed at 6pm. Many of the male population finished work at 5pm and would flock to the pubs and gulp down as much strong Victorian beer as possible, and on an empty stomach. An hour later, well inebriated, they would emerge to drive home. Road accidents were rife. The problem was referred to as the 'six o'clock swill'. Ian's father was a great upholder of the six o'clock swill. We were amazed at how he managed to manoeuvre the truck up the narrow, tricky lane without hitting any fences or cars, particularly as when he stepped out he could barely walk. Mr Andrews was not in a state to lock up his truck on these occasions so Dad would roll it to the bottom of the lane out of the way should he wish to use the XK.

The thought of moving to another area was quite unacceptable to me. I could not envisage my survival without Ian and Heather to play with. But move we did. The disappointment lasted just a short while. There were new hilly streets, parks and lanes to explore – quite a vast area without busy main roads to cross. The footpath at the bottom of our new road presented a new challenge with its sweeping corner. I practised and practised to travel as fast as I could down the hill into the corner without braking, and to position the bike so I could take the corner in a controlled drift. Quite a feat on a three-wheeler! More often than not the drift became uncontrollable and I ended in the gutter. Many times I frightened old ladies as they were walking along the footpath but fortunately contact was never made.

A year after we moved house Dad decided to sell his business and the engine reconditioning works was bought by Repco, who were looking to start a branch in Geelong. The arrangement suited both parties, as the town most likely did not have enough trade to support two such outlets.

Winter in Victoria is fairly cold. After the sale the family decided to head north for the winter months, to laze on the warm beaches of tropical Queensland. A special arrangement was made with the teachers at school, who prepared exercises for me to complete and post back every week.

With the caravan hitched to the XK120, we began our journey to territory unknown. After visiting friends in Sydney and Surfers Paradise, we kept travelling north and eventually found an idyllic small town called Noosa Heads, about 200 miles north of Brisbane, situated on the edge of a sandy lagoon. We pitched our camp under the shade of some tall trees and remained there for two months. The water was safe and I spent most of the days swimming, sometimes in the company of pelicans. We would throw in a fishing line and before long the night's dinner was hooked. Once a fish had been landed every pelican in the area appeared, hoping to get some of the leftovers when we cleaned the fish, or perhaps they were protesting at us humans stealing their catch. There were other Victorians escaping the winter, camped nearby, so I was never lonely. At night the barbecue was lit and locals and foreigners like us would cook our spoils and exchange stories. On my bike, up at the general store, I met other kids, which led to a few invitations to parties. For two months I never wore leg-irons. In those days not many Queenslanders wore shoes and I didn't either.

Too soon it was time to return home, however, and go back to school. After two months of shoeless bliss my feet did not take kindly to the big heavy boots and my legs chaffed with the clumsy leg-irons. Thoughts of running away to Queensland became attractive, but to a youngster a 1,200-mile journey on the bike was rather daunting. There was no alternative but to settle down to classwork.

Now that my father had retired at age 36, he wanted to fulfil the dream of competing in a new racing car. There were no Australian companies making racing cars then – Britain was the hub of motorsport. He ordered a D-type Jaguar from the factory in England, but every month seemed to bring some communication stating that the delivery would be delayed, so eventually that purchase was cancelled. Instead he contacted the Cooper Car Company in Surbiton, England, and ordered a Formula 3 Cooper Mk 9.

Some time later a big wooden box arrived and the nice, new blue Mk 9 was unpacked and parked in the garage at home. Locating a Manx Norton motorcycle engine proved difficult. But before the Cooper arrived, Dad had purchased a crashed Norton motorcycle and the engine was removed and rebuilt, ready to fit into the Cooper just after arrival. Great haste was needed as Dad had entered the Cooper for the 1955 Australian Grand Prix, to be held at Port Wakefield, South Australia, in three weeks time.

The joy of acquiring a new Cooper rapidly turned to dismay, however. The gearbox seemed rather second-hand and the suspension appeared to have been hammered together rather than assembled with care and precision. Most days and evenings were spent rebuilding the car and fitting the Manx Norton engine. Little time was left for thorough testing before Dad left for South Australia but he managed a few short runs up and down a country road near Geelong. The throbbing sound of the Manx Norton was fantastic.

The grand prix drew a mixed entry including homemade specials and Formula 1 and Formula 3 cars. Practice went well and Dad was pleased with the handling of the new car. It was a vast improvement on the Mk 4, which had a habit of swapping ends when driven with verve.

During the race Dad was lying in thirteenth place when suddenly he had no drive and stopped. One of the rear drive shafts had broken and when the rear suspension was stripped he discovered that both drive shafts appeared to be second-hand. Several years later, visiting England for the first time, Dad became good friends with Charles Cooper, the founder of the Cooper Car Company.

'We often put second-hand parts in new cars,' said Charles when Dad complained about the drive shaft incident. 'Go and get some new shafts out of the stores if you want, boy.'

'No thanks,' said Dad. 'I won't bother. I've modified the car since then. Anyway that was four years ago.'

To make room for the Mk 9 in the garage, the Mk 4 Cooper, minus its engine, was relegated to the veranda of our new house to await resale. Joan, my new friend – a bit of a tomboy like myself – and I used the Mk 4 as our plaything, jumping in and out, pretending we were racing. Before long the excitement of pretending wore off and we started to push the car up and down the drive, taking it in turns to steer. But that was exhausting for two young girls. Our real excitement came when we pushed the car up the road and then took turns to coast it down the hill, turning sharp left into the drive through two tall brick pillars, without braking. The winner was the one who coasted up the drive the furthest. Terry, our dog, also enjoyed sitting in the Mk 4 and liked to sleep in the cockpit at night – although after chewing the steering wheel he was immediately banished back to his kennel. Just as kids and dog were becoming accustomed to the new toy, it was sold and excitement had to be found elsewhere.

My other favourite pastime was swimming. We spent hours swimming in Corio Bay and surfing on the many beaches surrounding Geelong. As swimming was good exercise, Dad decided to build a swimming pool in our front garden. Swimming pools in private houses were unheard of in the fifties and when word spread that one existed, people began to park their cars in front of our eight-foot high fence, stand on their cars and peer over. Even as a youngster I felt that this was an invasion of our privacy. Being mischievous children, when we saw a strange face peering at us over the fence we would grab the hose and spray the spies until they fled. After school and in the holidays I spent a lot of time in the swimming pool or riding the bike. Only once did the bike end up in the pool, when I miscalculated how close the rear wheel was to the edge.

Secretly I began to walk without leg-irons when out and about. Instead of riding through department stores, I parked the bike outside and went in on foot, browsing. My greatest fear was being caught out by my mother, but she soon became aware of what I was doing and eventually I only wore the leg-irons to school and on outings that required walking a considerable distance.

The Cooper Mk 9 was campaigned successfully by Dad on many weekends throughout the year. He was unbeatable in the Formula 3 class at Templestowe and he won the first ever race on the new Phillip Island circuit in 1956. Phillip Island became my favourite venue. The Island is situated in Western Port Bay about 60 miles south east of Melbourne. A bridge connects the Island to the mainland. At dusk the fairy penguins would return to the beach from the sea: we spent many hours watching this spectacle.

We travelled to all race meetings in a convoy of two. The Cooper was towed in its new fully enclosed trailer by a Holden FC, and the XK120 towed the caravan. Camp at Phillip Island was set up in a middle part of the two and a half-mile circuit. The setting was magnificent, surrounded by tea-trees, with a fantastic view over the rugged coastline. You could see a good part of the circuit from here but it was much more exciting spending the day in the paddock area. I loved to feel involved with the team and all the racing and paddock activities that took place.

Our team consisted of mechanic Ron Davey, who had been Dad's apprentice since leaving school ten years before, and Ron Watson, assistant, and married to Davey's sister. Dad had total faith in his mechanic's ability and was known to say 'he approaches his work with the care, cleanliness and skill of a surgeon'. My mother looked after all our culinary needs and made sure that the competing cars were immaculately polished. Not a driver herself, she might have preferred a quieter lifestyle but always supported my father's – and later my own – speed exploits, and still does.

From our fully enclosed pit we could see the racing directly in front of us and by looking out of the rear door we could see most of the back part of the circuit. The circuit was very demanding, with fast sweeping and slow corners, long and short straights. My father excelled here and rarely left without trophies. He dominated the Formula 3 class. Quite often the F3 event was combined with a 1,500cc race and the Formule Libre race. Dad always provided excitement for the spectators at Phillip Island, usually finishing well ahead of cars three or four times the engine capacity of his little Cooper.

We would all be cheering Dad on. From a distance the Cooper looked as if it was flying but as he passed by the front of the pits, hearing the single-cylinder beat of the engine compared to the roar of the bigger engines, we thought he had slowed. We realised our mistake as Dad overtook larger cars right there in front of us!

From 1956 to 1958 most of the Formula 3 circuit races were won by my father – at Ballarat, Fisherman's Bend and Darley – as well as the 500cc Hill Climb Championships. He was unbeatable. On 14 April 1957 Dad broke the class record at Templestowe Hill Climb by a massive 1.5 seconds and he was five seconds in front of his nearest rival.

Despite Dad's success, the Light Car Club of Australia would send back any entries he submitted for events it was organising.

What seemed to be a clear case of discrimination appeared to have been sparked off by an incident in 1952 at a Ballarat car race meeting. Dad had entered for two races in the XK120. The layout of the circuit at the air force base incorporated two long straights, one short straight on the two runways and separate road, and six slow 180-degree corners at the end of the straights. Dad had brake fade on the XK on previous occasions and decided to ventilate the backing plates and to drill eight large holes in the brake drums to coincide with similar holes in the pressed steel wheels. On the aluminium brake discs, which had elongated holes, he bolted about two inches of metal strips cut in the discs and then bent the metal back to about 45 degrees. All these modifications were carried out to create turbulence to suck the air out of the brake drums and to keep them cool. After the modifications were finished in the workshop, the XK was jacked up and the engine revved in gear – the draught created felt like a minor hurricane.

At Ballarat, for the first time the XK did not experience brake fade and Dad was fastest in practice. This was remarkable as the two other XKs competing were on 8 to 1 compression ratio while Dad's was quite standard at 7 to 1. The event organisers seemed unhappy with Dad's pole position and decided that the race was to be changed to a Le Mans style start. This required the drivers to line up on the opposite side of the circuit and, when the flag was dropped, sprint to their cars and start. Dad agreed but asked that his mechanic run on his behalf: he would stand by the XK and jump in when the runner arrived. The organisers refused, excluded him from the race and would not refund his entry fee. My father replied that he did not care what they did with the fee. After that he was excluded from the rest of the meeting and ordered to leave the circuit.

When my father telephoned the Australian Automobile Association (AAA), governing body of motorsport in Victoria, to report the incident he was promised that the matter would be investigated. Two weeks later a notice appeared in the *Sporting*

Globe newspaper that the AAA had withdrawn its support for all motorsport. With no motorsport controlling body anymore the Light Car Club was apparently running events to its own regulations without the sanction of the RAC in Britain.

Some weeks went by and another notice appeared in the *Sporting Globe* stating that a meeting was to be called in Sydney by a Speedway Association to form a new body to govern all motorsport in Australia. This caused quite a stir within the car clubs of Victoria so my father proposed to call a meeting in Melbourne to pre-empt the one in Sydney. He hired the Shell Company Hall and placed a notice in the newspaper.

Dad had no experience of setting up this sort of organisation but received a telephone call from Donald Thompson, the motoring correspondent of the *Herald* newspaper, who had a copy of the FIA rules and volunteered to attend the meeting. Thompson subsequently took over from my father, and thus the Confederation of Australian Motor Sport (CAMS) was formed.

In 1956 Dad was running third in the Winter Cup Hill Climb Championship, behind Lex Davison and Bruce Walton. The events alternated at Templestowe, organised by the Sporting Car Club, and Rob Roy, organised by the Light Car Club. As for several years Dad's entries for any Light Car Club event had been returned to him, he decided not to waste time with that round. Several days before the event he received a call from the secretary of the meeting to ask why his entry had not been received. He explained. Some minutes later there was a call from Lex Davison, the Club President, to say his entry would be accepted. Perhaps Davison felt a conflict of interest as he was the leader, at that time, of the Winter Hill Climb Championship and would in effect be excluding a rival. Dad agreed to take part but only if his entries for all future events would be guaranteed. When Davison refused, so did Dad. Davison gave the guarantee.

My father drove at Rob Roy Hill Climb, smashing the 500cc record and winning the class, his nearest rival three seconds behind. At a subsequent meeting there he broke the class record.

Towards the end of 1957 Dad needed a new challenge. The field of Formula 3 cars was diminishing, with many competitors fitting twin-cylinder engines of double the capacity to put them in another class. Instead of following suit, he decided to supercharge his single-cylinder Manx Norton.

Attempts had been made all over the world to fit a supercharger to a single-cylinder engine but none was successful. Engineering experts like Phil Irving, who was involved with the design of the Repco engine that propelled Jack Brabham to a World Championship win in 1966, told Dad he was crazy to waste his time on an engineering impossibility. Perhaps that condemnation hardened the Rainey resolve! Supercharge the single-cylinder he did – and very successfully.

The main problem of fitting a supercharger to a single-cylinder engine is the character of the engine, which has a time lag between strokes. Dad was able to overcome this to a certain extent. The induction pipe from the supercharger must necessarily be big and Dad decided he needed a pipe that would hold at least two and a half litres. This presented another problem. When the car was approaching a corner and easing the throttle, the pipe would still be full of fuel for about five strokes of the engine and in theory the corner would have to be taken at full power. On leaving the corner, a good thrust on the accelerator would not produce the desired effect until the pipe had filled again. Dad designed a butterfly arrangement inside the induction pipe to control the flow of fuel. It worked in conjunction with a blowout valve as a safety measure. The compression ratio was stepped down from 14:1 to 8.5:1. When the engine was run for the first time the characteristics were amazing. It idled at about 300rpm and then produced so much power that it would reach 6,000rpm in a very short distance with the highest gear ratio that my father had.

An event in April 1958, at Phillip Island, was looming fast but there was little time to test the supercharged engine properly on the road. Dad decided he would go ahead anyway and use the race weekend as a trial. He was also leading in points for the KLG Trophy, presented at the end of the season to the most successful driver of the year, and if possible wanted to add to his points.

What an amazing performance we witnessed! Still with bugs to iron out, the Cooper achieved a lap time six seconds quicker than its previous fastest lap. The supercharger was not working at maximum efficiency and Dad could only get off the start line slowly. In the 1,500cc racing car scratch race he had caught the front-runners in half a lap, but in challenging Bill Patterson's Cooper Climax for the lead he spun yet still managed to catch him again in three laps. Dad lowered his best lap time to 2 minutes 22 seconds that day. Considering that the outright lap record held by Lex Davison's 3-litre Ferrari single-seater was 2 minutes 17 seconds, the performance of this little single-cylinder engine was quite remarkable.

The most outstanding race of my father's career was the Racing and Sports Car Scratch Race at Phillip Island in June 1958. He started on the second row of the grid behind Tom Hawkes's Repco Cooper, Doug Whiteford driving the ex Jean Behra Maserati 300S sports car and Ron Phillips in a Cooper sports car fitted with a D-type Jaguar engine. Hawkes took the lead and remained there unchallenged. On lap 2 Dad overtook the two big sports cars going into Lanes Corner on the back part of the track. Down the straight the power of the sports cars came into its own and both were able to retake Dad. On the tight parts of the circuit Dad once again overtook the sports cars and managed to hold off the Jaguar-engined Cooper, finishing 24 seconds in front. The Maserati finally got past and cut the corner tight, sweeping back a shower of stones. My father, when cornering, always rested one arm on the outside of the body and the stones hit his hand, causing so much pain that he had difficulty changing gear for the rest of the race. The crowds were cheering wildly. We all thought he had won, from the great acclaim that greeted him when the race had finished.

After selling his business, Dad became more involved with the local Western District Car Club. He had been instrumental in setting up the club as well as organising the Grampians Trial. Now he started to look at organising a sprint meeting at Ritchie Boulevard, along the waterfront at Geelong's Eastern Beach. The idea was to equal the prestigious Brighton Speed Trials, one of Britain's oldest events which had been held along Madeira Drive, in the south coast seaside town of Brighton, since 1905 and only ever interrupted during the war years.

Geelong offered an ideal setting of a quarter mile of bitumen road with the beachfront and Corio Bay on one side and a hill covered in lawn on the other side. This provided a natural grandstand. Permission was sought from the Geelong City Council and in 1956 the first Geelong Speed Trials were held. The entry list was impressive and included a variety of competition cars and motorbikes. This became an annual event and is still held to this day, despite some opposition and interruptions.

When Dad was not racing, we spent time at our farm, purchased after we returned from our trip to Queensland. The 77-acre property was situated at Grassy Creek, about 35 miles south of Geelong, along the spectacular Great Ocean Road. The road from Geelong travels through eucalyptus forests to Anglesea and then climbs a hill to give the most breath-taking coastal view of the wonderful sandy, surf beaches. After more forests the road follows the rugged coastline to Eastern View and turns into a valley surrounded by eucalyptus-clad mountains. This is Grassy Creek.

Our property was named The Black Stump. The house was situated right by the road, rather too close to the traffic. Dad devised a method of moving the house 100 feet back by laying down telegraph poles and pulling the house over the poles by tractor, bit by bit, until it was in the right position. Then he built an enormous front room with an impressive fireplace and chimney using rocks collected from the creek. Behind the house was a fairly flat paddock of several acres stretching out to the edge of the creek before the land rose abruptly. The road continued past Grassy Creek and climbed up to the mountains surrounding our valley.

Sometimes after swimming in the creek we would go round the corner and swim in the surf. The farm was an ideal playground for kids and dogs. When not in use the Ferguson-Ford tractor, which had push-pull levers to steer, became my new toy. It was the first time I had been in total control of a moving mechanical object.

Most times we travelled to The Black Stump in our other family workhorse, a Holden FC. It was in the back paddock that I learned to drive. I was permitted to take the Holden round a half-mile track I had devised with four right-hand corners, one with a large tree on the outside, and another quite tricky one which led onto a long mound of earth and then back down to the flat. I wasn't quite sure what to do with the clutch pedal. I pushed it in and let it out briskly, crunching the gear and setting off with a jerk – it got smoother, however. The gear lever was situated on the steering column and before long I managed to change into three gears as I sped round my private racetrack. At first the crunching of the gears brought tears to my father's eyes but quite soon my technique improved. Early on I gave myself quite a scare as I raced round the corner with the tree. The rear of the car stepped out and I lost control. Not knowing what to do I watched in horror as the tree loomed closer – we missed it by inches.

One day as I watched my father painting a large mural at the back of the house, we heard a loud squeal of tyres. A Triumph Herald had missed a corner on the road about 100 feet up and was flying through the air. The action appeared to be played in slow motion until the car crash-landed in the creek. We rushed down and miraculously found the two occupants still alive, and only one had broken limbs.

Another time Dad went down to The Black Stump during the week when I was at school. Someone had stopped by the road above our valley to admire the view and noticed a car in the creek below, then drove to tell Dad. They found the remains of the car and four dead bodies. Most likely they had been there for several days. What with that and my own near-accident with the tree, I was happy to curtail my driving ambitions.

Time heals most things, however, and soon I was in the driving seat of the Holden again, lapping the circuit. Back in Geelong I started filling in hours of boredom by reversing the Holden to the front gate and then taking it the length of the 50-foot drive. When friends came to visit they would pile in as if we were off on a trip and the afternoon would be spent driving back and forth. Many times I was dared to drive the car to the top of the street – I was tempted but just could not bring myself to take the risk. It seemed OK to my young mind to push the Cooper up the hill, hop in and coast down, but there was a definite no-no to driving the Holden up the hill under its own power. The police, I am sure, would have viewed both situations in a negative manner.

In 1958 Dad started harbouring ideas of taking the Cooper to Europe for a season of racing. Plans were soon being made.

Chapter 2

THE EUROPEAN TOUR

Enjoying the culture of circuits and history

Plans were finalised. We were to leave Melbourne in February 1959 on board the *Castel Felice*, with Dad's Cooper and my bike travelling in the hold. Normally the ship, part of the Italian Sitmar line, travelled via the Suez Canal but at that time the Canal had not been finally cleared after the Suez Crisis. The ship was scheduled to sail to Sydney, Auckland, Tahiti, Panama Canal, Curacao and Lisbon, finally arriving at Southampton six weeks later. All the ports of call sounded exotic to me but the thought of a year off school was even more exciting.

After all the bookings were made Dad was notified that the rules for Formula 3 racing in Britain had been changed and cars were required to run on petrol for the 1959 season. This news caused quite a stir. Both the Norton engines for our Cooper ran on Methanol and major engineering changes would be required to convert to petrol – time was short before our departure.

My father knew that the latest TT Norton engine had a 90mm cylinder bore but in Australia neither engines nor components were available. However he heard that an Australian rider had brought back from England a cylinder head from a 90mm bore engine and wanted to sell this. Dad managed to find a 350cc Norton engine in a crashed motorcycle and, after purchasing both engine and latest cylinder head, he set about making a special barrel of 90mm bore. The end result was a 500cc short-stroke engine capable of high revs and running on petrol.

Little time was left for thorough testing before the car and trailer had to be delivered to the Melbourne docks for loading, but several runs on a road just outside Geelong had demonstrated that the engine went quite well. It appeared that with some further development it would be very quick indeed.

The day of our departure soon arrived and as the ship slowly pulled away from Station Pier, Port Melbourne, to the emotional sounds of 'Auld Lang Syne', our party – my parents, me, and Dad's mechanic, Ron Davey – waved farewell to friends and family until they were out of sight. The run down Port Phillip Bay was smooth, but once we were through the Heads to Bass Strait the sea became rough. I felt fine and rather excited at the start of our eleven-month world trip but, waking after my first night on board, I felt like death warmed up and could not lift my head off the pillow without wanting to vomit. After the second day, however, I had found my sea legs and began to explore the ship.

On the third day we sailed into Port Jackson Bay, escorted by a shoal of friendly dolphins. Standing on deck, we could see Circular Quay in the distance, with ferries coming and going across the bay. As a typically territorial Australian, I thought that any city, harbour, mountain, scene, food or drink was much superior in Victoria, the state of my birth, and therefore the harbour view of Melbourne or Geelong could never be beaten. But I have to admit that Sydney harbour, with its famous bridge, on that fine, sunny, calm morning certainly left a favourable impression. The hills rolled gently down to the many inlets and you could see big houses overlooking the water. What views they must have had.

After docking at Circular Quay – almost in the centre of Sydney – we were met by Ron Tauranac, who was to take his family to England the following year. In partnership with Jack Brabham he started designing and manufacturing Brabham racing cars, finally winning the Formula 1 Championship in 1966. Ron had already built and raced a 500cc car with his brother Austin Lewis, hence the name of the car – RALT, an amalgam of their initials. There was no sightseeing for us that day, but he took us to see a motor race at Mount Druid, a circuit we had read about but never visited.

Then, for the first time for each of us, we were leaving Australia en route to New Zealand. Auckland did not leave any long-term impression on me at the time. The buildings and layout of the city appeared quite similar to those at home. Even the people almost spoke the same language, perhaps with a slightly different accent. Maybe the attitudes were different there though. A New Zealand passenger one day asked me if I was excited at returning home to England. I replied, 'I was born in Australia and Australia is my home.' My response appeared to surprise him as he said, 'well, I'm a third generation New Zealander and I always refer to Britain as home.' How odd, I thought, particularly as he had never visited Britain before.

Six weeks is a long time to keep oneself occupied in a confined space like a ship, particularly as we were just travelling from A to B, not on board to experience a cruise. Life for some passengers became one long party and their behaviour appeared to be quite unrelated to normal life. Fortunately the ship was only half full so there was ample space. Some passengers were Australians, off to Europe for a couple of years of adventure, as was becoming the fashion then. Others were Britons returning home after their two-year stint in Australia – which had initially cost £10 each – not happy with their adoptive new country. They were referred to as 'ten pound poms', 'dissatisfied poms' and other derogatory things. At times some of the verbal exchanges I witnessed between 'fair dinkum Aussies' and 'ten pound poms' were rather exuberant, not to say educational.

There were other passengers about my age and we began to occupy every minute of the day with activities. Vera became my new friend. Although she was born in Australia her parents were German, and her mother was taking her to meet the grandparents and other relatives in Germany.

Various entertainments were organised for the passengers. There were gala balls, twenties charleston parties, a crossing-the-line ceremony, talent quests, opera evenings, jiving contests, bingo, general knowledge contests, treasure hunts, fancy dress parties and so on. Much time was spent scrounging materials to make costumes. My own fancy dress required little ingenuity: I borrowed my father's crash helmet and visor and appeared as a racing car driver.

As the ship neared the equator I was asked if I would like to be involved in the crossing-the-line ceremony. My adventurous spirit would not allow me to refuse, but I did not realise what I had let myself in for. Firstly, the prisoners (participants) were locked up in a prison cell made of rope. One by one we were taken to appear in front of King Neptune, a formidable character dressed in a long flowing robe and sporting an impressive beard, to hear our charges and then receive the appropriate punishment.

I was charged with crawling up and down the aisles of the dining room stealing all the food from the serving trays, every day. My punishment was for my stomach to be operated on to remove all the stolen food. I was to take a spoonful of medicine to assist in the operation. As the King held out the teaspoon with what looked liked white powder, I hesitated and he whispered 'Don't worry, it's only sugar.' I swallowed it back and then just about choked. The 'medicine' turned out to be salt. As I coughed and spluttered, trying to catch my breath, the crowds roared with laughter and I wished one of them was in my place. The guards carried me to the operating table where I was laid out and covered with sheets. The 'surgeons' arrived, equipped with their very precise surgical instruments such as large carving knives, forks and axes, and proceeded to operate. From under the sheets long strings of sausages, potatoes, bones, chickens, every large vegetable imaginable and scraps of food were brought out and thrown into the air, all supposedly extricated from my stomach. After this I was forced to sit up when suddenly a deluge of freezing water soaked me from the shower mounted above the 'operating' table. At least the other passengers were amused.

The sea from New Zealand to Tahiti was smooth. When needing some space of my own I would spend hours at the bow of the ship watching the flying fish or gazing at the changing patterns of the waves. As the ship slowly sailed through the coral reef surrounding Tahiti, the view was phenomenal. The volcano rose abruptly out of the wonderfully opalescent blue lagoon and there were tropical trees and plants, and flowers I had never seen before.

Crowds thronged the pier as we disembarked. Attractive, scantily dressed Polynesian ladies placed shell and flower necklaces over our heads and showed such a warm welcome. This was all quite overwhelming. I had never experienced such affection from strangers before. For a nominal figure we were offered a sightseeing tour round the island by a taxi owner. Roads were deserted as we skirted the base of the volcano. Unusual scents from the tropical flowers permeated the air. The sight of the traditional houses – thatched roofs held in place by poles, perched within a few yards of the water – gave me ideas of running away to live in paradise.

The coral atoll surrounding the island kept out sharks and any other species harmful to man, which made the sound of living here even more attractive. When I was four I was paddling in the shallow surf near Barwon Heads, not far from Geelong, when I noticed a flat object riding the waves. I called to my father on the beach to look. When he saw that the floating 'bag' within a few feet of me was a stingray he came charging down, yelling at me to run. Several stingray fatalities are recorded every year. A month before we had left on this world trip, a lifesaver was attacked by a shark at my favourite beach near The Black Stump. Those were dangerous waters, yet I used to swim there quite happily. I couldn't wait to get into the water at Tahiti and throughout the day, while we stopped for refreshments, I managed to swim without even checking if dangerous fins were racing towards me.

The night's entertainment at the Tahiti Hotel, a traditional building on the edge of the water, provided us with a spectacle of traditional Polynesian dancing and unusual food. Raw fish and wonderful salad was a treat, while the Polynesian girls and chaps gyrated their hips, accompanied by the hypnotic, rhythmic beat of the drums. I was dragged onto the stage and the male Polynesian dancer tried to encourage my hips to move rhythmically like theirs but in comparison it was as if mine were locked.

The following morning before the ship departed we were watching the bustle of the flower and necklace sellers below on the pier when I noticed John, our taxi driver from the previous day, beckoning us to go down. As we went ashore to say farewell, people kept placing shell necklaces over my head until I could hardly keep my neck upright because of the weight. What a wonderful place Tahiti was. I really did want to return.

After a couple of days at sea there was a large swell that caused the ship to roll. Many passengers were ill again and we were told to turn our mattresses lengthwise in the night cabins so that we felt the ship's motion as head-to-foot rather than side-to-side. The rolling seas continued for over a week, during which time a lot of glasses and crockery got broken in the bars and dining rooms, but at least the sleeping method seemed a success as none of us was seasick.

Travelling through the centre of America, from the Pacific Ocean to the Atlantic Ocean, was amazing. At school I had recently written an essay about the Suez and Panama Canals. To be experiencing one of man's greatest engineering feats first-hand was rather incredible, especially remembering that thousands of the largely Caribbean workforce had perished from malaria and yellow fever while building this very same area we were now passing through. The 51-mile Panama Canal is a lock canal and the upper level is over 80 feet above sea level. With about 50,000 people involved in the construction and the removal of 360 million tons of earth, finally in 1920 the canal was opened. Our trip through, although fascinating, encountered a problem. The rudder of the *Castel Felice* was damaged and we had to spend a day at Colon, the Atlantic end of the Panama, while repairs were carried out. Seven of us hired a taxi and spent the day sightseeing at Panama City. For seven previously untravelled Australians, used to fairly modern buildings in wide, clean streets, the tackiness of the place was quite shocking.

Lisbon, our first port of call in Europe, turned out to be overwhelming in a positive way. It was difficult to believe that buildings, some hundreds of years old, were constructed so long before white man had stumbled on to the shores of Australia. The word 'conservation' had not yet reached the Australian dictionaries. Back home the usual practice was to knock down any building over about 50 years old in the name of 'progress', the meaning of which I am still trying to understand at my mature age.

It seemed such a short hop from Lisbon to Southampton after nearly six weeks on board. The skies were grey and miserable, reinforcing my pre-formed ideas of the British climate. Many of us felt so sad that the trip had come to an end, saying fond farewells to people who had become so important over such a short period, and who we were probably never to meet again.

Dad had ordered a Bedford camper van, fitted with a tow-bar, to meet us at the docks, but to our surprise a Volkswagen Caravette was waiting without tow-bar. There was quite a rush to get the tow-bar fitted. We were running behind schedule, the ship having arrived a day late. It was Easter and Dad was entered for his first race at Brands Hatch. By the time formalities were sorted out and the tow-bar fitted, we headed straight for the circuit. As we drove I looked at the streets of terraced houses and came to the conclusion that England must be a very poor country indeed. I had never seen so many 'slums'. That initial assessment was through the eyes of a young Australian, used to seeing streets of terraced houses being demolished to make way for more spacious modern buildings but it took some time and much travelling before I began to appreciate the quaintness of the English architecture.

The drive to Brands took longer than anticipated. We were used to calculating our journeys based on 60 miles to the hour on the normally straight Australian roads – motoring on such narrow, winding roads through the English countryside and towns was a totally new experience. Practice had finished by the time we finally arrived and Dad was not permitted to compete the following day.

As I stood near the startline it was possible to see most of the circuit. The layout was like a natural grandstand, with the track at a lower level than the pits. It is exciting for the spectator to be able to see all the activities during a race.

At Phillip Island, my favourite track, quite often we missed my father's most spectacular overtaking moves, as they were just out of view.

It was mind boggling to see so many Cooper 500s. At an Australian race meeting, even a few years earlier than this when Formula 3 was in its heyday, there would be fewer than half a dozen 500s, and on most occasions races were combined with cars of a bigger capacity to make up the numbers. Yet here at Brands there were so many entrants it was necessary to have two qualifying races before the final.

After finding a house to rent in Banstead, Surrey, the next race scheduled was at Oulton Park in Cheshire. The Mk9 started well in practice and was lapping quite competitively, when suddenly it phut-phutted to a standstill. Nothing seemed to be going right on our overseas trip. The piston had broken and we had no spare. The piston for this new petrol engine had been manufactured specially by Repco just before our departure from Australia. It was meant to be robust enough for racing use but Dad discovered that the aluminium for the casting was only suitable for road cars. There had been no time to find an alternative, however, so it was fitted anyway.

The day after Oulton, the search began for a piston suitable for a 90-degree bore Norton engine. Off we went to Hepworth & Grandage in Sheffield, well-known piston manufacturers. They could not sell us one, but told us that motorcycle rider Bill Bodice had a supply. Next stop, the Midlands. Bill was not home so we waited in front of his house until he returned from work. He demonstrated wonderful Midlands hospitality with cups of tea and, of course, the purpose of this meeting, the rare Norton piston.

After the piston was machined to specification the engine was re-assembled, ready for the next race meeting, at Mallory Park in Leicestershire. We arrived the day before practice and set up camp. At the social club we met the owner of the circuit, Clive Wormleighton, and a number of locals who frequented the bar. Everyone was so friendly that we immediately felt at home. We started to understand and enjoy the British dry sense of humour, at times at our expense as Australians. Clive took us to Rothley Hall, a property he had recently purchased to convert into a country hotel. At the rear of the main building was a small 13th century chapel where, in the Middle Ages, Crusaders had attended services before setting off on their sacred mission to deliver the Holy Places from the infidel. I had difficulty believing that buildings of over 700 years old were still standing – and that I was actually visiting places I had read about in history books 12,000 miles away.

Dad's Cooper ran reasonably well in practice but during the race he ran out of brakes and had to stop. The short stroke engine appeared to experience a high frequency vibration, which very quickly affected the push rods in the brakes, rendering them inoperable.

During May, Dad had entered for a race meeting at Crystal Palace. The entry was late and he was placed on a reserve list. Right at the last minute permission was granted to race, but Dad had to start at the back of the field, even though he was fourth fastest in practice. The weather was very hot. When the race started, Dad was carving well through the field but after coming out from under the bridge at Maxim Rise he was trying to overtake two cars when he lost control going through some melting tarmac. He ended up in a pile of straw bales, damaging the front end of the car quite badly. My father had not experienced an accident before – he was not injured but we were all in a state of shock when we saw the state of the car. It would need to be taken back to the Cooper factory and put on the jig to straighten the chassis. First thing next morning Dad arrived at the Surbiton works only to be told by Charles Cooper that they were too busy with the Formula 1 programme and could not possibly fit in this job.

'Well, the Formula 3 jig is not in use,' said Dad. 'Perhaps we could do the work ourselves if you'd let us use it?'

'No boy', said the hard-nosed Charles. 'Not possible. Got to go. I'm very busy.'

As Dad was about to drive away in the VW, one of the mechanics came out.

'Charlie's going away in a couple of days time to the Dutch Grand Prix. Bring it over then and we'll repair it.'

After starting the job, it was discovered that the transverse springs required were not available in the storeroom. Milling around, Dad found some wishbones that would fit, so they decided to make the suspension like a miniature current Formula 1 car, with coil springs. Everyone was quite enthusiastic about this new project, but before it was finished Charles arrived back early from his trip and ordered Dad to take his car and leave, but gave him a couple of hours for finishing. During that time Charles brought several visitors to view the project, and in a short time became so enthusiastic that he told Dad to take his time and repair the car properly.

Later, Dad took Charles a list of the materials used and the help given by staff. Expecting the bill to be in the region of £200, he had taken a wad of cash. Charles hardly glanced at the list and said the bill was about £70. At that moment John Cooper walked into the office and Dad, unrolling the pound notes, asked who to give the money to? Both men yelled 'ME', so my father threw the notes into the air and was amused to see them diving onto the floor to grab what they could. Charles later remarked, 'I got more than 'im!'

The next race entered was at La Chartre in France. The thought of travelling through Europe was exciting, particularly as we had been given all the right sort of tickets to stop off en route to watch the French Grand Prix at Reims. This was the first time we had been to a Formula 1 World Championship race and I could hardly wait to look at all the cars that I had not seen before, and perhaps to meet some of the drivers.

After setting up camp near the centre of Reims we ventured out to the circuit. Practice started on the Wednesday before the race on Sunday and we were able to spend several days mingling with the teams and talking to the drivers. As we walked into the pit area, where the team cars were parked, I was almost overcome with emotion at the sight of the five bright red Ferrari Formula 1 cars. The weather was extremely hot and the long red bonnets gleamed as the sun shone directly above them.

As we stood to admire the Ferraris, we heard a very friendly 'Ah! Bonjour!' The greeting came from none other than the number one Ferrari driver, Jean Behra. Jean had visited Australia in 1956 to race in the Australian Grand Prix, and came out to Templestowe Hill climb when Dad was competing. None of us could speak French and his knowledge of English was similar but we developed quite a rapport and communicated with sign language, mime and dictionaries. He must have thought I was a sweet little kid as he so patiently and enthusiastically showed me the cars, allowed me to sit in his Ferrari and introduced us to everyone in the team.

Over the three-day period we spectated from many vantage points at the circuit. To watch Stirling Moss howling down the long Soissons Straight in the lime-green BRM, emitting such a unique exhaust scream and clocking 180mph before braking for Thillois hairpin, was an experience for me that has not been equalled. But it was Ferrari drivers Tony Brooks and Phil Hill, and Jack Brabham in the Cooper, who finally ended up on the front row of the three-car grid, with Moss and Jean Behra on the second row.

The temperature on race day was blistering. Before the start the drivers were soaking themselves with water and fitting drink bottles into their cockpits, hoping to be able to survive the gruelling 50 laps that lay ahead. Waiting for the starting flag to be dropped, I secretly wished that Jean Behra would win.

The roar of all of those Formula 1 cars created such an atmosphere that my heart was pounding. Into the lead went Brooks and as I looked back to the start there was my friend Jean Behra still sitting on the line with his engine stalled. The Ferrari mechanics push-started him but it was obvious he had no chance of success as the rest of the field were way ahead. What a disappointment!

Unbelievably, Jean worked his way through the field and by the halfway stage was up to third place. The race was closely fought throughout, but it was Brooks who finally took the honours, followed by Hill and Brabham. My friend Jean retired with piston problems on lap 32.

After more than two hours of intense rivalry in the heat of 110°F, many drivers were nearly collapsing with exhaustion. Some did. What surprised me was the stamina of a few. Next in the programme was a 25-lap Formula 2 race and some of the same drivers were entered. Stirling Moss won. He had been disqualified (push start after spin, in order to drive back to the pits) seven laps before the end of the grand prix, and perhaps this extra time had helped him revive enough to endure another stint. But it was a remarkable achievement.

The journey to La Chartre took several days to allow for sightseeing. When we stopped for refreshments the French people appeared to us to be rather strange. Although none of us could speak the language we would attempt to communicate and ask for things in French but there was no willingness to try to understand us.

After setting up camp near the town we went to find the circuit. To our surprise a normal road was partitioned off and used for the race meeting. The circuit was only about one and a half miles long, with two longish straights and a couple of slow corners. Here everyone was so friendly, and again it was frustrating that we did not speak French. Every time we met anyone involved with the running of the event they would shake our hands. For three days most of my time seemed to be spent shaking hands. I was impressed with this style of greeting, and decided that our Australian 'G'Day', without the physical contact, was a lot less personal.

My father's Cooper had not been tested on the road since the rebuild at the factory. During practice he noticed different handling characteristics and wanted to acclimatise. The track had a certain amount of gritty debris on the surface and there was not much grip. Practice was quite chaotic, with workmen still building the grandstands. But by the end of the session my father was satisfied with the handling and felt confident that, driven at ten tenths, the car should be reasonably competitive.

The entry list was international. Drivers from many European countries were competing in various races in saloon, sports and racing cars. Sten Bielke, a Swedish count who was racing his Saab in the saloon car race, delighted in practising his English. He had never met Australians before and was intrigued by our accents and turn of phrase – and by my mother's cooking. Each night, instead of returning to the hotel, he appeared at our camp with his mechanic to sample the barbecue. I had not seen a Saab before. He drove me up the road in it one day – I had never experienced such extreme angles when cornering and held my breath with fear as I thought he had lost control, but we always emerged facing the right direction.

As the flag dropped for the Formula 3 race my father, starting from fifth on the grid, overtook two cars before the first corner. My mother and I were jumping up and down, barracking at the top of our voices. On the third lap, at the corner near us, he appeared to go straight on and the car got stuck. He frantically gesticulated to the marshals to give him a push but they did not notice. My mother ran down as fast as she could go and began to push him out. The marshals then noticed and he once again set off, but in last position.

Dad worked his way through the field and was clearly the fastest car in the race until – in the penultimate lap, by now in third position – he was about to challenge for second when suddenly the engine lost power and he crossed the line third. It turned out that the carburettor had sucked in the stocking stretched over the bellmouth to keep the grit out, so was starving the engine of fuel. I also wanted to know why Dad had run off the road. It was not like him to make a mistake. With the independent suspension fitted, the anti-roll bar was too firm, he said, and when racing under fast conditions with slow corners, the front end would not pull in sufficiently.

In the evening a civic reception was held in the town centre. Sten drove me there in the Saab. The square was packed with thousands of onlookers. To be surrounded by thronging crowds was a totally new experience. I felt like royalty. An official opened the car door and escorted me to a long table covered with every culinary delight imaginable. I was seated next to the Mayoress, both of us unable to communicate apart from smiles and gestures and, to start with, a hand-shake. After we all enjoyed a wonderful meal and listened to speeches we could not understand, the winners were presented with their trophies. The evening was memorable. I had felt rather self-conscious eating, watched by the crowd, and unable to speak their language, but I certainly managed to perfect my hand-shaking technique.

Now it was time to forget motorsport for a while as we were heading off to Italy. Our next Formula 3 race, at Roskildering in Denmark, was three weeks ahead, which left just enough time for sightseeing. On the *Castel Felice* I had started to pick up some Italian as few of the crew spoke English. By the end of the voyage I was developing a fascination for the language and for the historic sites I'd learnt about at school. At Lyon we found a car-parking garage and left the trailer and Cooper in storage. Driving along narrow roads and through medieval towns was much easier without those in tow.

Our first Italian port of call was San Remo. We were to meet Reno Benassi who was visiting his family after being in Australia for ten years. Reno had lived at The Black Stump for some months as the builder involved with moving our house to its new position and constructing the magnificent front room. Reno was proud of his work and after he had finished we all remained friends. He reminded me of the character in the publication *They're a Weird Mob*, by Nino Culotti, a parody of the life of an Italian immigrant to Australia in the fifties who became involved with the building trade.

As a beach-loving Australian teenager, I was excited at the thought of sampling what I perceived to be the best beach in the world, the Italian Riviera. Schoolbooks and tourist guides about European history and geography had always implied that anything European was far superior to the Australian equivalent. So after finding the Benassi family in the middle of eating their pranza – and insisting that we sample the homemade pasta – I was keen to get down to the sea. Imagine then my horror to find miles and miles of pebbles. This was the Italian Riviera! Nice blue Mediterranean water, but pebbles, pebbles and more pebbles. No sand. Despite this, we rented a beach hut just near the water's edge and spent the next few days swimming, eating and enjoying the sun.

The evening before our departure we took the Benassis to the restaurant on the rooftop of the Casino. While Diana Dors entertained us, I was happily trying every Italian culinary delight from the buffet table. Every time I piled the plate high, an image of King Neptune flashed into my mind. I hoped that he would not make an untimely appearance.

Reno wished to visit a friend in Parma so decided to hitch a lift with us in the VW as we were going close by, on our way to Florence and Pisa. The roads were narrow and winding and late at night we decided to pitch camp out in the countryside. At the side of the road we found a small shelter consisting of a roof supported by poles. In the dark, thinking that the construction belonged to a farmer, Ron and I decided not to erect our one-man tents there but to put the camp stretchers under the roof beside the VW. Reno hopped into his sleeping bag and crashed out quickly, straight on the ground. At dawn, in a deep sleep, I became aware of voices quite close. As my eyelids grudgingly opened, I got the fright of my life. There, standing under the shelter, were ten people, just waiting. We had camped at a bus stop.

Next, we visited the Leoncini family in Castel Fiorentino, not far from Pisa. Guigno, a member of the Western District Car Club in Geelong, had emigrated to Australia some years before and insisted we visit his mother and sisters during our trip to Italy. The family were so pleased to meet people who knew Guigno. His mother became extremely emotional when we produced photographs of her grandchildren. She did not believe she would ever meet them. In fact years later she spent some time in Australia before Guigno so tragically died. The Italian people were so friendly and helpful. Quite different from the French.

Pavement cafés fascinated me. Australia in those days had not introduced dining al fresco, apart from barbecues. Here, the Lambrettas and Fiat Cinquecentos, sounding their horns, screeching their tyres and gesticulating rudely at each other, was entertainment unequalled. Every time the need for refreshments arose I always wanted to find a trattoria or café with pavement tables so that we could enjoy the macho Italian sideshow. Pollution was as yet unheard of so we endured the fumes of these noisy vehicles without concern.

In Rome, visiting the historic monuments evoked such a sense of wonder. I stood in the Coliseum, imagining the spectacle of the lions killing Christians in front of thousands of baying spectators. Wandering through San Pietro and gazing up at the ceiling, I could almost see Michelangelo, the 16th century artist, perched on his scaffolding painting those famous frescos. I was so overjoyed to experience these treasures first-hand. The famous Shakespearean speech came to mind while visiting The Forum, and under my breath I began to recite

Friends, Romans, Countrymen, lend me your ears;
I come to bury Caesar, not to praise him.
The evil that men do lives after them,
the good is oft interrèd with their bones;
So let it be with Caesar.

At last my school history lessons started to take on some meaning. The teachers most likely would not believe the transformation.

I felt regret at leaving Italy. The melodic language, and the interested, volatile nature of the people, made me vow to return, but next time with the ability to communicate. Travelling back through Switzerland en route to Lyon to pick up the Cooper, we could not help noticing the cleanliness of the streets and the orderly behaviour of the traffic and population. To me, already missing the excitable chaos that was Italy, life there appeared monotonous.

One day as we were descending a mountain in France, it was time to boil the billy. You would never expect to be entertained so sensationally whilst drinking a cup of tea in a lay-by. Most of the traffic was driving as though in the last lap of a Grand Prix. The squeal of the tyres was unbelievable, so was the body roll of the Citroën 2CVs. I expected the cars to let go and end up with their wheels facing the sky, but not so. After the first exhibition we all thought the driver must be crazy, but every 2CV, and there were many in half an hour, was the same. This must be the normal style of driving, we concluded.

Progress through France with the trailer attached became much slower. While travelling north we saw in a newspaper that Jean Behra had been killed at Avus. I was devastated. It was only three weeks since we had met at Reims. As we passed through

Germany we went to Avus and saw the tyre marks that went over the edge of the banking. We all felt so sad that we would never again see that very amiable and kind gentleman.

At Roskildering Dad had been promised £90 start money but, after signing on, he was informed that he was not to receive the payment. As the organisers acted in rather an arrogant manner, Dad decided not to compete. We chatted to Stirling Moss and other drivers we had previously met and then boarded another ferry bound for Sweden, to visit our friend, Count Sten Bielke.

His house, on the edge of a lake, was similar to Australian houses, with no upstairs, just ground floor living. The water in the lake was fairly warm and, as usual, my first priority was to run down the private pier and dive straight into the clear, blue, fresh water. Sampling Swedish food, and living in the bungalow, instead of under canvas, and was quite a pleasant diversion for several days. It was a luxury to sleep in a proper bed.

Soon it was time for the next adventure and this time a definite start in a motor race. Saxonring, in East Germany, was to play host for combined motorcycle races and Formula 3 car races. The ferry from Denmark arrived at Rostock near midnight. The terminal appeared to be a railway shunting yard, with steam engines coming and going. Guards with dangerous-looking weapons were everywhere. It was dark and scary. The trailer and all our documents were examined but, without any difficulties, we were allowed to proceed. It was very dark everywhere. No cars, no street lights, no house lights. We decided to travel through the night and find somewhere to pull in at dawn when we could see our surroundings. The roads were deserted. The darkness felt eerie. Our headlights lit up the trees at the side of the road and often we would see people scrambling out of sight. At regular intervals we saw one or two people in areas that appeared to be miles from any town. It was hard to imagine what they were doing.

The information we had read about East Germany described people disappearing or being tortured. Just before dawn, when we saw a number of Russian tanks and military vehicles crossing the road in front us, we became quite frightened. Soldiers waved guns, signalling us to stop, which we did, until all the tanks had crossed. At this point my father was beginning to regret that he had entered for the race in East Germany.

Just after dawn, it was time for a brew-up. Finding a lay-by at the side of the road we began to boil the kettle. Out of nowhere a man appeared holding a bicycle. He spoke some English and told us about the dreadful living conditions East Germans had been forced to endure since the politicians divided Germany some 14 years earlier: the fear, the oppressive regime, no future and no escape. As he spoke, our informant kept looking around to see if he was being spied on. We noticed a strong smell of alcohol, quite unusual for early morning. Perhaps it was to numb the grimness of life under these conditions? The other shadowy figures we had seen in the countryside may have been trying for some sort of temporary escape too.

We had to make several trips to East Berlin to collect the permit that would allow us to travel to Saxonring. Each time we went to the office of the car club we were informed that the permit had not arrived. The contrast between the two sides of the city was stark. In the East every street seemed to have piles of rubble where buildings had once stood. It was as if the bombing raids of the Second World War had finished just the day before. Streets were deserted, with very little traffic. It felt so frightening.

West Berlin, in total contrast, was vibrant, with people living as if there would be no tomorrow. Tables at sidewalk cafés were always fully occupied, with bands playing melodious German music, and there was traffic everywhere. Laughter could be heard – the townsfolk were enjoying themselves.

The permit eventually arrived and with some reluctance we drove through the Brandenburg Gate for the final time into East Germany, bound for Saxonring and the Formula 3 race. Near where we thought the track might be we stopped to ask some youths for directions. They decided to escort us on their mopeds and bicycles. It was near midnight when we set up camp. At first light we explored the track and facilities. My father was not very enthusiastic. The track was extremely rough and, he thought, quite dangerous. A temporary grandstand had been constructed. When the officials arrived they did not seem to be very efficient and Dad quickly decided that he would not race there. He weighed up all the pros and cons and looked at the worst scenario. Should he be injured in an accident he did not feel confident about the medical expertise. And there was us to consider too. If he were in hospital what would we do? He made his excuses and we left, anxious to cross that border back into the West.

At the checkpoint heavily armed guards examined our passports and the carnets for the VW and trailer and then, after a lengthy discussion amongst themselves, took all our documents to an office a hundred yards away to be checked by a supervisor, who spoke some English. After what seemed an age, we were informed that our visas were correct to enter into East Germany but we did not have the right paperwork to leave. All our fears seemed to be realised at once. I couldn't imagine spending the rest of my life living under such oppressive conditions. The thought of school in Geelong felt attractive for the first time, certainly compared to the mental image I had about life in East Germany.

After haggling for two hours we were suddenly allowed to go. The sighs of relief didn't start until we were well out of sight of the border. We found a campsite with a lake at Bad Hersfield and went swimming. That was a memorable lesson on what living in a democratic society really meant: the privilege of having the freedom to choose how to live. I did not ever want to visit a communist state again.

During the afternoon we noticed a number of men with limbs missing who were swimming in the lake. They were rather friendly and most spoke quite good English. All were victims of the war. Camped next to us, a German family enjoyed their annual holiday. The woman's face and body were severely disfigured. She told me how she received the injuries from a bomb blast during the war. I did not hear one word of criticism from her or any of the disabled men. Having only read about the war at school, I was now seeing the results and began to wonder whether it could ever be worth all the grief and devastation. What really amazed me was that these people, who were so kind and nice to us, had not so long ago been the enemy.

Bad Hersfield was thoroughly enjoyable but as Dad had entered for the Brighton Speed Trials the following weekend, we did not have time to stay more than one night. Late at night we arrived at the Belgian border bound for the ferry crossing from Ostend. After examining the documents the guard would not let us through as he insisted that we needed a carnet for the Cooper as well as the trailer. We had not encountered any problems on previous border crossings but the guard would not listen and told us to return the following morning. It took all day before we were allowed through and we missed the last ferry crossing to England. The day's delay meant we were too late for the Brighton Speed Trials. The motor racing content of our overseas trip was becoming a disaster.

The final straw happened at Mallory Park. After problems with the Cooper in practice Dad scratched from the event. The four of us were watching the race, however, when right in front of us we witnessed a horrific accident that seemed to take forever to finish. One of the competitors was killed, a chap we had found friendly and helpful. My father suddenly said, 'that's it'. He never drove the Cooper again.

Before returning to Australia we visited the Cooper Car Company to say farewell to the Coopers and their staff. As we walked towards the double doors we heard quite a high-pitched engine noise, a bit like a motor mower. Bruce McLaren came speeding out of the garage mounted on a small device, the likes of which I had never seen before. That was my introduction to go-karts.

Bruce and John Cooper had built the kart as a diversion and this was the first test drive. As 'Mr Charles' (Cooper) was absent, a track was hastily cleared down between the lathes, round a Formula 2 jig, through the door into a terrazzo floored showroom, the area used for assembling racing cars, and down the main straight past the milling machine.

After the first drive Bruce complained that he could not make the tail break away when cornering. 'We'll soon fix that!' muttered Cooper's chief mechanic Noddy Grohmann when Bruce was out of earshot, and he sloshed the entire terrazzo floor with a bucket of soapy water. The tail certainly broke away when Bruce came hurtling round the makeshift track. After three complete spins he cannoned into a stack of packing cases. Everyone laughed – all, that is, except Bruce.

As I pored over this miniature 'racing car' I realised that my small stature would be absolutely ideal for this new form of motorsport. During the four-week trip back to Australia, I couldn't get the idea of racing out of my mind. I kept hoping that go-karts had been introduced to my home country by then and that a driver's licence was not necessary. In Victoria you had to be 18 to apply for a driver's licence and I still had years to wait.

It seemed like forever.

Chapter 3

FLAT-OUT OR STOP

Karting, controversy and my first road car

The timing was perfect. As we arrived back home, school was about to break up for the long summer holidays. A whole seven weeks before I had to return to lessons. At least that would allow me to 'recover' from the trip and mentally prepare for the academic year. I was kept very busy catching up with friends, swimming and riding the bike all over Geelong.

Several days a week Joan rode her bike to my place, arriving at 4.30am. We would head off to ride the two-mile trip to the Eastern Beach, dive off the pier into the salt water of Corio Bay, swim half a mile in the shark-protected pool, get dressed and ride home exhilarated. After breakfast we spent the rest of the day swimming at our pool and sun-baking. Who wanted to return to school? I certainly didn't.

Some weeks after our return I noticed an article in the *Geelong Advertiser*, the local newspaper, about a go-kart club that had just been set up, with a graded dirt track under construction just outside town on the way to Drysdale. I could not believe my luck! The president of the club was the owner of a motorbike shop just a few doors down from where Dad's engine re-conditioning works was situated and my father knew him quite well.

After just a little persuasion Dad took me to look at a go-kart and I became a member of the club. During the weekend we visited the new track and watched a number of people lapping. What surprised me was that there were men's races and women's races but no mixed races. Men and women were only permitted to drive together in practice.

I was old enough to compete and a road driver's licence was not required. Everything was definitely in my favour. I would need a go-kart, however. I was offered a trial run but very reluctantly could not accept, as there would have to be modifications to the pedals so that I could reach them. The solution of course was to have my own go-kart. 'Please Dad,' I implored with great passion. 'No, I won't get fed up with it, honestly, please, please.'

It did not take too much persuasion or whining. Before long we were looking at a basic chassis built by a local exhaust pipe manufacturer. Dad was not impressed with the design but after some consideration he relented and purchased one, together with the components to assemble a go-kart. Convinced that my interest would not last long, he did not want to put too much money or effort into this new project.

As we had just purchased a new motor mower, the old one was stripped of its 98cc Villiers engine and, after a quick rebuild, this was mounted in the new toy. Soon the kart was ready for its first test-drive. The night before, I was so nervous that I would not be able to drive properly that I had difficulty sleeping. I did not want to disappoint my father.

The track at Geelong was quite an interesting design, with a long straight, a right-hand 180-degree corner, a short straight to a left-hand 180-degree turn, another short straight, then a right-hand long sweeping corner leading into the start of the long straight.

As I was push-started, the engine sprang into life and I shot off down the straight. It was petrifying! The first corner arrived so quickly. I tried to get round it but immediately spun right round. What an idiot. Another push start and another spin. Dad wasn't too impressed with my driving and told me to try to drive slowly to get the feel of the steering and the power of the engine. After several more attempts I managed to lap slowly round the circuit without spinning and, before long, began to improve the driving technique and drive with some verve. My cornering needed improvement. At first on the dirt track I would either putt-putt slowly round the corners or, trying to achieve a nice smooth slide, overdo the technique and spin. With a number of practice laps I began to develop a feel for the steering and throttle and my cornering became more controlled. After the end of that first test I felt rather pleased with myself, although apprehensive about my first race, the following weekend.

The day before the Sunday race, the track was open for free practice. I seized this opportunity with great enthusiasm as I had not driven with other competitors. I needed to learn about overtaking manoeuvres, rules and regulations – that is, if I were competitive enough to overtake other drivers. My apprehension turned to fear when we arrived. There were quite a number of go-karts, many more than anticipated. The track looked crowded. Both men and women competitors were lapping and queues were waiting for the next practice session. I wanted to go home.

I was sure I would make a fool of myself and be an embarrassment to my father. Before we had gone on our overseas trip, nearly every week the *Geelong Advertiser* ran articles about his motor racing achievements. There was a reputation to be lived up to and I did not want to ruin this with one foul swoop.

The hour of judgement arrived too soon: I could not find any more excuses to wait for the next practice session. The track was rather crowded with 100cc and 200cc karts, both men and women lapping round. The bigger-engine karts belted past me in the straights, which was overwhelming at first, but at least I managed to keep facing the right direction. In the second practice session I started to keep my right foot hard down and discovered that the larger capacity karts, although quick in a straight line, did not corner any faster than my own kart.

All the other competitors were adults with drivers' licences, and this I found intimidating: my only driving experience was reversing out of the front drive and back in again, and belting around the back paddock at Grassy Creek.

When we arrived at the track on race day, queues of spectator cars were beginning to arrive, waiting to sample this new form of motorsport.

'Oh well,' I thought. 'If I make a fool of myself, then there sure will be a lot of people who'll know about it.'

Official practice for the 100cc women's race lasted for ten laps, with eleven participants. My kart would not start. It was about halfway through the session before I managed to get onto the track. One lady spun in front of me going into the corner at the end of the straight. I managed to just avoid clipping the front of her kart by frantically steering onto the grass. Practice finished before I wanted to come in, thinking that my recorded time would not be good enough. How surprised I was to discover that my kart was the fastest. Unbelievable! Suddenly my confidence shot up. Perhaps after all I might not be an embarrassment. On the other hand, there was the official race to come and who knows what the outcome of that might be.

That day the fastest in practice had to start at the back of the grid. All the karts were push-started and we made a lap on part of the track in formation, for a rolling start. The Australian flag was dropped and we were away, three abreast in each row. I was placed on the inside of the last row and managed to overtake two karts before arriving at the corner in a prime position to sneak through on the inside. Passing the pit signals each lap, I noticed Dad urging me to go faster. After eight laps I was in the lead and on the tenth lap the chequered flag was dropped and I was the winner.

My pit crew were so excited and I could not believe my luck. But the day was not finished: there was one more race to attempt, a combination of 100cc and 200cc karts. The smaller-engine karts were positioned on the front rows of the grid and off we were flagged. I took the lead but during the second lap the old Villiers engine suddenly coughed unhealthily and came to an abrupt stop. 'Never mind,' I announced. 'There will definitely be another time.'

Dad appeared quite pleased with my performance – 'not a bad first attempt' – and announced that he was going to make me a proper go-kart. How exciting! The seeds were beginning to be sown for the next project, the Rainey Kart.

After the races were finished the presentation of trophies took place. At last I would have a trophy of my own to place on the shelf next to my father's collection.

Each race winner was presented with an impressive silver cup. The standard of trophies looked much better than some of the cups that Dad had previously won in his racing car.

My turn came and I proudly stepped forward to collect my cup and a handshake from the president's wife. I do not know if my jaw dropped with shock but it felt like it. My trophy was an embroidered set of sheets. Undoubtedly beautiful top quality sheets. *But, sheets.* How could I put those on the mantelpiece to show off my first win in motorsport? I was so upset. My mother thought they were wonderful and anyway she was fed up with the never-ending job of cleaning Dad's trophies so why would she want another trophy to add to the burden? Unfortunately, to a girl in her teens and an aspiring racing driver, not the slightest bit interested in feminine niceties, it felt like a snub. But with the benefit of many years of hindsight, I fully understand the thought behind the gesture: that females would prefer practical trophies. This female did not, and has never subscribed to the norm, but I am still trying.

Dad spent some time at the drawing board planning what he thought would be a good design for a go-kart. His idea was to follow a proven racing car design of the time and produce it in as simple a form as possible. It would have a light but strong chassis, a racing car driving position so that the driver felt part of the kart for better control, correct steering geometry, a low centre of gravity and neat appearance. The space frame chassis was to be constructed out of 3/4in square steel tubing and the first task was to make a jig.

The steering was to be in effect a 'rack-and-pinion' type, with a bobbin on the steering column and aircraft control flexible cable operation and aluminium tubing for the track rods. The king pin angle presented a problem. If the available production wheels were to be used, the king pins would have too great an angle. Dad decided to make a pattern and cast our own two-piece aluminium wheels. He was not happy with welded up stub axles and made patterns so these could be manufactured in one piece from solid steel. Even the seat, to be built of fibreglass, needed a pattern. As the planning progressed further, Dad realised that the cost of building one go-kart would be phenomenal and decided to make a batch of 12, for sale, the prototype of which would be mine.

Being rather impatient I would have liked my go-kart immediately. I was raring to go. But, as school had just started, the delay was probably beneficial: at least there was no justifiable excuse for not doing homework. I had difficulty settling back into school. Most of the girls in my class were a year younger than me and had been a class lower before I went overseas. I felt rather isolated.

A lot can change in a year of absence. As well as the situation at school, Ian had started work and Heather was now living in Ararat, about 100 miles from Geelong. Although we had not met up that often after my family moved house, we always managed to get together on birthdays. The fact that our lives had now gone in different directions was hard to adjust to.

As summer changed to autumn, I started to settle into study. The new go-kart was taking shape after the patterns for all the components were finished. The ultimate 100cc engine to use was the McCulloch, an American import, originally used in chainsaws. Dad, having put so much into the new go-kart, did not want to spend yet more money so decided to carry out his own experiment using a locally made Villiers engine. This was quite simple with a non-detachable head. He parted the cylinder head off with a long thin parting-off tool, fitted four cylinder bolts and raised the compression ratio to 9 to 1.

One day when I got home from school, there was my new go-kart waiting on the veranda. I'd already had fittings for positioning the seat, pedals and steering wheel but to see it all finished and painted was more than exciting.

A few days later, on Saturday morning, we tested on the track and it felt wonderful. The steering appeared to be much more positive than the previous example and the engine more powerful. There were a number of other people testing and as I began to familiarise myself with the handling of this wonderful new toy, I started to push quite hard and overtake some of the bigger capacity karts.

'Perhaps it was a fluke,' I thought as I pulled into the paddock area. 'The other drivers might have been having problems.'

Dad checked everything and we set off again. My confidence must have overflowed as I spun right round on the second corner. After a few more laps my chief mechanic and kart designer said I should come in and not wear the go-kart out but save it for the following weekend's race meeting.

All the karts in the first 100cc women's race were powered by Villiers: no-one in Geelong had yet purchased the expensive and more powerful McCulloch engines. The race went very much like my first race of some months back, but I took the lead in just a couple of laps and went on to win by quite a margin, even lapping two slower karts before the finish. My engine seemed to be putting out quite a bit more power than the others. Every two weeks there were races and I was not once challenged. I started to think that the other ladies, usually driving their husband's machine, were not as serious as I was about competing.

Some months later, at the Saturday test session before the Sunday race, I was lapping quite quickly on a crowded track. As I came round the top-sweeping corner into the straight, closely following two karts having a scrap between themselves, I took the inside line, swept past them and fell in behind a 200cc kart just before the sharp 180-degree right-hand turn. I was flying. I braked but she braked so hard she almost came to a standstill and I ran into the back of her. I could not understand why she had braked so violently and felt furious. Fortunately there was no damage to either kart and we were pushed off again but I pulled into the paddock area still shaking. We watched the other lady lapping and discovered she approached every corner the same way. Fast down the straight and just crawled round the corners.

The following day in the combined race I had started on the back row and was driving flat-out to try to win this race as well as the 100cc race and, like a replay, as I overtook a kart in the long straight I came upon a 200cc kart which braked like hell and bingo, into the back I went, my kart riding right on top of her engine and then down again. I had forgotten all about her 'driving style' in my determination to win. There were complaints to the organisers that I should be banned as a dangerous driver. I argued that no driver should brake so violently going into a corner and that we were racing for positions.

The following week the president of the Geelong Go-Kart Club called an extraordinary meeting to decide whether to exclude me from competition. To this day I maintain the incident was not my fault, that this particular lady was an incompetent driver and I was unfortunate to be behind her on two occasions. I was not banned but reprimanded and told that if it happened again I would be excluded. I felt humiliated, particularly as some people at the meeting were arguing that I should be forbidden forever from competing at the circuit, so I decided to stop driving for a while and concentrate on schoolwork. Exams were imminent and my minimalist approach to study might not achieve good results.

I had meanwhile started to consider travelling to Melbourne to see what the competition was like there. I expected it to be tougher in the big smoke and anyway perhaps they presented silver trophies to lady competitors! My mother was accumulating quite an interesting array of my 'trophies'. The items included a plastic picnic set and cutlery for six, a hand-painted casserole, a woollen rug, sets of teaspoons, sets of cake-forks, a set of anodised aluminium mugs, a large Pyrex casserole, small Pyrex casseroles, sets of six Pyrex mugs and sets of towels – but still no silver tankard, cup or anything that could be put on the mantelpiece.

Two of the production Rainey Karts were regularly campaigned successfully in Geelong and at least six in and around Melbourne. All the Melbourne karts were fitted with McCulloch engines, some with the 100cc version and some with twin engines for the 200cc class. Rainey Karts always finished in the top places.

At that point, although there was no controlling body of go-karting, clubs issued their own rules based on US regulations, so there was some uniformity throughout Victoria. One day Dad received a phone call from the president of the Geelong Go-Kart Club to inform him that the Rainey Kart was banned from all competition at Geelong because the steering arrangement was dangerous and infringed the regulations. Furthermore, clubs throughout Victoria were to be informed of this decision. Checking through the rules that were available, Dad could find no evidence of an infringement and requested more information. It was an unbelievable situation to be in, as no person in the Geelong club would clarify the position.

Next morning we received a telephone call from the secretary of a go-kart club from the eastern suburbs of Melbourne, inviting us to become honorary members and to drive at their meeting the following Sunday. We were informed that several Melbourne clubs were in the process of trying to set up a Go-Kart Association as the controlling body of the sport in Victoria. When they heard about the ban they had objected to the Geelong Club, to no avail, hence their invitation, as a protest. I felt much more reassured about my future as a competitor, particularly as these people were total strangers and they were concerned. Immediately, I resigned my membership of the Geelong Go-Kart Club and never drove at my home town again.

At such short notice I was not able to accept the invitation to compete as some new modifications were under way on my go-kart and there wasn't time to get them finished. Dad had just fitted out a go-kart however so he drove instead. Most of the production Rainey Karts were there and all passed scrutineering without any problems, although as yet no modifications had been made to the steering mechanism. Soon after this the Go-Kart Association of Victoria was formed and Geelong could not maintain its ban on the Rainey Kart.

Dad drove in a number of races when an innovation he had designed needed testing. Some successes came his way but he did not take go-kart racing very seriously and thought that most of the drivers were barking mad, some driving more dangerously than the competitors in Formula 3 – almost as if there was a World Championship at the end of each race.

The first 'foreign' event I contested was at Dandenong, just outside Melbourne. There were many more competitors than at Geelong, with two qualifying races before the final of the 100cc women's race. When I saw that most of the karts were fitted with McCulloch engines I guessed the competition here would be tough. I was right. In practice, after familiarising myself with the circuit I began to push quite hard but could not manage to fly past any of the others. Qualifying, I was rather surprised to find myself second fastest and on the front row of the grid.

At the rolling start a young lady took the lead in her McCulloch powered kart and I was right on her tail going into the first corner at the end of the straight. Through the series of slow corners I felt that if I could get an inside line I could get past, but she drove with good blocking capabilities. As we swept round into the straight the McCulloch showed its superior power and cleared out from me, but going into the corner I advanced right on to the rear of her machine. We continued in this fashion for ten laps.

At one point I thought I could get past and nearly did so on the last corner before the straight, but as we came out side by side, once again the power of the American engine took over. As we drove past the pit area each lap I could see her father and my father both jumping up and down barracking and signalling encouragement. She deservedly took the chequered flag first and I was second. Even now, decades later as I write this, I remember that it was one of the most exciting races I ever drove.

My father seemed inspired by the race and told me he was intending to experiment more with the Villiers engine to see if he could get it to put out as much power as a McCulloch. He said the measures he was about to take were quite drastic. After opening up the ports he tried to raise the crankcase pressure by filling the inside of the piston with cork. First he acquired a block of cork and cut an old piston in half and made a plaster cast mould of the inside. Then he shaped the cork to the inside of the piston, allowing room for the con-rod to be fitted. The cork was soaked in boiling water until it became malleable and forced past the gudgeon pin bosses so that a good tight fit was achieved. After drying out it was coated several times with shellac. The next step was to fit a reed valve system. Using a reed end holder from a pulse jet model aircraft engine, Dad cast and made a housing with the same thread as the head of the pulse jet and welded it onto the side of the Villiers cylinder, over the inlet port. Four aluminium plates, the size of the crankshaft counterweights, were drilled and riveted onto the crankshaft. The crankcase pressure was raised quite a bit by these modifications and finally the flywheel was lightened substantially.

Time was passing and a fortnight later we were due to drive at the new Western Suburbs Go-Kart track just out of Melbourne. Dad thought the engine should be tested on a dynamometer before it was installed. As there were no suitable dynos about, he made one from a generator and components acquired from an aircraft disposal firm. After some testing the engine appeared to run well and was developing a favourable horsepower, comparable to the McCullochs.

At the race meeting I qualified on the front row. As the flag was dropped I planted my right foot as far as the pedal would go. Half expecting one of the other karts to overtake me, I looked back to find I had pulled ahead of everyone. After eight laps of the ten-lap race I started to lap some of the back markers, the only overtaking necessary, and at the tenth lap the chequered flag was dropped and I was the winner. We were all rather surprised at the outcome and excited that the Villiers engine had beaten the McCullochs.

Dad was aware that he had stretched the Villiers to its extremities. At my next event, when I was in the lead, the power proved too much for the barrel. The engine went bang and blew the cylinder right off the crankcase by splitting round the bottom. Although I know he was half expecting the big bang, my team manager, chief designer and mechanic announced after this great disappointment that he would build me a super duper Grand Prix style go-kart and fit a McCulloch engine. What a surprise! To say I was overwhelmed was an understatement.

The new go-kart was to be much lighter. The tubular chassis frame, constructed with smaller diameter steel than my previous model, was stiffened with stressed-skin dural panels. The wheels were lightened. The steering was a similar rack and pinion arrangement but with dural tie rods. Even the rear large sprocket was manufactured out of lightweight dural with the machining of all the components painstakingly carried out by my father. The front disc brakes were made out of toggle clamp welding pliers, and worked very effectively, while the rear drum brakes were acquired from a NSU Quickly moped. Even the aluminium seat was formed to suit my shape and to give support when cornering. Dad couldn't leave the McCulloch engine alone and opened up the ports to give yet more power and fitted twin carburettors, designed to progressively open.

Out of the workshop emerged a brilliant example of engineering expertise as well as an aesthetically pleasing go-kart. I hoped my driving would be worthy of all Dad's effort.

At the first event I found the handling characteristics quite different from my previous go-kart and spun several times in practice. Not wanting to spin during the race, I was rather more cautious than usual and finished third. The first two ladies were very quick. They had been winning most of the major events in and around Melbourne, both driving McCulloch powered Rainey Karts. I realised that the competition was very determined and, even in my hot new machine, any successes I might achieve would be a lot harder won than in the past.

The next event I won with ease, however. At last I was presented with a silver trophy. It wasn't for winning a race though, but for having the best turned-out go-kart! The person responsible for purchasing the trophies obviously did not expect a female to win this award otherwise it would have been of the more practical variety.

After leaving school I started to compete more in Melbourne and other parts of Victoria, winning many races and occasionally losing.

The time was now imminent for me to take the driving test. Dad purchased a 1953 Morris Minor, owned from new by an elderly chap and used once a week for shopping. The speedometer read 9,000 miles and the car, with its grey gleaming exterior and red upholstery that looked as though it had never been sat on, could just have come out of the showroom.

I excitedly polished the car while Dad made the extensions for the pedals to enable me to drive. If cars had a soul, then this one was in for a shock. From a sedate life with an elderly driver, the Minor's life was about to be dramatically changed. The driving experience of its new young owner thus far was limited to driving flat-out in go-karts and belting the Holden round the paddock at The Black Stump.

I felt so thrilled that at last I had a car of my own. But first I had to learn to drive on the road with other traffic and pass the test. Dad accompanied me on my first test drive, with my mother sitting in the back seat. Memories came flooding back to when I was a youngster and Dad was trying to teach Mum to drive. A friend and I were sitting in the back seat, giggling at my mother's attempts. As we were driving along Dad told her to push the clutch pedal in and change up into another gear. Mistakenly, Mum stepped on the brake pedal – quite hard – and the car came to an abrupt stop with me finishing upside down in the front seat. That stopped the giggling. Mum never drove again.

As we started in the Minor for the first drive, I was taking my foot straight off the clutch pedal and stalling the engine. My only previous experience with the working of a clutch was taking off at high revs in the Holden, but then I was on the front row of the grid in my imaginary Grand Prix, so the technique was different. Dad persuaded me to get the feel of the clutch and feed it in gently. After a short time my technique started to improve.

On our second outing Dad was concerned that I was wanting to overtake every car in sight and told me 'take it easy, you're not in a race now.' A family friend, riding in the back seat that day, was amused at this instruction. He remarked 'Murray, how do you expect Joy to drive sedately when since she was a kid you have driven her at speeds of over 100mph, taken off with racing starts at every opportunity and always demonstrated to her that there are only two speeds, flat-out and stop!'

We all thought the comment hilarious at the time.

Part of the Victoria driving test included parallel parking. To practise I parked the Holden in front of our house and persuaded any visitor to risk parking their car in front, just leaving enough space to manoeuvre the Minor in and out of the space. I spent hours perfecting the technique. I definitely didn't want to fail.

When the day finally arrived I was a bundle of nerves. The policeman assigned to me for the test was a big burly man with a gruff manner, which didn't do anything for my confidence. For three-quarters of an hour we drove through the busy streets of Geelong. At one traffic light I stalled the engine and thought that had put paid to my result. The parking test was the last component and instead of parking between cars, two steel poles on a stand had been placed in front of the Police Station. As I reversed into the area I lost sight of the pole and *crash*, I bumped into it. That's done it, I thought. It couldn't have happened at a worse time. The policeman went inside and I followed and waited, and waited. Then he came to tell me I had passed.

What a relief!

It was a wonderful feeling to have my own driving licence and be able to drive anywhere without an instructor on board. I felt as though I was suddenly an adult, liberated, with the world at my feet.

Chapter 4

MINOR KEY, MAJOR CHANGE

Heartache, E-types and a British winter

Adulthood usually means getting a job. My ambitions did not extend to any great academic career after I'd only just managed to scrape through school exams by the skin of my teeth. One of the last school excursions I went on was to a laboratory at the local Institute of Technology, where we watched tests being carried out on wool and other fibres through every stage of manufacture to the end product, fabric. Intrigued, I applied for, and got, a job at the Commonwealth Scientific and Industrial Research Organisation (CSIRO) Division of Textile Industry as a technical assistant grade 1.

Life now took on a new meaning, driving myself to and from work everyday and college once a week. There were annual holidays of three weeks, a three month long service leave after ten years of employment, and perhaps promotion. All this to look forward to!

The Morris Minor was driven with some verve every time it ventured out. At traffic lights I waited impatiently for the green light and took off as though it was the race of my life. Maximum revs were reached in every gear before changing up. The poor Minor! There were only two speeds, flat-out and stop. When my father was witness to this treatment he would tell me off.

'For goodness sake Joy, do you want to wear out the Minor? Stop racing all the time.'

'Yes Dad, just like you used to drive the XK,' was my cheeky reply.

Quite often I commuted thirty-five miles to work from The Black Stump, along the magnificent Great Ocean Road. After several trips I became aware of a girl driving a VW, who appeared along the road at about the same time each morning. We started to race each other, which provided some excitement to the morning trip. The VW pulled up hills much better than the Minor, so if I was in front she overtook me. We continued for miles in this manner, until we reached the outskirts of Geelong where I filtered off into the office car park. This became regular entertainment. I never met the driver. Some mornings if I were a few minutes late she would be waiting at the side of the road.

One morning, just a few miles short of my destination, the Minor appeared to be performing better than normal. It seemed to pull up the last hill with much more vitality and I managed to overtake the VW in spectacular style. Feeling quite smug I pulled into the car park. The engine started making strange noises as I switched off the ignition. Steam and oil came gushing out from underneath the bonnet, with loud sizzling. I knew I had cooked the engine – and I also knew I would really be in for it.

In some respects I was unlucky. The fan belt had broken and sheared off the tap of the radiator, allowing the water to leak out. The engine, with no load from the fan plus draining water, had indeed got hotter, in both respects. Dad was not impressed!

A good proportion of my wages was tied up for some time. New pistons and valves were necessary, but at least the head was OK. After the rebuild the Minor was driven in a much more sedate manner. For a little while.

Dad was kept busy farming at The Black Stump and I travelled to many parts of Victoria to race the go-kart with my friend Max. He raced in the men's 100cc races with a Rainey Kart. Some weekends we returned home laden with trophies for both the men's and women's races, he with the silver trophies and me with the practical ones.

Life began to change. The things that once seemed so important, like motorsport, became less compelling. Perhaps it's due to growing up. One begins to place more emphasis on a career and relationships. Max became central to my life. Our backgrounds were extremely diverse but we both had an interest in racing. Now, with the benefit of hindsight, I realise that must have been the only common interest and our ideas even on that one subject were not similar. But, both being young and naïve, we entered into a conventional partnership of courtship and engagement, followed by the life-long commitment of marriage. School friends and work colleagues were travelling down the same path so it didn't appear unusual. I had some doubts early on in the relationship, but my young optimistic mind decided that after the knot was tied the 'bed of roses' and 'happiness' would appear from all directions.

Life became more ordinary. Emphasis was placed on the important things in life such as food supplies to the household, and matching the colours of curtains and carpets. At least there was no worry about matching towels. My supply of 'trophy' towels was so numerous we could take our pick.

In sixties Australia the male population tended to expect their womenfolk to lead a life totally absorbed in domestic duties, without outside interests or friends. Mistakenly, I had chosen a husband who fitted nicely into that category. Go-karting had to stop, friends were not to be contacted and my career had to be terminated.

Life became difficult. I wasn't suited to this docile existence. I felt isolated, and my self-confidence was dwindling. My parents, unaware of any difficulties, decided to return to England for ten months. Life became even more lonely. Secretly I started to visit Jeanette, a friend from my early teens whose relationship was also going through a sticky patch. For an hour or two a week we reminisced and laughed a lot. Other days, my dog Terry and I spent hours walking along the beach. This was the only sense of freedom I had.

After three years the relationship came to a bitter end.

I was devastated. I had failed in my life-long commitment. I felt so ashamed and embarrassed. I did not know what to do.

With no strict timetable to adhere to, no job, or indeed anything to look forward to, the days and nights passed so slowly.

Self-reflection and guilt filled my time. Terry and I walked every day in the country or on the beach. After a week of this misery Terry became so listless I took him to the vet. Cancer was diagnosed. The vet operated immediately to remove a large growth. I brought him home the next day as he had a fear of the vet and would rest better at home. He was placed on cushions in the sunroom.

The next morning at daylight I woke suddenly to find Terry standing by the bed watching me. I helped him back to the sunroom where he lay down and died in my arms.

There was nothing left in life now. Terry had been my constant companion since I was twelve.

What the future held I did not know. Or care. The present was too painful. I drove in my car and sat looking out over Corio Bay for several hours. There were no tears left, I felt cried out and very alone.

The next day something made me go to the travel agents and I booked the first available flight from Melbourne to Heathrow. Within twenty-four hours I was sitting on a Boeing 707 on my way to visit Mum and Dad. Thirty hours later Dad was driving me up Box Hill, Surrey, to Shoushan, the house lent to my parents by Mrs Elsie Cooper.

Dad had kept in contact with 'Mr Charles' over the years. In 1964, when his health was deteriorating, Charles said 'why don't you come over for the 1965 season, boy, and drive me to all the Grands Prix?' My parents decided a season travelling to the European races would be a nice break from the Victoria winter. And when, in October 1964, Charles Cooper suffered a major heart attack and died, they decided to come to the UK even so.

As we drove in past the Shoushan gatehouse, there it stood, a magnificent house, tucked away on the side of a hill. I had not slept the night before flying out of Melbourne and was unable to sleep on the plane. Late afternoon I went to bed and did not wake up for fourteen hours. When I did emerge it felt unreal: here I was unexpectedly in England again, with my life in tatters.

Healing is a slow process but this was the perfect environment to start. Visitors kept popping in, some from the Formula 3 days. There was never a dull moment. After a few days Dad said 'come on, we'll go down to the car auctions at Farnborough and get you something to drive around in.'

We were looking for some small, cheap heap capable of getting me from A to B during my stay. As we walked by the rows and rows of cars trying to decide which one was worthy of our bid, I stopped in my tracks. There stood a bright red magnificent E-type Jaguar FHC. My upbringing in the XK120 had left me totally biased on the subject of sports cars. There was only one make worthy of any mention and that, of course, was Jaguar. I'd seen only two E-types before this, so it was hard to believe that a mechanical object could evoke such passion. It was the most aesthetically pleasing, elegant masterpiece I had ever laid eyes on. Perfection!

I felt captivated by this one at Farnborough. The owner had not given loving care and attention to his wonderful E as he should have. But with a little bit of effort the new owner could have a wonderful car. I felt envious. To my great surprise Dad said, 'I think we'll put in a low bid. We probably won't get it, but if we do, we'll take it back to Australia to sell and perhaps make a few quid.'

In a short time we were the owners of a 1963 Jaguar E-type 3.8 litre fixed-head coupé Series 1. What a delightful surprise! Over the next couple of days Dad made up some extensions for the pedals, while I happily stripped out the seats and carpets to give it all a thorough cleaning. Under the bonnet, engine cleaner was painstakingly applied to every area, including the suspension. After several days of hard slog the E started to look as it should.

Neither Dad nor I had driven an E-type so we were both excited at the prospect. At home, quite a number of them had been written off during the first few weeks of ownership. It had been told to me that an E-type could give a false impression of speed, if the new driver was not accustomed to a silent low revving fast car. On Australia's straight roads, drivers might think they were

FAST LADY

travelling at a reasonable speed until they arrived at a corner. Then disaster happened.

After my first few drives in the E, I began to understand how one could be misled. You needed to acclimatise to that slow, revving purr and responsive acceleration – particularly in my case after driving a Morris Minor, usually with the accelerator pushed to its limit. The E was astounding. I convinced myself that it was definitely designed with me in mind. When I opened the driver's door I just glided in, not having to hoist myself up into the seat. Perfect height! The adjustable steering wheel and controls, apart from the pedals, were all within reach. No other car had felt so custom-made. I knew I would enjoy this.

When the three of us went out, Dad drove and I sat perched between the two seats, reminiscent of XK120 days. If feeling lazy I sprawled out horizontal in the rear section. On my own forays I was usually alone.

I had met a group of very sociable people living in a small village surrounded by woods in deepest Surrey. Parties at different houses each week became the norm. Cider at Wilf's farm on Sunday mornings before lunch at Sally's house, followed by afternoon tea at Tony's place. Mid-week pub night, then coffee and late-night chat and laughter back at Sally's. Life was becoming interesting again!

The sixty-mile round trip provided the opportunity for the E and me to get used to each other. I loved it and jumped at any opportunity to drive. My driving style was very 'Australian' of the time – aggressive.

1. Never give way to cars trying to enter a main road from a minor road.
2. If a car does manage to sneak out of a side road in front of you then give the driver a hard time by sounding the horn, waving your fist and any other gesticulation you think is appropriate.
3. Don't stop for pedestrians unless they're about to step into the road, and then only to avoid them denting your car.

4. Always take off flat-out at the green traffic light. (The fact that the British didn't always follow these rules must, I realised, be a result of the reserved nature of their characters!)

The possibility of making a few quid by selling the E back in Australia persuaded Dad that he should take two back. So began the new search. Eventually one was found similar to mine but grey in colour, the two to be shipped home when we left England in October.

The brakes on the 3.8 E-types were prone to fade, particularly after cruising along at high speed. My heartbeat increased somewhat in such situations. The new 4.2 E-type was easier to stop, however. After arranging with the factory Dad decided to purchase the parts to upgrade our own two cars. We had not travelled on the M1 motorway before and the trip to Brown's Lane provided the opportunity to drive at speeds of over 100mph. Dad was so impressed by the new 4.2 E-type that he decided to order a new white one, to be shipped to Australia for his own use. There was a waiting list of about nine months, which meant that it would arrive about six months after my parents got home.

I began to think of spending the winter in England. I'd only left Australia three months before and, although life was easier now, the prospect of Geelong felt lonely. A room came available in the Surrey village so, after some pondering, I decided to take it. I couldn't seem to get away from motorsport connections though. The previous occupant of the room was Peter Walker, winner of Le Mans with co-driver Peter Whitehead in 1951, in a C-type Jaguar. Peter had decided to move from the village and, as it turned out, that was hardly surprising – if he had any wish for comfort! The house, if one could call it that, was in reality a wooden building, condemned to demolition but still lived in by an elderly married couple. To supplement their income they let the one spare room. Their mode of transport was motorbike and sidecar. The Isle of Man TT had been their holiday destination for many years and the rent helped finance the trip.

Over the past few years I had regularly been accused of being born with a silver spoon in my mouth. There had also been taunts of 'think you're clever because you went to a posh school'. A spell of roughing it in a condemned house in the heart of a British winter might be good for the soul, I decided. When the time came to move my belongings into the lodgings, my mother came with me. She was horrified and there was a brisk exchange of views!

'Joy, you can't possibly stay in that dump!'

'It'll be OK, I've got my own bedding and I won't be eating meals there.'

'You must be mad. You never know what diseases you might pick up.'

'It's fine, really.'

I wouldn't give way, determined to demonstrate my new independence. As autumn approached, the temperature dropped. On the first night at the new 'palace' doubts started to enter my mind. No heating at all! The toilet was situated twenty yards down the back yard. The bath, placed high on a stand in a lean-to shed at the side of the house, could be used by prior arrangement, once a week. Twenty-four hours notice was necessary so that the fire could be stoked ready for the big event. Being Australian, used to walking into a hot shower at least twice a day at home, and fresh from the luxury of my own bathroom at Shoushan, I found the contrast stark. I only used the facilities once. It was too much of an ordeal. Sally insisted I use the bath at her place instead. Towel, soap and toiletries were carried about in the car as part of the kit.

As I was about to leave the house on my first morning I heard a car approaching down the drive. Out jumped one of my new friends, calling in to welcome me to the village. After I'd said 'Good Morning' he was almost falling over with hysterical laughter. I thought I must be missing something as no-one had ever been so amused before when I said this. It turned out that he was tickled by the incongruity of having the nice shiny red E-type parked beside this dump of a house, particularly after seeing it parked at Shoushan.

Soon, every day and evening became fully occupied. One day I was leaving Tony's house after an enjoyable tea. He, an avid MGB owner, was trying to wind me up by saying how gutless the Jaguar was and how slow they looked. Not one to resist temptation I took off in rather a spectacular manner, laying a trail of smoking rubber up the village street. That night Tony told us that as he was crossing the road on his way to the pub, he tripped and fell – on the rubber the E-type had left. Just like my father showing off years before in Minyip, I was never able to live that down.

Some days when I felt in need of motoring connections I headed off to visit Leonard Reece at Carshalton. A friend of my father, he was a manufacturer of camshafts and in the process of developing the Fish Carburettor. This was an unusual type of carburettor as, apart from having a float feed, it had no choke tube, taper needle, jets or air strangler like conventional carburettors, and the fuel level was relatively unimportant. The only moving parts were the throttle spindle, needle valve and leaf valve. And more important, it was meant to use much less fuel than the 'normal' carburettor.

Other times when I wished to hear some fascinating stories I visited the Watson family at Streatham. We had met Dave at race meetings in 1959, when he competed in a Kieft Formula 3 car. After Dad's race accident at the Crystal Palace circuit that year, the *Daily Express* published a photograph of the impact of the Cooper as it went into the straw bales and sleepers. In the background was Dave in the Keift and it was always a joke that he got fame because of my father's crash.

Dave was a brilliant raconteur. How much each story related to the truth was hard to judge, but one could spend hours listening to him, unaware of time. Stories about his time with famous racing drivers, film stars and royalty were the starting point. He was later involved with supplying cars for several films, including *Monte Carlo or Bust*, and he proudly showed me a photograph of himself with Juan Manuel Fangio, standing before a panorama of

Monte Carlo, looking as though they were both deep in conversation or, as Dave liked to joke, 'me giving Fangio advice on how to drive'.

In the depth of winter, when the temperature plunged below freezing, I had some difficulty getting up in the morning. Sleeping under ten blankets I'd still felt cold, but it was even worse trying to get dressed. The glass of water by my bed froze solid. One morning I noticed the sun shining through quite a large area of the wallpaper and realised that only the wallpaper was separating me from the outside elements.

In February I decided that it was time to go home. Four months of roughing it, especially in winter, was enough. I felt much more positive about myself and the future, although I did not have any serious thoughts about the direction I should take. The E-type was booked on the first available ship and I headed off to Colorado on my way home. Kathy, my American pen friend from when we were both nine years old, was waiting at the airport. Although we had never met we had regularly exchanged photographs from childhood to adulthood and written about our joys and sorrows. In fact we knew everything about each other. Immediately we recognised each other and for a week I had the pleasure of experiencing life in Denver and seeing the spectacular Colorado mountains. Then I left on the last leg of my journey back to Geelong.

Relatives and friends were waiting at home when I arrived from the airport, which gave me a sense of belonging. After all this time away I had mixed feelings about what the future held but knew that I wanted to find a worthwhile career. In some respects I felt that the past four years had been wasted. What I hadn't realised then was that all experiences, successes and failures, are valuable, and can contribute to a more balanced perspective on life.

Dad had been invited by Win McGuire, the former president of the Phillip Island Auto Racing Club (PIARC), to fly with him in a Cessna, piloted by his son John, to Phillip Island the following weekend. There was a spare seat and Dad insisted that I come along.

The circuit at Phillip Island had started to fall into disrepair and the club could not find the funds for an upgrade. It was bought by Len Lukey, whose racing exploits in a Ford Falcon saloon car and a Cooper Bristol single seater were well known in Australia. Lukey had an exhaust manufacturing enterprise with branches in every city and nearly every town in Australia and this gave him funds for the purchase.

A press day had been arranged so that the European drivers, who were in Australia for the Tasman series, could fly to Phillip Island on their way from Melbourne to Tasmania for the next race. The visit of motor racing celebrities was meant to help generate maximum publicity for the upgraded circuit and perhaps attract sponsorship.

Our own flight from Geelong, on this fine warm day, was without problems.

We landed in the centre of the circuit, just near the spot where we used to set up our camp. It was now a grass runway. To my utter surprise Graham Hill came running over and opened the door of the Cessna, jokingly acting as doorman. Jackie Stewart, Jim Clark and a number of Australian drivers soon joined us.

A reception had been staged near the new building and swimming pool. Everyone was driven there in a convoy of cars. I was one of the first to arrive, walking in with Jackie Stewart and Jim Clark. As we passed by the pool Jackie paused and, when Clark walked by, pushed him in, fully clothed! None of the press photographers had arrived and, camera in hand, I started clicking away enthusiastically. Jackie was highly amused at his actions and kept well away from the pool in case Clark reciprocated. When the photographers finally arrived all the fun had finished and I felt rather pleased that my pictures would be exclusive. At the reception I took yet more snaps.

The next day I took my films to the camera shop to be developed. It was difficult waiting two days before they would be ready. When I eventually went to pick them up I thought I must be having a nightmare. The shop owner said that both films had been duds and contained not even one photograph. I'd got the films in Fiji airport the week before and felt like going straight back there and strangling the person who sold them to me. Whether they really were duds or just ruined in processing I'll never know, but I can never forget the disappointment.

After the E-type arrived I travelled quite a lot, meeting up with my childhood friend Pamela Wade in Melbourne before we ventured further afield. It felt strange driving an exotic car in my home town, far removed from the Morris Minor. Now I didn't need to be first off at the traffic lights – in fact it might have been rather demeaning for a car of this class to be pitched against 'hot' Holdens and Fords, with loud sports type exhausts. The E-type, with its unpretentious soft purring sound, did not have to be proven to anyone.

I was not impressed with the reaction of some Australian drivers. Often on the dual carriageway, when I went to overtake, the driver in front blocked me. This I found quite frightening as I was usually travelling alone. Eventually I came to the conclusion that it must be sour grapes. A case of 'if I can't have one why should you?' Leaving the E-type parked gave me some anguish as well. There were many incidents reported of car paintwork being vandalised in the streets. Bottle tops were a favourite weapon. I started to think that the British were much more appreciative of interesting cars. In England people would often come and ask what the E-type was like to drive. Not so in Australia.

The grey E-type very quickly sold after its arrival in Australia. The new proud owner, from northern Victoria, informed us that he was used to driving fast cars as he owned a 'hot' Holden. Within five days of buying the car, he ran out of road, missing a corner on a country road, and the E ended up in three sections, engulfed in fencing wire. When we told Vern Schuppan, a fellow go-karter who was later to win Le Mans in a Porsche, he purchased the wreck and painstakingly rebuilt it.

My father was keeping himself busy with the restoration of a 1933 Morgan JAP three-wheeler he had purchased in England on one of his previous trips. It was totally stripped and, to start with, he built a new wooden frame. But then my parents began to talk of returning to England once again, this time for two years. Dad wanted to find and restore a pre-war straight eight cylinder car, possibly a Bugatti or Alfa Romeo. Before long the talking became serious and a decision was made. The family house and cars, except the Morgan, were all to be sold. The Morgan was to be finished in England. Dad's new 4.2 E-type was quickly sold, with very few miles on the speedo, not many more than 'running in' miles. My E went to the owner of a dry-cleaning business, but not before I had competed it at a sprint meeting at Calder Raceway, just out of Melbourne, and won the class. What surprised me was that I was presented with a silver trophy, engraved as well. At last, something to put on the mantelpiece – but just as the house was to be sold!

I felt rather lost, not knowing what to do. I kept asking myself whether I should return to England or stay in Australia? Then out of the blue I was offered a job in Melbourne. Paul England, Australian Hill Climb Champion, was expanding his crankshaft grinding and balancing business, moving from a small workshop to large purpose-built premises in North Melbourne, and I was to be the first receptionist.

It was emotional when the family house was eventually sold and we drove through the gates for the last time. This had been my home since I was ten, and now everyone was going in different directions, my parents to England and me to Melbourne. Memories came flooding back, happy and not so good. When life went wrong I always came running back to 6 Hermitage Road. For the first time, there would be no refuge.

My childhood friend Joan worked in Melbourne and commuted each day from Geelong. Her parents asked me to stay at their home and Joan and I began commuting together. Her fiancé was serving in Vietnam with the Australian Army. As we were both at a loose end, we spent weekends surfing and sizzling our fair skins in the hot sun, oblivious to the damage we might be inflicting on ourselves. After a few months, however, I did not want to outstay my welcome, winter was upon us and the length of time spent commuting each day started to bother me. A cheap bed and breakfast was found just opposite the beach in a suburb of Melbourne.

Work was fairly straightforward – typing, answering the phone, calculating the wages, greeting customers, nothing too taxing, even listening, grudgingly, to some of the male employees' marital problems.

Many of the customers were familiar faces, involved in motorsport when my father was competing. The owner of Dad's Cooper Mk 9 arrived one day supported by crutches. He had only driven the Cooper on two or three occasions and each time managed to crash, the last time breaking both legs. He couldn't get the hang of the power of the supercharged Norton engine.

Paul England was just finishing off his new hill climb special, a single seater, four-wheel drive, powered by two Volkswagen engines, each engine driving one pair of wheels. A number of people were sceptical of this project, but when the bugs were ironed out he was unbeatable and won the 1972 Australian Hill Climb Championship.

Before setting up his own business Paul was employed by Repco Research at the start of the Formula 1 Repco engine project. His engineering abilities were supreme.

One customer from Sydney, five hundred miles away, rang regularly about progress on his various jobs. An Englishman, he had lived in Australia for some years, accumulating a collection of cars and clocks. Every year he returned to England to drive his supercharged Bentley in vintage races and hill climbs. I had heard of Jumbo Goddard's eccentricities and when I first met him his trousers were held up by rope and his feet were clad in tartan slippers. 'Very comfortable for driving in,' he said.

In conversation he told me he owned a D-type Jaguar, among other cars. Most likely he grasped that I was a Jaguar fanatic. It would be difficult not to notice. Several months later as I looked up from typing, there, pulling up outside, was a D-type Jaguar. That was quite a rare sight, especially in Australia. Jumbo had driven it five hundred miles just to show me. I felt very honoured.

My social life became rather hectic, from meeting people involved in motorsport and from the twice-weekly Italian evening classes that I attended. Quite by chance, one evening as I was taking my clothes to a laundrette, I noticed Reno Benassi in a small Italian restaurant, opened just a few months previously. Reno, who we met when he worked on the rebuilding of The Black Stump, was now a restaurateur. I became a regular customer, after evening class, so I could further practise my faltering Italian.

Several people I knew had studied Italian at Perugia in Umbria, home of Università per Stranieri (University for Foreigners). Since our trip to Italy, my desire to learn Italian had not diminished. I came to the conclusion that to learn properly I needed to be totally immersed in the language, without knowing anyone who could interpret. Of course that meant living in Italy.

After a year in Melbourne I had managed to save a good proportion of my salary. Deep down I was beginning to feel that I wasn't achieving anything. What I wanted to achieve I didn't know, but a job, socialising and spectating at hill climbs just wasn't enough.

Time to uproot again. The destination, England, and possibly Italy. Rather than fly, I wanted to retrace the trip via Tahiti and the Panama Canal. The *FairSky*, the ship in which we had returned to Australia in 1959, was following that exact route. Once again I set sail for England.

Chapter 5

LONE TREK TO PERUGIA

Learning Italian and self-reliance

O n board the *FairSky* I was treated like royalty. Some of the crew from nine years earlier were still working on the ship. Noticing that I was travelling alone this time, the stewards paid me unexpected attention. Every time I walked into the main bar a seat was reserved at the bar and, before I could utter a word, a nice cup of cappuccino was placed in front of me. As I started to meet other passengers the jokes about this special treatment caused much amusement.

An elderly Mancunian couple, Albert and Mabel, took me under their wing. Returning to England after several years in Australia, they were slightly at odds with one another. Mabel wanted to remain in Australia but Albert preferred his homeland. For six weeks Mabel poured her heart out. I felt so sorry for her. I told them about the fascinating twenty-four hours we had previously spent in Tahiti and, when the ship arrived there this time, asked them to join me in a taxi ride round the Island.

As we disembarked, the Polynesian girls placed leis and shell necklaces over our heads. Albert was lapping up all the attention. Suddenly, out of the crowd emerged John, the taxi-driver.

'Come on, I'll show you round the sights again,' he called out.

I asked him what the cost would be, but there was no reply – he just grabbed my hand and started leading me to the car. Albert and Mabel thought they were witnessing a kidnap! The first port of call was the new airport. After parking the car we followed John into the terminal. To me it looked like any small airport building, but he felt so proud that Tahiti had progressed into the twentieth century. Nine years earlier, entry to Tahiti was only by sea and tourism had not really started.

As I was becoming interested in environmental issues I felt rather shocked at seeing tarmac and modern European buildings where once tropical trees and plants had thrived. That was just the beginning. Hotels were now built down to the water's edge and construction sites were everywhere, providing evidence of the power of the dollar. The price of a glass of tropical fruit juice was now exorbitant. Local snack bars had been replaced by sophisticated restaurants. The small hotel where we'd previously enjoyed our evening out was now a large European-type building. John took us to the centre of Papeete, the capital, and into the telephone exchange where we met his wife, who was a telephone operator. That, anyway, was not state-of-the-art. It was fascinating to watch the Polynesian women taking and transferring calls from around the Island, and the world, via this antiquated system.

Papeete to me appeared rather tacky. I often wondered what the Island was like before Captain James Cook and his crew arrived in 1777, and before the French colonists had started building.

The ship was scheduled to sail at 7pm, denying us a night of Tahitian dancing and entertainment. On the way back to the quay we visited John's house where he piled us high with jars of jam made by his wife from local tropical fruit. I took these to England and none of the family had ever tasted such exquisite jam on our breakfast toast before.

When we arrived at the ship I asked John how much we owed him for the day's outing. Expecting the bill to be high, I held my breath.

'It's free,' John replied.

We all argued, but he was adamant.

'You'll offend me if you give me any money. I have enjoyed showing you Tahiti.'

From early morning to late afternoon he spent with us without charge.

The three of us were rendered speechless. It was an emotional farewell. We waved until the ship had passed through the coral atoll and the people were just dots in the distance. I wasn't sure if I was as determined to return to Tahiti again. Should there be a next time, then I would like to visit more of the Polynesian Islands, particularly those without an airport.

The remainder of the voyage was one long party, swimming and lying in the sun all day and socialising for half the night. As we got closer to England the weather began to deteriorate. The sky was grey at Southampton. A drought had gripped Melbourne for nine months before I left. It was almost pleasant to feel rain beating on my face again – the novelty soon wore off, however. On board there was sadness as we bade farewell, but a group of us promised to meet in one month's time at the Overseas Visitors Club in London.

My parents were waiting at the docks as I disembarked and we headed off in the two-door Ford Falcon that Dad had brought from Australia, to the Rainey home at Wix Hill, West Horsley, Surrey. Wix Hill was just seven houses surrounded by fields. As a city girl I wondered how I could survive in such an isolated place, without all the choices for entertainment.

The restoration of the Morgan three-wheeler had been completed and Dad took me for a run up the road. What an amazing machine! My preconceived ideas of the handling characteristics of a car with just one rear wheel were quite wrong. I feared that, when cornering, the Morgan would feel unstable and perhaps topple over. It cornered as if on rails.

Soon I started looking for transport of my own. I was looking for a sports car, as it would be easy to get in and out of. In Guildford I found a six-month-old Triumph Spitfire Mk 2 and purchased it. This was not comparable to an E-type but at least it was low. The switches and gadgets were all within reach and I could easily lift the bonnet and reach the engine when maintenance was required. It was ideal for my needs at the time – easy to park and to wash, plus a nippy little 1,300cc engine.

To keep occupied I travelled quite a lot in the Spitfire, visiting friends from years back, but I couldn't dispel my desire to go to Italy to study the language. After much agonising I applied to the 'Università per Stranieri' for a three-month language course, from October to December. My parents were not too pleased about me travelling alone to a foreign country, especially as I couldn't yet speak Italian, and I must admit deep down I was rather apprehensive.

'What do you want to learn Italian for?' my father kept asking. 'You won't have any use for the language even if you do learn to speak it.'

Perhaps he was right! Eventually the acceptance arrived and no one could persuade me not to go. I was very determined. In the meantime it was time for the Overseas Visitors Club meeting. Rather curious to see if anyone from the ship turned up I was surprised to find about twenty people waiting at the bar. Jenny and Barbara, two Melbourne girls, were there. Both had been accepted for the prestigious cordon bleu cookery course in London, and this evening had brought along a friend from Melbourne who had been away for over a year. Pat Anderson and I hit it off immediately. Neither of us was interested in cooking or table etiquette and we drifted off to talk about other things. Pat was secretarial temping in London to save money for her next trip. We arranged to meet in London the following week for a theatre night. Until my departure for Italy, two or three times a week I travelled the 35-minute train trip from West Horsley to London where we saw just about every major theatre production, our seats the cheapest, always in the 'gods'.

The distance from West Horsley to Perugia was about 1,200 miles: quite a long trek alone. It was a relief to find I could transport the car from Boulogne to Milan on an overnight train. After an emotional family farewell, the ferry crossing over the English Channel and loading the car onto the train, I sank back in the carriage compartment and started to wonder why I had been so determined to go. For the first time in my life, there would be no familiar face waiting to meet me at the destination. I was overcome with fear. If the clock could be turned back, I would choose not to go.

Just as I was beginning to think that I was lucky enough to have the small compartment all to myself, in through the sliding door entered a large, well-dressed Mediterranean-looking gentleman, aged in his early sixties. It turned out that he was Italian, a Dover hotel owner on his way to Milan to visit relatives. He couldn't believe that I was off to Perugia to learn the language and became quite concerned about me driving the 350-mile trip without a companion. Perhaps he thought I was helpless or maybe he hadn't met many independent females before? I was, of course, feeling quite vulnerable but I tried to project self-assurance and confidence in what I was doing. In the morning he opened a hamper filled with every imaginable delicacy, that he was taking to give his family, and packed a hearty lunch for me to eat on my travels.

After being directed to a route that would avoid the early morning traffic I headed for Perugia. On the train I had repeatedly rehearsed the techniques for driving on the 'wrong' side of the road. Every conceivable situation had been practised. At a roundabout do everything in the opposite direction. Always think right not left. At the first roundabout, not far from the railway station, I momentarily paused, then carried on, leaving the roundabout to my left, not my right. Soon my confidence started to increase and in no time the Spitfire and I were speeding south on the Autostrada del Sole.

Travelling at a steady 70 to 80mph I had calculated that arrival time at Perugia should be about lunchtime or just after, which would be ideal as I had to find accommodation before the end of the day. Not many miles out of Milan a car overtook me, full of Italian men, then when in front they slowed down forcing me to overtake. They were waving and gesticulating and I started to feel frightened. Wondering how to handle the situation I decided to completely ignore them and hope they would get fed up with the game. After several overtaking moves I kept looking ahead impassively as though they did not exist. After a while they got bored and sped off into the distance. Just a few miles on, another car appeared with similar antics. Perhaps the locals weren't used to blonde girls driving sports cars! Whatever the reason, I was feeling intimidated and convinced myself that, without any doubt, I would be back in England within a week – another failure to add to my list.

By early afternoon the Spitfire and I reached the outskirts of Perugia. As we wound our way through the picturesque mediaeval streets, I saw the Università per Stranieri and was lucky to find a parking place fairly quickly. The Università was easy to spot. I'd seen photographs and the building was relatively modern compared to other buildings in Perugia. Built in the Baroque style as the Palazzo Gallenga in 1740, it was the residence of the noble Antinori family for many years. Just across the road was a 2,000-year-old Etruscan arch, forming part of the old walled city. I felt in awe as I walked through the impressive marble arches into the entrance hall of the University, with its eighteenth and nineteenth century frescoes, paintings and stained glass windows.

The accommodation office was closed. I'd forgotten all about siesta from 12 to 4pm and didn't want to waste three hours just hovering about waiting. I was hoping to find somewhere to stay on the outskirts of the town, where parking would be easier. I also wanted a place with no other English-speaking foreigners in the household so that I would be forced to speak Italian all the time.

Feeling quite bewildered, I stood at the door of the office wondering what to do next, when a German girl, speaking English, asked if she could help. When I explained my predicament she suggested taking me to the Secretary of the University, in his office upstairs. As we knocked on the very ornate tall doors a bespectacled man answered and informed us it was not his job to find accommodation. I explained that I was looking for a room on the outskirts of the town. He replied, 'rooms are hard to find, I can give you one address but it is near the central Piazza so you had better take it.'

The German girl, accompanying me to act as interpreter, and I, arrived at a small apartment. The spare room was actually part of a hallway, with a single bed placed on one side. Round the bed a curtain had been hung to give the impression of privacy. All the traffic to every room would need to pass by this bed. I was horrified at the lack of privacy, but was told that there was no alternative accommodation. My desire to return to England was being reinforced. I knew I could only stay here for one or two days. Just as the financial terms were being explained to me the telephone rang and I was given a message to return to see the Secretary immediately.

'What now?' I thought. 'Have I done something wrong?'

The anxiety must have shown on my face. As I entered the office once again, the Secretary was reassuring.

'I have remembered a woman with several rooms at Monteluce, about two kilometres away, on the way to the hospital. I've spoken to her and she has a room available with space for the car as well. If you are interested I'll call her and say that you will come down now.'

'Yes please.'

Feeling much better, I looked around the extremely large room as the Secretary telephoned and noticed a young chap at another desk filling in a form.

'What part of Australia do you come from?' asked the stranger.

'Geelong.'

'I'm from Sydney. My name's Denis, what's yours?'

What a surprise! A fellow countryman. Suddenly I didn't feel so isolated.

Denis, who already had a room organised, offered to come with me and unload the car.

La Signora Luccarelli was waiting outside as we pulled up at the end of Via delle Clarisse, a very narrow cul-de-sac cut into the side of a steep hill. Numero 24 was a block of pre-war flats, five stories high, all owned by her. The Luccarellis lived on the ground floor and let out two rooms to students. When the old lady from the first floor flat had died a few years earlier, Signora decided to turn all the rooms into bedrooms for letting to students. Even the kitchen was in the process of being converted to a bedroom.

My room in the first floor apartment was enormous and grand, with a magnificent view down the hill over the exquisite tiled roofline of the small houses below, to the green hills and olive groves in the distance. What a contrast to the previous room. My mind started to change: perhaps I wouldn't start driving back to England tomorrow.

Signora Luccarelli was aged in her seventies and dressed in black, with grey hair pulled back into a bun. She spoke no English and, using the little Italian I knew, I enthusiastically agreed to stay, and paid for one month's rent in advance, as required.

Oh well, I thought, I'm now committed to stay for a bit! La Signora cooked a meal every evening for those who required one and I signed up for one month. Denis was quite impressed with my digs, commenting that he wished he had found the room before I did, as it was ten times better than his.

Denis and I decided to walk into the centre to explore. As we were about to enter the central Piazza Quattro Novembre, an attractive girl stopped us to ask for directions to the Università. That was Sandra, another Australian, from Melbourne.

The first day of lectures Sandra and I were assigned to Professore Baratti and Denis to Professore Lorenzo. The classes were enormous, about 100 students, of every age group and nationality conceivable, all with the same aim, to learn the Italian language.

I was under the impression that a class so large could not be successful and might be boring. The Melbourne evening classes I had attended were quite monotonous – but in just twenty

ABOVE LEFT *The SS1 with my mother, Norma, and me posing on the bonnet.*

ABOVE RIGHT *My first set of wheels – a British-manufactured tricycle with pneumatic tyres.*

BELOW *The Wylie Car, my father's first racing car. That's me in the driver's seat, fantasising about becoming a racing driver.*

ABOVE LEFT *My father, Murray, in his Jaguar XK120, just after he finished converting the car to a fixed-head coupé, before the factory version was introduced.*

LEFT *Dad, in the XK120 leading an XK140, at the start of the 1958 Geelong Speed Trials.*

ABOVE *Dad's second racing car, the Cooper Mk 4 JAP, competing at Templestowe Hill Climb, near Melbourne, in 1954.*

RIGHT *The Cooper Mk 4, just before it was sold. My friend Joan and I used to push the car up the hill, hop in and coast down the road, then turn sharp left into the drive, trying not to brake.*

Above left *Dad's Cooper Mk 9 outside the Cooper Car Company after its front-end rebuild with independent suspension. Charles (left) and John Cooper pose with my father.*

Above right *One of my first go-kart races at Geelong.*

Below *The Rainey Kart that Dad made for me, and his Cooper Mk 9.*

My first race outside Geelong, at Dandenong. One of the most exciting races I have ever driven, and I only came second.

The Triumph Spitfire Mk 2, just before I took the car to Italy for nine months.

ABOVE LEFT *The 1968 Morris Minor that performed so reliably, through Europe and Morocco, loaded to the hilt with camping gear and four Australians. That's Pat Anderson and me fooling around for the camera.*

ABOVE RIGHT *The television celebrity Leslie Crowther still smiling after I took him for a ride in our 1933 Morgan three-wheeler.*

BELOW *Captain George Eyston, land world speed record holder, recounting some of his exploits to friends Brian Maxwell-Muller, Paul Finn, my father and me.*

The Brooklands Society track clearers, dressed up in their finery for the 1974 annual dinner. That's John Wall, the clearers' organiser, kneeling next to me at the front.

Dad driving the 1933 Morgan three-wheeler at the Coppa Monza in 1970. Unbelievably, crash helmets weren't mandatory in practice.

The three Raineys loading the Morgan three-wheeler on to the trailer at Monza after the flywheel came loose during the race.

Taking Dad for my first drive in the Morgan.

My first competition in England – a sprint at Gaydon in the Morgan.

My favourite car – 1970 Jaguar E-type FHC, Series 2, which I still have.

Competing at Shelsley Walsh in the Jaguar E-type in 1975.

My first drive at Prescott Hill Climb in the Dastle twin-cam, in 1977.

minutes on that first day in Perugia we covered all the language that I had spent months practising at home.

Far from being boring, Professore Barratti was amazing. An entertainer who kept us all captivated and amused while he so brilliantly recounted his life through mime, gesture and simple language, interjected by amusing stories of the problems foreigners encounter before they can understand the language. We saw hilarious, skilful demonstrations, complete with props, of how not to eat spaghetti, we heard how his wife had died and, with three children to bring up, he employed an American nanny, called Guilia.

Guilia became the love of his life. He adored her, showering her with gifts and affection. With great emotion we heard how Guilia was not sure if she wanted a permanent involvement and returned home. Heartbroken, our Professore found difficulty coping with life, packed in his job and headed for the US. Without much knowledge of the English language he could not find a job. Guilia had found another amorante and our dejected Professore returned to Perugia to rebuild his life. Il Professore brought tears to our eyes with his performances, had us laughing uncontrollably, and all the time we were learning. Such brilliance!

After the first week of lectures I couldn't wait for the second week to begin. If this was hard work then I was enjoying every second of it. It was like being personally involved in a fascinating performance, every day. When morning lectures finished at midday, Sandra, Denis and I explored all the trattorias and cafés for lunch. Before leaving for Italy I had been determined not to socialise with Australians or any other English-speaking student, such was my wish to immerse myself fully into the Italian language. Now it did not seem important anymore.

After cena in the evening I retired to study in my room. Some evenings, after finishing her chores Signora Luccarelli came up to talk to me. She patiently picked objects in the room and constructed simple sentences, then questions, forcing me to speak.

'Questa è una lenzuola' (this is a sheet).

'Queste sono lenzuole' (these are sheets).

'Quale sono queste' (what are these)?

'Faccio il letto' (I am making the bed).

About the third night of my stay Signora brought some visitors to my room. The handsome male was Dr. Sandro, a newly qualified doctor from Perugia's Medical College, and his parents. Sandro used to live in the room next to mine while he was studying and was just returning for a month while he finished off some project. Keen to practise his limited English, although it was much better than my Italian, he said, 'Joy, you have really bella fur'!

Although there was just one bathroom to service the five bedrooms, I hardly ever saw the other occupants, apart from Dr. Sandro. One day I noticed the door open on the room two doors from mine. It was just a small room but appealed to me as it had a large window opening onto a balcony. With such a magnificent view I fancied the option of walking onto the balcony instead of being cooped up inside.

The occupant was a French girl called Sylvia. I had only caught a fleeting glance of her. Signora informed me that she would be there for another six months so I gave up hope of moving. Several nights later I was awoken by screams that went on for some minutes. Feeling too frightened to go rushing out, I found it hard to determine whether the screams had come from outside or inside. In the morning no-one mentioned any strange happening and I began to wonder if I'd had a bad dream.

The next evening when I arrived home from University, Signora informed me that I could move into the small room as it had suddenly become available. Feeling rather pleased, I moved my belongings in. When Signora came to visit later I asked her what had happened to Sylvia. With my very, very basic knowledge of Italian I gathered that Sylvia had been besotted with the handsome Dr. Sandro for some time.

Whether he returned the same desires I could not grasp, but I don't think so.

When he came in the previous evening, Sylvia had been standing at the top of the stairs, naked, with a knife in her hand, threatening to slash her wrists if he forsook her. I never managed to hear the full details of the story, but Dr. Sandro reappeared a couple of weeks later and Sylvia was never to be seen again. 'Returned to France,' I was told. Oh well! I certainly enjoyed my new room.

On waking every morning I opened the wooden shutters and stepped out on to the balcony to soak up the glorious atmosphere. On the right, up the hill, La Chiesa di San Pietro could be seen. On clear mornings, on the left one could just see Assisi. Che magnifico! Before long the people from the flats above started to speak from their balconies.

'Buon giorno signorina, che bella giornata.'

'Ah, buon giorno signora, si e bella.'

Some mornings I drove the Spitfire to University, but finding a parking space proved difficult and increasingly I walked. The October days were beautiful, warm and sunny. With the distinctive sounds of the Lambrettas, the Fiat Cinquecentos and the chaos on the roads, there could be no mistaking what country this was. So uniquely Italy!

After a month I was beginning to be a little more confident about speaking my new language, but I felt too much time was spent communicating in English with Denis and Sandra. Sandra's parents were Italian and, although the family had always spoken English at home in Melbourne, she grasped the language much quicker than Denis or me, which sometimes dented our self-belief.

A four-day Saints Festival was held at the beginning of November. The three of us were planning a break in Venice but at the last minute I decided not to go. My time would be better spent here, studying and speaking Italian. With my textbooks spread across the bed on the Saturday morning, hard at work, I heard la Signora knock on the door.

At the Saints Festival, a market was set up on the outskirts of Perugia. La Signora asked me to drive her there. What a good way to practise, I thought. There were many stalls with clothing, local food and delicacies from Umbria, embroidery, carvings, such a vast array of objects and produce. Signora was in her element, rifling through the products on every stall. But how embarrassed I felt! I'd never experienced bartering like this before. Raised voices, arms flying everywhere, la Signora stomping off the particular stall in a huff, only to be almost dragged back, supposedly unwillingly, by the stallholder. Unbelievable circus! At times I thought la Signora was going to land a punch on the stallholder's face. In amazement I watched as she eventually paid for the goods at the price she originally offered and shook hands as though they were friends for life. Then the whole bartering process started all over again at the next stall.

At the end of the day I felt exhausted just watching this spectacle, but less embarrassed, as I'd got used to the routine. Next day I headed back to the market alone to shop for Christmas presents for the family. Using the same bartering techniques as la Signora, but probably not as dramatic, I ended up with some fantastic bargains and compliments about my use of the language. Above all, my confidence received a big boost and from then on I was never shy when trying to express myself in that very musical language. Apparently I was even using my hands in an expressive Italian way now when speaking.

A few days after I moved into my new room, a student arrived and rented the converted kitchen. Katrina, aged just seventeen, came from California. After spending several months travelling round Greece, all alone, she decided to learn Italian. The peace of our apartment changed immediately. Katrina liked to spend hours in the bathroom and, when she left it, the place was like a swimming pool. Hearing la Signora uttering very expressive Italian words at rather a high and excitable pitch, I thought a murder had been committed. Katrina became la Signora's target for anything that was out of order. But no matter how much she screamed at Katrina the bathroom was always an absolute mess after her use.

My room became a meeting place. Often I'd arrive home to find Katrina or Denis or other people from University waiting there. Social life was hectic, with invitations from the occupants of the flats above for afternoon café or Sunday pranza. None of them spoke English so my new language improved in leaps and bounds.

When I drove the Spitfire round town, quite often I was tailed by another driver. This I found rather annoying. I did not want to give away the address of my digs so drove hard round the back streets until I threw off my pursuer. I got to know Perugia well. One evening on my way back to Via delle Clarisse, a car started following but, after trying every trick in my book, I was unable to shake it off. Eventually, as the traffic lights changed I managed to get ahead of the traffic and the car became caught up and I disappeared. Denis and Katrina were waiting as I arrived home in rather an annoyed state.

'I'm fed up with being followed just about every time I go out.'

Denis decided to come out with me to prevent any further problems. He donned one of Katrina's large floppy felt hats so that he looked like a female. Just two streets away a Fiat sports car started following. To make sure we weren't imagining things, I drove fast up some of the narrow streets. Sure enough, right behind came the Fiat. After quite a spectacular drive we headed down Via delle Clarisse to the end and switched off the engine. The Fiat parked nearby and as the two male occupants eagerly emerged, Denis sprang from the Spitfire, throwing the felt hat off at the same time. When they saw he was a man and not the gorgeous foreign girl they were expecting, they rushed to get back into the Fiat, reversing as rapidly as they were able, while Denis taunted them about their heroism and masculinity.

My driving style suited the conditions in Italy. I hadn't been in England long enough for the Australian aggression to ameliorate. Here the rude gestures and comments were appropriate and given plenty of use. The route from the University to home went down a street and in through another Etruscan arch where two other roads entered into the main road. Not once was I able to enter freely into the main road. No one would give way and, nearly every time, the traffic on the main road came to a standstill, with horns blowing and hands waving. There was always chaos. I used to think that if only one person would give way then the traffic could start flowing. But, when it came to motoring, fair play and tolerance did not seem to be part of the local culture. Even at pedestrian crossings the drivers would not stop unless they were about to hit someone. I must admit that while driving the Spitfire I employed the same techniques. But when the roles were reversed, I took great precautions and wouldn't step on to a road until there were absolutely no cars in sight.

After a month, when the rent for my room became due, I decided not to pay for cena at la Signora's but instead sample the small cafés and trattorias dotted round Perugia, often with friends. Life had certainly taken on a new meaning. My confidence as a member of the human race started to rise. Without knowing one person, or the language, on arrival in Perugia, I now found that every minute of the day was fully occupied interacting with people. The contrast was enormous from just a year or two before, when I felt right at the bottom of the social heap.

There was so much to do. I found that seeing the Palazzo Comunale, built between 1293 and 1297, and the amazing collection of paintings and sculptures belonging to the National Gallery of Umbria, and the collection of paintings by Pietro Perugino and his pupils in the Collegio del Cambio, for the first time, was too overwhelming to grasp. But by living in the town and making countless visits to art collections, churches and buildings, I started to understand and to feel extremely grateful that I had the opportunity to experience such culturally rich treasures.

There was so much to explore round Perugia that it was some time before we had any desire to venture outside. Our first trip was to Assisi, just 12 miles away.

With just two seats in the Spitfire, Denis gallantly offered to squeeze in the back. Thereafter he was stuck with that position as Sandra refused point blank to travel anywhere unless she was in front.

Assisi was the birthplace of both St. Francis, founder of the Franciscan order, and St. Clare, who started the religious order known as the Poor Clares. The town has such narrow, winding streets surrounded by mediaeval walls, that it is difficult for cars to pass, so we parked the Spitfire on the outskirts and walked in. Sandra had a fascination for the relationship between St. Francis and St. Clare. She was convinced that their association was more than just professional and we spent the day wandering around looking for evidence of a romance. Firstly, scrutinising frescoes by Giotto, Cimabue, Lorenzetti and Martini, in the lower church of the Basilica of San Francesco, where St. Francis is buried, then in the upper church – and not surprisingly, all the depictions were of highly moral and religious subjects. Despite examining the Basilica of Santa Chiara, the Cathedral and every church and convent building that we could visit, there was no startling evidence to support her theory. A fruitless exercise undoubtedly, but it provided a framework in which to analyse the fine art works and kept us intrigued for the day.

When a room became available at my apartment block, Sandra snapped it up, and before long Denis had moved in as well. 'Australia House' is what I started calling numero 24. Robyn and Margaret, two girls from Sydney who were in Denis's class, visited us regularly. Often the five of us, or more, went off in the evening, walking from Via delle Clarisse to the centre for cena and entertainment: 'Denis and his harem'. We all treated him like a little brother. Sometimes I wondered why he stuck around, but he must have liked it.

As we were all keen to learn the language we recognised that some of the socialising needed to be with Italians. Robyn and Margaret had Italian friends from the mainstream University, Denis had friends, and I visited the upstairs flats regularly. Sandra decided she would learn more Italian if she found a job. She applied to an agency for a nanny's job and almost immediately accepted a position in Rome. Denis and I were shocked. It dawned on us that the exciting life we were leading was limited, not for always, and we had just four weeks left.

On the stairway of the flats I quite often passed a large lady, possibly aged in her mid forties. At first she was not friendly but gradually she started speaking. One day she invited me to her flat for a cup of coffee. Silvana lived on the very top floor, sharing a tiny flat – one bedroom, kitchen, bathroom and sitting-room – with her mother, an even larger lady who always wore black. Silvana's brother was married to Signora Luccarelli's daughter and they lived in a very large apartment on the same fifth floor. I discovered later that there was no love lost between the two matriarchs, but that is another story.

This particular day I was let into the flat by both Silvana and her mother and told that I was the first foreigner who had visited them. I felt flattered until I discovered that neither of them liked foreigners. They seemed to lump all foreigners into one category regardless of their nationality. Most likely they meant non-Italian and if you were non-Italian then you must have defects. As they spoke rather quickly and in local dialect, I had to concentrate hard, but they appeared to be venting their frustration on me.

No foreigner they had met previously was worthy of an invitation to their casa, I heard. Foreigners were all dishonest. Foreign women were immoral. They had seen me going out at night with MEN. From this observation they had come to the conclusion I was immoral. Rather than listen to this harangue, I tried to explain that any male I had been seen with was most likely another student who was, like me, here in Perugia to study the language. There was no romance between us, just friendship.

'Solamente amici,' I kept repeating.

Guffaws from Silvana and snorts of disapproval from her mother.

'Men and women cannot be just friends,' I was informed.

'Oh how wrong you are,' I kept insisting.

Both of them seemed to believe that if a man and a woman were in a room all alone without the chaperone, then some uncontrollable forces would take over and, bingo, sordid behaviour was inevitable.

For a while I thought I was in cuckoo land. The women's attitude must be about 100 years behind what I was accustomed to. They couldn't seem to grasp that we foreigners living on the first floor respected each other as human beings, regardless of gender.

I couldn't wait to finish my coffee and get back to my room. But that wasn't the end. Perhaps they felt guilty. Next day when I arrived home there was a gift of Perugini chocolates left in my room and an invitation for Sunday pranza. I quickly said I had other arrangements. But the invitations kept coming, and eventually I went up for an evening meal. This time the conversation was less accusative and more welcoming and they appeared to want to hear what life was like in Australia. Perhaps this foreigner was becoming more acceptable?

Despite the fun we had in Perugia, now and again most of us suffered a short dose of homesickness. One day when I woke up I felt cheesed off so decided not to go to the University but to stay in bed, at least until lunchtime. During the late morning as I was dozing, Katrina came in.

'Gawsh, what are you still doing in bed? Why aren't you at Uni?' she asked, surprised.

'I'm fed up, can't be bothered going today,' I replied, 'and may I ask you the same question?'

'I'm also fed up.'

'What are we going to do about it?'

'How about driving the Spitfire out to Lago Trasimeno and I'll buy you a seafood lunch.' Katrina insisted.

Just 10 miles from Perugia, this was a fishing village lined with trattorias specialising in seafood dishes, and was a popular bathing resort in the summer. I had not yet been there. The lake covers an area of 49 square miles but is fairly shallow, its maximum depth only 20 feet. It was here, in 217BC, that the Roman army, led by Flaminius, was ambushed by Hannibal and his troops. A bloody battle took place and it is said that 15,000 Romans were killed and ended up in the lake, with Hannibal the victor.

We found a trattoria at the edge of the lake and settled into an impressive plate of local fish.

'I really miss walking along the beach every morning,' said Katrina. 'We live right on the beach in California.'

'I miss the beach too,' I said. 'Pity we are so far away from the coast here in Umbria.'

Katrina suggested we drive to the sea that afternoon and, although it was winter and would be dark in a couple of hours, and we had no map, she pleaded and, after pondering for a few seconds, I agreed.

'As we are about in the centre of Italy, would you prefer to go east or west?'

'You choose,' she said.

I decided on Viareggio, mainly because I had never been there and neither had Katrina.

'It'll be quite a long drive over the mountain roads, so we'll have to sleep in the car and travel back tomorrow.'

Off we headed in a westerly direction. There were many trucks on the narrow, winding mountain roads and progress was slow. It was quite late when we arrived and I felt tired. Parking right beside the water's edge we tried to get comfortable in the limited space of the Spitfire. Without any spare clothes, rugs or any covering we soon got cold.

'Let's find a hotel,' said Katrina.

'I hardly brought any money with me, seeing we were just going out for lunch.' I felt quite fed up at having agreed to this trip.

Katrina thought she had just about enough for a cheap room and we were lucky – out of season a hotelier was glad enough to rent a room at a bargain rate. In the morning, after sleep, I felt much less cynical about our jaunt and suggested that we continue travelling to San Remo, just near the French border. I had suddenly decided that I wanted to see Reno Benassi's father and step-mother. It was more than ten years since our family visit, I wanted to see them again, and this time I would be able to speak their language.

Katrina was enthusiastic, but first we had to pool our money. There was just enough for petrol to get us to San Remo and then back to Perugia, with one cheap meal thrown in. Oh well, you only live once, I thought. The scenery was spectacular as we sped along the mountainous coastal road. With very little traffic about, we managed to put the two hundred odd miles behind us, arriving about midday.

Like a replay of my first visit, la Signora Benassi had just placed the pot of water on the stove for the lunch-time spaghetti bolognese as we rang the front door bell. Both Papa and Mama Benassi were more than surprised to see me again, and now we could exchange news without the aid of an interpreter.

While we ate the spaghetti, Papa Benassi expressed his concern that I was about to drive all the way back to Perugia, after coming from Viareggio in the morning. He told me I was mad and suggested that we stay for a few days. The offer was tempting but I explained that we weren't on holiday. As we drove off, waving frantically, I couldn't help thinking he was right. Who in their right mind would drive more than 900 miles just to say 'buon giorno'?

The return trip seemed never-ending. My eyes felt irritated, as if someone had thrown sand in them. After by-passing Genoa in the early evening, we stopped for a while and spent our last few liras on snacks. With no money left there definitely was no alternative but to get all the way back to Perugia, and I'd already had enough of driving for the day. Perhaps it was the combination of determination and necessity but we arrived in Perugia at 5am. That day I had driven more than six hundred miles.

Walking through the main door of numero 24, I felt such a sense of relief that I suddenly acquired a 'second wind'. Noticing a key in the front door of la Signora's apartment, we went in and set about raiding her refrigerator, giggling like naughty children. Although we had sent her a telegram from Viareggio in case she got worried about our 'disappearance', I was woken first thing in the morning by her yelling and screaming at me. She couldn't believe that we set off on such a monumental trip without any prior planning and was upset that she had not been warned. No matter what Katrina or I said she would not be convinced that we had gone on the spur of the moment. Three days passed before la Signora started speaking to us.

Robbie and Margaret had introduced me to a small trattoria just near the mainstream University, patronised by Italian national students. Every lunchtime the three of us spent our four hours of siesta in conversation, debating many issues, all in Italian.

Several weeks before the end of our course a notice was displayed about a 'bridging course', to be held from the end of January to the end of March. The next main course for foreign students did not start until April. I decided to enrol for the new course and found a student flight from Rome to Luton for just £20, so I could return to England just for Christmas. Robbie and Margaret decided to stay in Perugia for the festivities and we planned a trip in the Spitfire to southern Italy when I returned from England in the first week of January. Denis booked a flight as well; he liked the idea of spending Christmas in England and wanted to purchase a car to continue his travels in.

Christmas in West Horsley was to be an all-Australian celebration. Joining the three Raineys were Jenny and Barbara, the 'cordon bleu' girls from Sydney, Barbara's brother newly arrived from Australia, and Denis. The weather was rather cold and miserable when we arrived home on Christmas Eve. Denis talked incessantly about wanting a white Christmas.

'You very rarely get any snow in this area at Christmas,' I told him with great authority.

At 9pm as I glanced out of the window I could not believe my eyes. It was snowing. The enormous snowflakes were settling quite rapidly. Denis had never seen snow before. I'd had one experience on my previous trip to England, but it was exciting for both of us. Running outside we behaved like kids, making snowballs to hurl at each other.

Waking early the following morning, I pulled back the curtains and there was a large snowman. Denis had spent until 3am building snowmen all round the outside of the house. What a crowd! By every window a snowman was standing. It was a wonderful white Christmas. I have not experienced one since.

The pleasurable two weeks in England passed quickly but I was keen to return to Italy to travel with Robbie and Margaret. The Spitfire performed magnificently, as we climbed mountain roads on our way to the south. Feeling confident about our ability to communicate, we enthusiastically tried to strike up conversations with the locals in Calabria, only to receive strange stares. They couldn't understand us and we couldn't understand them. In Perugia we were taught the pure form of the language and it sure was difficult to get to grips with the southern dialect.

Every night we stayed in first class hotels for cheap pensione prices. Our bartering techniques worked well. At that slack time of the year hotel managers were pleased to have some rooms occupied. From Salerno to Sorrento the scenery was breathtaking. The Spitfire was in its element following the road as it twisted and turned along the Amalfi coast. I'd seen films of famous people speeding around this unique road with views of the crystal blue sea below, spectacular rocky outcrops and tiny fishing villages in the distance. The sporty note of the Spitfire exhaust, bouncing back at us from the unusual rock formations, added to the amazing atmosphere. Feeling like film-stars we booked into the poshest hotel, perched on the side of a hill over-looking Sorrento. Although the air was chilly we sat outside on our private balcony with a bottle of local wine, admiring the view and saying how lucky we were.

Back in Perugia the new course started in a low-key fashion. Perhaps it was lacking the engaging personality of Professore Baratti. The new lecturer could not hold my attention for long, but lectures finished at midday and the rest of the day was spent in practical work or, to put it another way, socialising. Time passed so quickly that suddenly we had reached the end of this course too.

It was decision time: whether to enrol for the next course or return to England.

The new intake of foreign students had already started arriving in Perugia and I happily conducted people around to my favourite haunts and trattorias, but I couldn't decide whether to stay or not. I attended the new course for the first week without enrolling but still I kept agonising. I wanted to continue my studies but I also needed a break from the excitable Italian temperament – to experience some English calm.

As I was returning to Via delle Clarisse one afternoon, a Fiat Seicento started following. As usual I sped off in a different direction, trying to shake them off. This time I mistook one of the streets I turned left into: it was a cul-de-sac. Feeling quite frightened I turned the Spitfire round in the narrow space and was blocked by the Fiat. I stopped and stared impassively, hoping they would let me through. After no movement I wound down the window and, in a very controlled and confident way, asked if they would kindly let me through.

To my utter surprise they obliged.

That incident made up my mind. There was a weekly train service with car-carrying facility, from Milan to Paris and I immediately booked. This gave me just three days for the farewells. Leaving numero 24 for the last time, I cried profusely. Signora and some of the neighbours from the upstairs flats were standing waving as I drove off. Those past eight months had been one of the most satisfying, happy and interesting periods of my life. Above all, for the first time I felt independent and self-assured, well prepared to endure life's trials, whatever they might be.

Chapter 6

MORGAN AND MARRAKECH

A summer of travel, on three wheels and four

Life back in West Horsley couldn't have been more different from the carefree student days I'd enjoyed in Perugia. When I returned home at Christmas, Dad was still searching for his ideal straight eight vintage racer. I went with him to view what to me looked like a pile of bits on wheels but was in fact an 8C Alfa Romeo. He'd agonised for a while and then decided to purchase this, the intention being to restore it to its original glory.

To help finance such a major project Dad had returned to Australia and brought back three vintage cars to tidy up and sell on. A Fiat 501, an Ansaldo and an American car called a Gray now graced the garage space in a totally unrestored condition. I helped by cleaning, polishing and preparing the cars for resale and acted as general dogsbody. Several people involved with motorsport in Australia wanted racing bits sourced, which meant that a lot of my time was spent travelling about, collecting and packaging components. At night, I started to translate the 8C Alfa manual from Italian to English. This was a major project, as I'd not had experience with mechanical vocabulary and technical engineering terms, but the exercise certainly extended my knowledge of Italian.

One day I noticed an advertisement in the local paper wanting vintage car entrants for a concours d'elegance charity fund-raising event in Guildford and we decided to enter the Morgan three-wheeler. There were about seventy veteran and vintage cars of all makes and persuasions, lined up in different categories, nicely polished and shining. Our previous involvement with motor events had been racing – in other words, very active. To park next to other cars and wait around all day until a judge came to check on whether every nut and bolt was authentic seemed amusing. Other competitors appeared to take the competition more seriously, however. Plaques were given out at every event and some people arranged these on wooden shields that were placed in a prominent position for passers-by to see.

In the middle of the afternoon we had to parade our cars around an arena. It felt like a dog show, the only talent needed being the ability to avoid running into the car in front. I was sitting in the passenger seat next to my father who was managing to putt-putt at slower than walking pace without stalling the engine, when out of the crowd emerged a familiar figure, Andrew Cruickshank, who shook our hands with great enthusiasm. Andrew – a household name, from playing Dr. Cameron in the 1960s BBC television programme *Dr Finlay's Casebook* – was the invited celebrity.

At the end of the day, the entrants were waiting around to hear the results of the judging. Surprisingly, our Morgan won one of the classes. Walking to collect the prize from the famous actor, I couldn't believe my eyes. Handed to me was a silver trophy of medium size and a small plaque inscribed with the date and event. Passing this on to my father I acknowledged the hard work involved in restoring the Morgan – but the preparation put into the Cooper and Go-Kart had been every bit as arduous, and was never-ending. Furthermore, when racing you had to drive yourself and the car to the absolute limit – and even then, the trophies were smaller (and in my case, regrettably practical)!

We entered a number of similar events around Surrey, Hampshire, Berkshire and Sussex, all usually associated with fund-raising for good causes and sometimes part of an annual village fete. Most of the other competitors were a friendly bunch. Everyone took a picnic basket and we treated each event as a day out for a bit of a jolly, the exciting part being to drive the Morgan to and from the showground. Mostly we came home with a trophy or two and the mantelpiece at Meadow Cottage started to fill up well. Sometimes the judges did not like our Morgan, however. One judge at Windsor was highly critical of the restoration and failed the Moggy because the slots in two of the screws on the body panels were not in the same position as the others.

Now and then the local mayor presented the trophies, and would wander round in robe and chains, shaking hands with the competitors. But more often it was a celebrity who did the honours. Once, at Bisley, blonde bombshell Diana Dors was the guest. After the daylong activities were finished she had still not made an appearance and the trophy winners, including me, were hanging about waiting. One wag commented, 'she's probably visiting her husband in Wormwood Scrubs and we'll have to wait until visiting hours are over.' The amateur comedian kept us amused till eventually the star arrived, hopped out of her chauffeur-driven limousine, rapidly presented the trophies, then hopped straight back into the car and drove off.

Showbiz all-rounder Leslie Crowther treated his celebrity status more seriously. He arrived as the invited guest at a village fete in Sussex in the early afternoon and visited every stall, sampling the goodies and chatting to the stallholders. He appeared to be thoroughly enjoying himself. When it was time for the vintage and classic car owners, he was rather fascinated by the Morgan and kept bending down looking under the rear of the car, much to the amusement of the crowds.

'What's it like to drive with just three wheels?' he inquired.

I told him that it was really quite stable.

'Fancy a spin up the road?'

'Yes please,' he replied, 'but are you sure it won't topple over?'

Off we drove as he waved to the cheering crowds.

After so many concours d'elegance events, Dad must have had a hankering for some real competition. When he read about the 'Coppa Monza' in Italy he applied for regulations and entered. The annual event, then in its eleventh year, was held at the

Monza circuit in Italy, and consisted of a series of races for vintage cars. It was a year since my return home from Perugia and I felt rather excited at the prospect of being in Italy again.

My father had another purpose in going to Milan. With the restoration of the Alfa Romeo 8C well under way, he had been corresponding with the Alfa designer, Cavaliere Luigi Fusi. Fusi had retired and was now the Alfa Romeo historian, in the process of setting up an Alfa Romeo Museum at Arese, just outside Milan.

Fusi had provided Dad with the blueprint of every component, chassis and part that he required for the re-build of the 8C. Dad had submitted a design of what he thought the body should look like and Fusi validated this. With so much correspondence to and from Italy, my involvement was as the translator. When a letter from Fusi arrived, my father wanted the contents to be understood straight away: anything I was involved with at the time was to be immediately dropped. When Fusi heard my father was competing at Monza he arranged to come out to the circuit for the event.

With just two seats in the Morgan and three of us Raineys, the Morgan was to be trailered to Monza behind the Ford Falcon. In any case, there was a tendency for the flywheel to become loose on the Morgan, which meant that after several events it had to be towed home. A 2,000-mile round trip with that threat didn't seem attractive, but Dad thought he had cured the problem and a race or two round Monza shouldn't be problematic.

We crossed France in just one day, sleeping the first night in the Falcon in Switzerland, my mother and father on the layback front seats and me in the large boot compartment, with the boot lid partially open so that the fresh mountain air could circulate.

Passing over the border into Italy I almost felt I was coming home.

We found a hotel, quite by accident, right beside Lake Como and booked in. Both our rooms overlooked the water and the view was stupendous. In the restaurant that night I happily chatted away in Italian to anyone who was willing to talk. Then it was an early morning start, to arrive at Monza for the day's activities.

Entering the paddock area, we were amazed to see the number of participating cars – veterans and vintage as well as classics, giving a spread of years from the early 1900s to late 1950s. There was a very international flavour with entrants from England, France, Germany and Switzerland, although of course the majority were Italian. Dad was excited to see a few Alfa Romeos. For the past year, his whole life had centred on the re-build of his 8C. To meet Count Johnny Lurani, a famous Alfa driver of the thirties, also competing here, was an unexpected bonus.

As we unloaded the Morgan from the trailer, quite a crowd gathered. Some were laughing, saying that it must be a special. Using my best Italian I explained that the Morgan was not a 'speciale' but a well-known English marque – indeed, that the factory now made four-wheeled cars and had a two-year waiting list for these. Of course, some people had heard of Morgans, but no one was familiar with the original version.

A number of practice sessions were held in the morning and the proper event was in the afternoon after a formal lunch provided by the organisers. Before my father ventured on to the track, I went to the pit stand to watch some of the other competitors practising. I was astounded to see cars lapping – some of the drivers without crash helmets. Crash hats had been mandatory in both my father's and my own experience in competition. But the biggest surprise was to see passengers in the competing cars, both in the front seat and rear seats of the bigger cars. As soon as I had noticed the passengers, I hotfooted it back to my father and told him the news.

'So,' he said.

'Well may be I can be a passenger with you in the Morgan?'

'Oh all right, go and see what the organisers say,' he conceded.

As quick as a flash I was in the organiser's office and in the politest Italian I could muster, I asked if I could be a passenger with my father.

'No problem, signorina.'

Rushing back, I arrived just in time as Dad was getting ready to go out for the practice session. I hopped in. Soon we were lapping Monza. I felt so excited as we came to sections of the circuit that for many years I had seen photos of, but never thought I'd have the opportunity to experience in real life. I'd not been in the Morgan before, being driven at ten tenths. It was impressive the way it hung on to the corners. Other sports cars didn't corner any faster than us. Father appeared to be enjoying every minute of every inch of the circuit, and so was I.

Practice wasn't timed and we were allowed to go out as often as we liked. The next time I took the movie camera with me. Dad dropped me off on an interesting part of the circuit and while he lapped, I filmed. After several laps he stopped and picked me up. We'd not experienced such laid-back organisation before. This was of course great fun, but I couldn't condone it from the safety point of view. Luckily there were no incidents. If there had been they might have been very serious.

After practice, we all went to the dining room. A fantastic three-course lunch was served, along with as much red and white wine as everyone could consume. I found this more than unbelievable. In Australia, no alcoholic beverages were allowed anywhere near the paddock area at a motor racing event, and if a driver had been caught drinking any alcohol he would be just about hung, quartered and strung up – or in reality banned from driving.

Yet here at Monza many of the drivers were drinking heavily. Dad didn't partake. As I was only a passenger it wouldn't have mattered if I'd had some wine but it tends to make me drowsy and I was enjoying myself so much I didn't want to ruin the pleasure.

None of the English competitors had much knowledge of the Italian language so I found myself interpreting for them when any difficulty arose. Just after we arrived I had noticed an elderly gentleman walking past who was dressed in lederhosen (leather shorts with bib), a hat with small brim and feathers stuck in the band and long socks with feathers. He also sported a long drooping moustache. I wasn't familiar with national costumes and wondered if he was Austrian, German or Swiss. I kept noticing him all morning and felt rather surprised at being placed next to him at the dining table. When I heard him struggling to make himself understood by the Italian waiter, I asked if I could help. Imagine my surprise when I discovered he was an Englishman. This was Bunty Scott-Moncrieff, vintage car enthusiast and wheeler-dealer from Stafford or, as he was officially known, David Scott-Moncrieff & Sons, Purveyors of Horseless Carriages to the Nobility and Aristocracy. What an entertaining lunch it was, listening to all the stories of this amateur showman.

Soon it was time for the really exciting part, the races. The organisers came over and said that if I was to be a passenger then I had to wear a crash helmet. One of the English competitors said I could borrow his, as we were in different races. Then, just before our race, we were told that the Morgan had to run with the veteran and vintage motorcycles. The reason given was that, with its three wheels, the Morgan would not corner as fast as cars on four wheels and might therefore be a hazard.

I went to the organiser's office and argued that the Morgan could certainly corner as well as four-wheeled vehicles and indeed that motorbikes would be a hazard to us as they could not corner anywhere near as fast. This must have sounded convincing as we were allowed to run with the cars, but had to start on the back of the grid.

The Morgan was placed about twenty yards behind the last row of the grid and Dad was instructed to keep right on the inside of the track to allow the cars to overtake when we were 'lapped'. The instructions almost seemed insulting at the time, as if it was a forgone conclusion that we would be lapped. Waiting for the start, Dad managed to sneak right up close to the cars in front and when the flag was dropped, we were away, overtaking a number of them before the first corner. My heart was pumping for all its worth. By the first corner we were in third position, but on the back straight we were overtaken by an MG TC. We then out-braked him going into the corner before the main straight and overtook him again. Entering into the straight the TC overtook us once more. As we drew level with the grandstands, we could hear the crowds cheering. I held up my arms in acknowledgement and the cheers got louder.

The atmosphere was infectious. Going into the corner before the back straight Dad once again out-braked the TC and overtook him. Even the marshals on the back of circuit started to wave. Just like a replay, going into the main straight the TC overtook us. By now the crowds were standing and cheering and I couldn't help waving again, which raised the volume still more. Each lap was similar, but on the eighth, as we entered into the main straight, the MG missed a gear and we stayed in front. The cheering was almost deafening. Entering into the main straight to start the last lap, our JAP engine suddenly coughed, clattered loudly and stopped. The flywheel had come loose …

Dad coasted as far as the Morgan would go just short of the pits and we were both in a state of shock. I hopped out and started to push, and people appeared from everywhere to help. Strangers came up with tears in their eyes to express their sorrow. What an emotional people the Italians are! By the time we had the Morgan at the entrance gate, the race was finished and Luigi Fusi came out and said not to push the car through the gates as the crowds wanted to see it. Before the next race Dad took a bow before we pushed the Morgan through the gate and the crowds stood up in the grandstands and gave him a standing ovation. Even we had some tears.

At the end of the day, the cars returned to the circuit in convoy for the Grand Parade. We loaded the Morgan onto the trailer and paraded with the rest. The applause was as loud as for the race. Spectators lined the track and ran beside the Falcon to shake our hands as we leaned out of the windows. Both the Morgan and

Ford Falcon were red. Perhaps this colour, similar to Ferrari red, fired Italian passions? Whatever the reason, it was an unforgettable day.

Before heading back to England, we had been invited by Fusi to Arese to look at the collection of Alfa Romeos that were eventually to form the exhibits at the museum. There were many examples, some modern, some older, all under dust covers and many in poor condition. A lot of restoration work was required.

The sweeping lines of the Disco Volante appealed to me. The 158 single-seater was attractive. It had spent some time in a museum in Switzerland and was gathering rust quite quickly. The funds allocated for the museum were quite limited. With so much work needed on every car, it was fortunate that there were enthusiasts like Fusi, who volunteered their time. His whole life had been devoted to the marque and now his retirement was spent researching, writing and recording technical data, as well as setting up the museum. The author of a number of authoritative Alfa Romeo publications, he was also a kind and personable man.

After the excitement of our trip to Monza, the thought of entering more concours d'elegance events seemed tame. However Dad noticed that the Morgan three-wheeler club was to hold a sprint meeting at Gaydon, and decided to enter. He told me that I could enter as well. I'd not driven the Morgan much and never competed any car in England. Although a bit nervous, I couldn't resist.

This meeting provided some useful experience. Most of the other three-wheelers were competition models. As ours was road going, there was no chance of winning, but the surprise of the day was that I beat my father's time! He kindly informed me that from then on I could use the Morgan for competition. I felt flattered.

The restoration of the Alfa was coming along quite nicely, despite many problems. Dad had also purchased a Ferrari 250GT, which was to be his ideal classic car. Hearing the note of the V12 engine for the first time was an exciting experience. The body was in need of restoration. While Dad was beavering away on the Alfa, Vern Schuppan had come to England from Australia to try to advance his racing career. Both he and Jenny, his wife, stayed with us until they found a flat of their own just down the road. Vern spent a number of months restoring the Ferrari to pristine condition. Life at Meadow Cottage was rather active, with both major restoration projects happening at the same time. When Vern purchased his first racing car, an Alexis Formula Ford, I started accompanying them to his early races. Once again my life was occupied with motorsport, albeit on a passive basis.

Pat Anderson, the Australian I met before going to Italy to study, had returned and we arranged to meet in London again. She now lived in a flat with two Australians nurses, Dodie from Western Australia and Inga from Adelaide. Dodie was intending to buy a second-hand Morris Minor 1000 in which the three of them were to travel down through Spain, Morocco, back to Spain and then on to Switzerland to the Beerfest in Munich. Inga and Pat were then going to work in Switzerland while Dodie came back to England.

I was rather surprised when Pat asked if I wanted to join them. I'd never travelled with an all-girl team before. I also needed to work out my finances and decide whether the three-month trip would interfere with any other plans that were formulating. The transport costs would be minimal, I decided. The Morris Minor was an economical car and just a quarter of the running costs couldn't amount to much. The accommodation was to be in a tent, so the initial costs for a sleeping bag, air mattress and a quarter of the tent, as well as the share of the camping ground charges, would be all that was needed. After doing some sums and talking over the trip with my parents, I decided to go.

Dodie managed to buy a good second-hand Minor already fitted with a luggage rack on the roof. A second-hand four-girl framed tent in really good condition was easily found and we bought a new one-burner gas cooker with a pan, pot, four drinking mugs and four plates. They all fitted into a plastic washing up bowl.

The weekend before leaving on the trek we had a test run, packing the car and erecting the tent. The tent and frame were wrapped in the plastic ground sheet and loaded onto the luggage rack. The rest of the gear, including our small cases, fitted snugly in the boot compartment. We did not have much room for clothing, just necessities and one change, plus swimwear and a towel. There was not an inch of space free.

Off we set. Fully loaded, the Minor pulled reasonably well up the hills. We progressed steadily through France, some nights not bothering to put up the tent if we stopped late, as we were trying to get to Pamplona, in Spain, as soon as possible for the Fiesta de San Fermín, and the running of the bulls. The festival was in honour of Pamplona's first bishop. Dodie and Pat shared the driving. Dodie was sedate, while Pat had more of a lead-foot style.

After several days of steady driving, we arrived in Pamplona. Pat had been there before so she knew where to find the campsite, situated several miles outside the town. As we pulled in, we were surprised to find that it looked just about full. There were flags of many nationalities perched on top of tents including Australian, New Zealand and American ones.

We found a plot not too far from the toilet block and began to unload the tent and gear. The best method of erecting the tent, we had discovered, was to assemble the top part of the frame, place the canvas over, then each of us lift one corner of the frame and bingo it was up. All that was left to do then was to hammer in the pegs and tie the guy ropes. Just as we had lifted the tent to its final position, two males with South African accents appeared, looking as though they had spent the afternoon imbibing the local brew.

'Australians,' one of them said. 'We love Australians, you're all so friendly. We'll help you put up your tent.'

Despite assurances that we could cope fine on our own, they staggered about, insisting they help and then hopped into our not quite ready tent. The four of us were tired, travelling from very early morning, and asked them to get out so we could finish putting the bedding in. Despite much persuasion they would not budge. Pat and Inga then went into the tent, lifted each one up and deposited them both on the ground outside.

'You can't be Australians,' they yelled, 'you are so unfriendly.'

The next morning, before starting sightseeing we decided to get some washing done. I noticed the South Africans just a few rows away in the company of some Australian girls and we were amazed that they were already drinking wine and beer. By the time we were leaving, there was quite a gathering from the former colonies, all singing dirty ditties and getting stuck into el plonko. As we drove out, one of them shouted, 'There's those stuck up Australian cows. You're a disgrace to your nationality.'

'We love you too mate,' one of us replied.

We all thought the assessment of ourselves a bit unfair: we were friendly and clean-living, wanting to experience the culture of the country that we were visiting rather than standing around all day drinking ourselves into a stupor with fellow countrymen. What a waste of an airfare. We could do that at home.

Before leaving England, I had bought a Spanish language book and found that, with a bit of study, I could get by with some basic Spanish, thanks to my knowledge of Italian. There were some similarities – and differences. The joke about the two Italians in a Spanish restaurant, insisting that they wanted burro (butter) with their bread, always came to mind when we were eating out. The Spanish waiter, on hearing the order, looked at the Italians as if they were mad, but the Italians, by now rather annoyed, were adamant that they wanted 'burro'. After some time the Spanish waiter returned with a donkey (which is burro in Spanish).

We stayed in Pamplona about ten days, visiting churches and art galleries, and the fourteenth to fifteenth century cathedral situated in the medieval part of the town, but mainly talking to people, both local and foreign. Most people were in Pamplona for the festival, which was the scene of much imbibing. Locals with bodegas slung over their shoulders (a skin bag full of wine, fitted with a spout), offered anyone a sample drink.

The highlight of the festival was the daily bullfight. Each morning the bulls were driven through the streets, and ahead of them raced men and boys. Most of the runners looked as though they were inebriated, as they ran for their lives in front of the stampeding animals. I found the running quite scary and kept at a distance, knowing that many people had been killed in the past – trampled or impaled.

No-one could convince me to watch the bullfight. I've never believed that animals should be killed as sport for humans. I was always shocked in Australia when I heard of young male city-dwellers going out to the bush at night just to shoot kangaroos and then leave the carcass there, not knowing whether the animal had a joey in its pouch. I could never grasp that people can actually get a thrill from this.

Pat reprimanded me. Here I was in Spain, where bull fighting was part of the culture, so how could I make a valid assessment if I did not witness the activity. I was pre-judging the bullfight from an Anglo-Saxon perspective. Perhaps she had a point I thought, so I reluctantly went. The pomp and ceremony was colourful. The matadors were dramatic and skilful in their movements, but when the sword was plunged into the bull and he started to fall dying to the ground to the loud roar of the crowds, I had to leave quickly. I'd seen enough.

After all the excitement of the Festival it was time to pack up, say farewell to new friends and head for Madrid. I had spent many hours in the campground discussing the meaning of life with Richard Maldonado, a newly qualified doctor from California. Richard had decided to spend a year hitchhiking round Europe with Mireille, his new wife, before starting his medical career.

We had also met some friendly American GIs stationed in Madrid and visiting Pamplona for the weekend. As we waved goodbye, it felt as though we had known these people for a lifetime, not just a matter of days.

Madrid was hot – the temperature over 100°F. The campground was enormous and packed. Managing to find a site quite a distance from the toilet block, but with trees behind, we constructed our tent. We all felt thirsty and I set off for the shop, situated near the entrance gate, to buy some ice-cold soft drinks. As I was leaving the shop I heard a comment from someone sitting at one of the tables inside.

'Oh look, there's one of those stuck up Australians.'

Feeling rather annoyed I marched over to the South African and asked what his problem was. I explained that when we had arrived at Pamplona we did not know him, he was behaving in rather an intrusive, drunken and loutish manner, and we weren't unfriendly at all. Much to my surprise he apologised and shook my hand.

Everyday we went sightseeing but the going was tough, the temperatures so high that it was hard to find enthusiasm for cultural pursuits. Escaping into the Prado, one of the world's major art galleries, we became involved mainly in the art of the fifteenth to nineteenth century, particularly the works of Francisco de Goya and Diego Velázquez.

We saw the world's greatest collection of body armour, housed in the National Palace, including the sword of Hernán Cortés, the medieval adventurer. Just nearby, we visited Madrid's first cathedral. I was really impressed by the broad tree-lined boulevard, the Paseo, along which are located the parliament buildings, embassies, fine residences and up-market hotels. Some of the medieval street patterns still existed but very few buildings of that era. The architecture of the Plaza Mayor really stood out, one of the most interesting city squares I have seen.

The camping ground had a swimming pool. It was a relief to return at the end of the afternoon for a swim, but unfortunately most of the other campers had similar ideas and it was always overcrowded.

Returning one day, we found a message posted on the notice board from the GIs we had met in Pamplona, inviting us for a guided tour round the Air Force base. We arranged the trip for the following day. Entering through the checkpoint, it was as if we had left Spain. The whole atmosphere was American: the music, the food and the conversation. The cars fascinated me. Compared to Spain's small Seats that we were seeing everywhere, the Chevvys, Pontiacs and Fords seemed gigantic. The base was like an American suburb, with streets and houses, the yank tanks parked outside. We dined on hamburgers and other US delicacies and were given carrier bags full of tins and packets of food to take on our travels.

About this time in the trip our individual interests started to come to the fore. I felt like hitting the road south again. The soaring heat and crowds were starting to get to me. Although we had been travelling for more than three weeks together, I felt a bit like an outsider and wasn't very good at expressing my own private desires.

Then it became more complex. Pat and Inga started to spend time with two of the GIs and wanted to stay in Madrid to see how the friendships developed. Dodie and I were acting as taxi, ferrying the other two in the Minor. The atmosphere became rather tense and after a pow-wow we all decided to move on and leave the romances to fate.

The conversation for the next few days, as we ambled along in the Minor, centred on how wonderful the two American guys were, which for Dodie and me became a little wearing – that is, until we arrived at Granada and the start of another cultural pursuit. Granada is rich with Renaissance, Baroque and Neo-classical churches, monasteries, palaces and mansions. We were kept busy for days visiting places of interest and, in the Gothic Cathedral of Santa María de la Encarnación, saw the tomb of Ferdinand and Isabella, the visionary royals who brought about the Spanish Reformation.

One of the greatest excitements was visiting Alhambra, the palace and fortress of the Moorish monarchs of Granada, built on a plateau overlooking the city. When the Moors were expelled in

139

1492, many of the buildings were destroyed or re-built as an Italianate palace during the Renaissance period. The whole area was like a contained town, with grand reception rooms, halls and banqueting rooms overlooking courtyards and terraced gardens, pools and fountains. Such magnificence reflected an opulent life-style I had not seen before.

I felt very comfortable in Granada and was sorry to leave and I hadn't met a GI. Keeping away from tourist areas, we passed over the mountains. The scenery was spectacular and the Minor, although loaded to the hilt, was coping well as it chugged its way up and down the steep passes.

In the middle of nowhere we passed two hitchhikers looking desperate for a ride. It was Richard and Mireille. We stopped and the greeting was as if we had met two life-long friends. Unfortunately, there was not one inch of space left in the car to offer them a ride and we wished them luck as we drove on, secretly relieved that it wasn't us waiting by the side of the road.

Soon we were near the coast heading for Algeciras, on the southern tip of Spain, where we intended to cross the Strait of Gibraltar to Morocco. We could see Gibraltar in the distance. The border into Gibraltar had been closed for years, due to the dispute between Britain and Spain. Access to the island was by sea or air, but when we saw the border gates at the causeway crossing were manned, we decided to pull up. One of the guards came out and we said we wanted to drive into Gibraltar. He obviously thought we were mad and wouldn't even bother to speak to us. His must have been a lonely job.

The ferries from Algeciras to Morocco were fully booked for several days, so we hung about sleeping, eating and talking to others waiting for the crossing. Some we recognised from the campground in Pamplona and Madrid: it seems we were all travelling a similar route. I was told it was the 'hippie trail'. When a pleasant German started to talk to me we discussed our respective homelands, education, travels and so on. He had been staying in Algeciras for three weeks, camping in his VW Combi, waiting for a friend to come back from Morocco and then they would head back to Germany. I couldn't help thinking that the situation was odd. Why would anyone spend three weeks waiting? It turned out that the friend went to Morocco to buy marijuana to sell back at home, and that's how they earned their living.

My new 'friend' was afraid that the authorities had caught his colleague, trying to re-enter Spain. There were stiff penalties for bringing drugs in. As he talked, I realised just how naive I was. I'd read about drug running and people taking drugs, but had no first-hand experience – and didn't want any. I made my excuses and left.

At last, we were on the crowded ferry, crossing the Strait of Gibraltar to Ceuta, the Spanish protectorate in North Africa. I'd never been to a Muslim country before and felt rather apprehensive, wondering how I would be treated. Our plan was to avoid Tangiers and the hassles that tourists have to endure, and head west along the northern mountain range to Al Hoceïma, situated on the Mediterranean coast. It was the middle of the night when the ferry docked so, with two drivers at our disposal, we decided to head straight for the road up the mountains rather than try to find a campsite.

By sun-up we were just arriving at Tétouan, a small city perched on a rocky plateau a few miles from the Mediterranean Sea. We needed to stock up on supplies. As we emerged from the car, it felt eerie hearing the muezzin proclaiming the hour of prayer from a loudspeaker fixed to the minaret of the mosque. We saw the men, dressed in their jalabas, heading off for the first of five daily prayer sessions. Soon the city came alive, with stalls opening for the start of the day's trading.

People were friendly and did not pester us. Perhaps this small city was not used to foreigners. Most tourists headed south, we were informed. Noticing all the women wearing chadors, covering their heads, we did feel rather underdressed. The roads heading west in the mountains were quiet. We hardly saw a car;

just an occasional 'ute' packed full of produce, most likely heading for market. Mile after mile, the Minor trundled along without any problems. We had not seen any civilisation, villages or people for hours when we noticed a well, built at the side of road with fresh mountain water spurting out. It was just what we needed. There had been no public facilities since leaving Spain the day before.

The four of us rushed off in different directions to carry out necessary biological duties, behind a tree of our choice. Just as I was pulling up my knickers I heard, 'Psst, ya wanna buy hashish?' I almost jumped into the top branch of the tall tree, such was the fright I got. Trying not to panic I looked round and saw a fairly young face crouched behind some bushes. Not knowing how to handle the situation, all I could think of saying was, 'No spikka da inglish', then I took off as fast as my legs would carry me, flung open the door of the Minor and dived in, heart pounding.

Half expecting the interloper to appear, I kept looking but did not see him again. When the other three emerged from their trees, they wondered why I had such a nervous look on my face. After I'd told them the story they could hardly stand they were so crippled with laughter. It took me a while to see the funny side ...

The camping ground at Al Hoceïma, situated right next to the Mediterranean, was full, not of foreign tourists but Arabs. We must have stuck out like sore thumbs: females walking around with heads uncovered. But despite our infidel presence, dressed against Muslim law, particularly when we swam in the sea, nobody took much notice and everyone we met was extremely polite and friendly.

Travelling over the barren mountain range, heading for Fès, we were right out in the middle of nowhere when we came upon a large gathering of people, with hundreds of stalls. Not knowing quite what this was, we decided to stop and then find out if we were welcome. Some of the people were dressed differently from what we had seen before. The women were in bright, vibrant clothing and their faces were not covered. It turned out that these were Berbers and the occasion was a camel market and bazaar. People had come from hundreds of miles around for this special event. Wandering through the rows and rows of craft stalls, we watched artisans plying their trade, making jewellery, hammering out copper work – and we could even choose a camel, if we so desired.

A few traders spoke English and a young chap offered to show us around. He took us to a wooden building, a café, and ordered mint tea for us. While we were enjoying the flavour of the indigenous drink, an older man appeared, unusually dressed in an immaculate western suit, white shirt and tie. He only spoke a few words of English, but it was obvious that he exerted some influence as many people were subservient towards him. When he clapped his hands, one of the minions appeared and the man spoke to him in Arabic. A record player was brought in and I thought we would be hearing some local Arabic music, but no. Rock and roll, Elvis style, was soon blaring out. Ice-cold coke was placed in front of us and the man sat down and started to try to communicate.

What we heard was rather mind-boggling to four innocent Aussie girls. Our new friend was wealthy, owned many houses, cars and a fleet of fast sea-going boats. He was, of course, a drug baron. The product was purchased from the growers that, we were informed, were everywhere in the hills, right down to the coast, then when harvested the drugs were shipped worldwide.

The four of us, on hearing the finer details of the trade, started to get nervous. My imagination was running away with me and I thought that we might not ever be able to escape from where we were. Perhaps the police would appear and cart us all away and I would never see my mother and father again. Unanimously we must have had the same thoughts, as we all started making excuses as to the reason for our departure. After much persuasion from our friend to stay for more of his hospitality, we took our leave and kept driving for hours until we arrived in Fès.

The buildings on the outskirts of Fès are modern. Stopping at a café for refreshments, we were approached by a young chap. A university student, he was keen to practise his English. He lived in a modern flat with his father and the second wife. His mother, the first wife, lived in the Medina (the old part of the city) with his sisters. We were invited to visit his mother the following day.

The winding, covered streets through the Medina were no wider than a narrow passage. On each side were stalls packed with traditional crafts such as leather and pottery, and workshops with artisans making the products. I saw men dyeing bolts of cotton material in the gutters as we walked by. The smells and the dark, gloomy atmosphere were hard to take. It was as if we had been transported back to the fourteenth century.

Our guide stopped, pulled out his keys and opened a door. We walked through the entrance and suddenly we were standing in a well-lit courtyard. This was his mother's house, a traditional Arab residence. Surrounding the courtyard on two levels were the rooms. It was amazingly beautiful. I'd never seen a house like this before.

We were taken to a room on the ground floor where seven ladies of all ages were sitting drinking mint tea. Only the chap spoke English, but they were all so hospitable. One of the sisters was getting married soon and there was considerable activity with a dressmaking session in full swing. The girls were decorating the backs of their hands with henna in fine lacework designs. They were keen to adorn my hands with designs. These didn't fade for a fortnight.

I was beginning to like Morocco. The people we met had been so helpful and friendly. Pat had been to Morocco before and warned that the situation would be different in the tourist areas. Casablanca was daunting. Much bigger than any other city we had visited in Morocco. Miles and miles of shanties and modern urban sprawl spread out on either side, as the Minor ambled into the centre, dodging the chaotic motorised traffic and small horse-drawn trailers.

None of us was keen on big cities. It was dark and we decided to find the camping ground straight away and head off to Marrakech the following morning. With no food left, we stopped for a snack. As soon as we emerged from the Minor, young boys appeared from every direction, dressed in rags and begging. We could see poverty everywhere and wanted to give but agreed that none of us would be left alone if we did. The perception was, understandably, that all foreigners must be rich. I'd not seen begging before and felt distressed. I also realised how very fortunate we were to be brought up in Australia – our generation had never experienced this sort of deprivation.

Feeling too tired to erect the tent for just one night, we placed our air mattresses right by a secure boundary fence, under a tree in the camping ground and I sank into a deep sleep. It was still dark when we were woken by a very loud eerie sound and discovered that, just the other side of the fence, was the local mosque. The muezzin, before dawn, was calling the Muslim followers to prayer, one of the loudspeakers placed a matter of yards from our sleeping place.

The temperature in Marrakech, not far from the Sahara Desert, was well over 100°F. It was too hot for sleeping in the tent. Pat knew of a hotel, just near the centre of the Medina that was well within our budget. We parked the Minor in the main street. Pat directed us down a narrow alleyway strewn with rubbish, dog dirt everywhere and young kids begging. We came to a door.

'This is the hotel,' she informed us.

Once through a small passageway we were in a courtyard, a typical Arab building with rooms round the perimeter. In the centre of the courtyard a palm tree towered over the building.

'Yes, there is a vacancy,' the landlord said, 'the room over there on the left. It has four beds.'

We snapped up this ground floor room, which cost the equivalent of five pence each, per day. The shower was on the opposite side of the courtyard and the toilet next door to our room. As we entered the room, I noticed something scampering across.

'It's only a cockroach,' said Pat.

Managing to kick the intruder out into the courtyard, we examined our surroundings. The bed linen, once white, was looking well used, as if it had not been changed for six months. The Marrakech Hilton this was not. Our hotelier, called in to inspect the sheets, insisted that they were fresh that very morning. We later brought in sleeping bags and placed them on top of the beds.

For over a week we wandered about the Medina, socialised in the Jema al Fna Square, the heart of the old city, and walked around the twelfth century city walls. We ate a traditional Moroccan lunch at a local schoolteacher's house. Sitting in the middle of the floor with the bowls of food placed in front and no western utensils, we scooped the food out with our fingers, trying to appear as if we were expert at this style of eating.

But every day, no matter what we were doing, young men always approached us, offering to act as guide. Usually they would not take no for an answer, which became quite wearing. Back in our room to rest from the scorching sun, late one afternoon, Pat went off to the shop to get some cold drinks. As she walked through the door she said, 'Look what I found.' Dr. Richard was standing there. He explained that Mireille had picked up some bug and was in bed in a hotel just round the corner and he invited me to visit her.

She was moaning and felt dreadful. Leaving her to sleep, Richard said that he had found a stall in the Jema al Fna Square that sold cookies just like he ate in California and suggested we go and have a snack. We ate wonderful cookies, washed down with Coca Cola, while the snake charmers and water sellers entertained us. The next day Pat had arranged an outing with some young fellows to a village out of Marrakech. I did not like the idea of going off with strangers but I also did not want to wander round Marrakech alone. I was getting fed up with the hassling, and didn't feel entirely safe.

After I was showered and dressed I felt strange, rather light-headed, a sensation I'd not experienced before. At the café where we were to meet the 'guides' I felt so thirsty I drank a bottle of coke in a matter of minutes. My head started to spin and I just wanted to lie down. Explaining to the girls that I didn't feel well, I set off alone to return to the hotel. At times I thought I was going to pass out and had to steady myself against the walls. All day I was drifting in and out of sleep. I felt so thirsty but we had no bottled water in the room. In desperation, I drank some tap water. Every half-hour or so I had to stagger out to the toilet.

There were cockroaches everywhere and no water to flush the French-style hole-in-the-floor toilet. What a hellhole. How I wanted to be back in England. The day seemed to last for ever. I was delirious; convinced I was about to die. I would never see my parents again. There was no phone so I couldn't even call them to say goodbye. Late at night, the three girls came back. I was sure that they were never returning and I would die alone. They'd had a bad experience, but did not want to tell me the details.

Pat went and bought some soft drink, which I gulped back. All night I drifted in and out of sleep and when morning arrived it surprised me that I was still alive. Although terribly weak I changed my mind and decided that I would miraculously live to tell the tale. Dodie had felt strange the night before and on waking she had caught the dreaded disease.

'Let's pack the Minor and clear out of here,' suggested Pat. 'We'll head for the coast and some sea breezes instead of this overpowering heat.'

'Let's go,' we replied, in unison.

Pat and Inga loaded the two patients into the back of the Minor and off we drove. Most of the day I dozed. Opening my eyes, miles from anywhere, I thought I saw a red light on the dashboard. Just imagination, I thought. When I looked again, the red oil light was indeed illuminated.

'Stop the car,' I yelled, 'we must be out of oil.'

Fortunately, we had a can of oil in the boot. Despite a complete absence of oil on the dipstick there was no apparent damage to the engine. We were so very lucky. It didn't bear thinking about what might have happened had the engine seized, way out there in the desert, in the soaring heat and two of us feeling like death.

The fresh air from the Atlantic felt so refreshing after the oppressive heat of the interior. The camping ground was equipped with an enormous swimming pool filled to the brim with crystal clear water. We spent the day swimming and trying to relax in the shade. As soon as we emerged from the pool, however, young Moroccan males seemed to appear from nowhere spouting the familiar 'I show you around'. Diving back into the pool seemed the only means of escape.

By late afternoon, the four of us must have had the same idea. 'Let's go back to Spain,' someone said.

Another unanimous decision. Rushing back to the tent, we packed up the gear, loaded the Minor and drove all night until we arrived at the ferry terminal, eager to cross the Strait of Gibraltar again.

Only the driver was permitted to occupy the car on the exit from the ferry into Spain. Passengers had to embark by foot. All of our hand luggage was searched as we proceeded through the official customs area. Once outside the terminal building we stood waiting for Dodie to appear in the Morris Minor. Car after car passed by until finally there was no traffic. Still no Dodie.

Walking past the terminal building we looked through the high wire security fence. There in the distance was the Minor, surrounded by officials in the process of stripping out every seat and unpacking each piece of luggage. Our belongings were strewn everywhere. We could see Dodie, standing next to the car looking bewildered.

We couldn't understand why Dodie had been singled out from over a hundred cars for an inspection for drugs. Pat thought that her prim, Sunday school teacher appearance might have unnerved the officials. But this time the officials chose the wrong victim. There were no drugs hidden in the Minor. We shouted to the officials to let us in. We wanted to help Dodie re-pack the car. Eventually the gates were opened and it took us over an hour to get the Minor ready for the next leg of its journey.

Although we had all made disparaging remarks in the past about the British tourist on his package holiday to Spain, wanting British food and cheap Spanish drinks, with no desire to sample the local culinary or cultural delights, that last episode with customs had left us feeling thoroughly fed up with Moroccan and Spanish officialdom. Suddenly we had a yearning to experience some 'home' comforts and headed for the resort of Torremolinos to recover from our ordeal.

Dressed in our finery, the Moroccan long dresses purchased for about 50 pence in Marrakech, we sat down at a pavement café and ordered champagne cocktails. Soon a middle-aged English couple joined us. The conversation quickly turned to a comparison of prices of every commodity between Britain and Spain. Whingeing was rife, about the food in their hotel, not British enough, size of room, en-suite bathroom and so on. Later, choosing a Chinese restaurant for our nosh, we sat next to another two couples having a similar conversation. By the end of the evening we were conversant with the value of everything we weren't interested in at the time.

Instead of continuing our journey to the north, up the Mediterranean coast, Pat and Inga – drawn by love – started talking about returning to Madrid. I wanted to see new territory instead. So did Dodie. The decision was taken that the Minor was to continue on the coastal route as originally planned, and the other two would hitch-hike to Madrid and meet us in Barcelona, at the camping ground, in two weeks time. Should there be a change of plan, they would write care of the American Express office.

We ambled north, enjoying the scenery and visiting the places of interest that took our fancy at the time. The Barcelona camping ground was situated several miles out of the city, right by the beach. We hadn't bothered to erect the tent on one-night stops as it took much more effort for two. But in this pleasant area we pitched our camp and spent several days sleeping and swimming, with just a little sightseeing.

Near our tent I kept noticing two new Reliant three-wheelers, which seemed a long way from home. I couldn't imagine anyone driving such a car so far.

I was of course a convert to three-wheel driving after my experiences with the Morgan but felt that the Reliant, which had the single wheel located at the front, looked ungainly. The Reliant owners had a different view. Two delightful middle-aged couples from Yorkshire, they purchased new three-wheelers every two years. Neither of the drivers had owned any other make of car. Every summer they packed their Reliants with tents and belongings and headed off on the long trek to Spain and, I was informed with some pride, 'we sit on 70mph for most of the journey'.

Two weeks had passed since we parted from our two companions. They hadn't turned up at the campsite and no letter had arrived.

'May as well continue to Switzerland, as planned,' said Dodie.

Pat had previously worked in a hostel at Leysin, where she had arranged to work again, so we knew they would eventually turn up there. But in France, as we neared the Swiss border, I had a great longing to visit Perugia again. Dodie agreed, we changed direction immediately and set out for Umbria, driving there non-stop.

As Perugia appeared in the distance, perched on its hill, I felt as though I was coming home. La Signora Lucarrelli expressed such surprise as I walked into the kitchen and screamed in delight. We were made so welcome. One room was available for our use for three days. I showed Dodie all my haunts, trattorias, cafés, the university and places of historical interest. The time passed so quickly, I didn't want to leave.

Denis had visited Perugia with his parents just the week before, La Signora said. I would have liked to see him again. As we headed north on the Autostrada del Sole, my memories of that earlier time in Perugia, the study and sense of achievement I gained, started me thinking. Although I had been keen to experience the festivities at the Munich Beerfest, my enthusiasm was now beginning to wane. By the time we got to Leysin I had decided to opt out of the rest of the trip and return to England. Pat and Inga had arrived several days before us, were already working, and were going to stay. An English girl we met in Leysin wanted to experience the Beerfest and arranged to travel in the Minor with Dodie.

After a farewell Swiss dinner, the next morning I headed back to England by train and arrived at East Horsley railway station with just 20 pence in my pocket. I felt broke – but greatly enriched by my three months of adventure.

Chapter 7

ON THE BANKING
AT BROOKLANDS

Drivers, track clearance and Test Hill

After living in Italy my attitude to study had changed. At school it was a chore but at university in Perugia every minute was enjoyable. Back in England, wanting to continue as a mature student, I located a small language school in Guildford run by an elderly lady and booked in for weekly Italian lessons. Miss Bond-Nash spoke eleven languages and we hit it off right from the start.

She encouraged me to work for an A Level in Italian and in just four months I passed the examination. It was no easy ride, most of my time was spent in study and, for the practical side, I spoke with a waiter from Perugia who I'd met at a new Italian restaurant near where I was now living.

One day Miss Bond-Nash asked me to take over a class for two weeks while her regular teacher was on holiday. The six students of an advanced class in 'English as a foreign language' were preparing to sit the Cambridge University exam. Although I had taken regular beginners groups now and again at the school, I didn't feel confident enough to step in at short notice for such an important class. After much persuasion from Miss Bond-Nash, however, I relented. Professore Baratti's method of teaching was always in the back of my mind. My aim was to keep the students motivated and provide them with plenty of new material in an enjoyable way. In the classroom on that first day were six smiling friendly faces full of anticipation and at that point my heart missed a beat. I so hoped I would not let them down.

The two weeks was hard work. Every evening I planned the following day's lesson and corrected the homework. I was convinced that all of the students had a good chance of passing the exam if they kept working at the level that they had demonstrated to me. Their motivation was high, but as the teacher I had to introduce variety throughout the three-hour period, otherwise their concentration would naturally lapse. On the last day I was relieved that my stint had come to an end and the experienced teacher could resume her class. I wasn't particularly confident that the students thought they had benefited from my teaching, as I had no other class of this level to compare with.

Going into class that day, I thought my worst fears were confirmed. Everyone was whispering and I sensed an unusual atmosphere. One of the students apologised, telling me there was a problem and asked if we could start a few minutes late as they needed to have a short discussion with Miss Bond-Nash. After about ten minutes, I was summoned to see the Principal.

Walking down the stairs to her office, I just wanted to run out of the front door and away. I had experienced failure before. The strong feelings of humiliation started to overcome me and I know my face was flushed and my heart racing as I entered her office.

'Joy, sit down please, I have something to discuss with you,' Miss Bond-Nash said in a matter of fact way. 'The students have decided unanimously that they want you to take over their class. If you don't agree they have threatened to walk out.'

It was lucky I was sitting as you could have knocked me over with a feather.

After a short silence while I began to grasp the reality of the situation, I agreed to continue, at least until the examination. Soon I was teaching full-time, both beginners and advanced 'English as a foreign language'. Now with an enjoyable job and an income I started to feel reasonably secure, as I watched the savings start to slowly accumulate.

As I'm not really a creature of habit, it wasn't long before I looked around for a new challenge. I applied to the Open University and enrolled on a degree course in Social Science that would be keep me occupied for the next four years and, more importantly, give a BA to tack on to my name. I knew this would be demanding, so decided to work part-time, mornings only, and study in the afternoon and evenings. It took me a while to adapt to the strenuous schedule. At times I felt like tossing everything in but once I became accustomed to academic life and meeting other students on the same course, my determination hardened.

I drove the Morgan to more concours events around the area. It provided a necessary alternative to study. Dodie, now working in London, came down to Surrey in the Minor at weekends and sometimes rode pillion in the three-wheeler.

I always enjoyed the first event of the year. The Daffodil Run was more of a challenge than the concours. For this event, organised by the Bean Car Club, we set off early in the morning from Maidenhead, a riverside town in the Thames Valley, and wound our way through narrow country roads until we arrived at the beachfront at the south coast resort of Bournemouth, some five hours later. There, the concours was held, then we drove in convoy through the streets to the Town Hall. The Mayor and councillors fed and watered us with afternoon tea and delicate little cakes and, for entertainment, a speech or two.

The hosts were more formally attired than us vintage car drivers, kitted out for a demanding drive in unpredictable weather. Dodie and I couldn't help giggling at the incongruity of it all. After tea it was time to drive back to Surrey. I always needed a day to recover after the Daffodil Run. The Morgan had just half a turn of the steering wheel from lock to lock, which meant that a considerable amount of muscle power was needed on tight corners. A round trip of 300 miles, at the start of the season, with no physical preparation on my part, left my arms feeling as if I'd been lifting heavy barbells all day. It felt almost restful to resume study.

In most areas of Britain, the Vintage Sports Car Club held monthly pub meetings. Members would drive over in their vintage cars and socialise. The meet we started attending was held on the last Thursday of every month at the Phoenix Inn at Phoenix Green. The VSCC was inaugurated here in 1934.

It was a pleasant drive of about twenty-five miles through Guildford, over the Hogs Back to Farnham, then round some country lanes to near Hartley Witney. The re-build of the 8C was nearing completion and the monthly outings offered my father an excuse to escape from the workshop and meet like-minded people as well as give the Ferrari 250GT an airing. We shared the cars. I might drive the Morgan to the Phoenix, then Dad would drive it home, while I piloted the Ferrari.

The first time I drove the Ferrari I was, surprisingly, disappointed. Expecting to be absolutely overwhelmed by the power and aura of such a famous make, I thought that my long love affair with the E-type would be over, but no. In my view, the E-type was easier, pleasanter and more exciting to drive. And as for looks, nothing could equal the aesthetics of the Jaguar.

We always looked forward to the meeting. A wonderful sense of camaraderie prevailed within the vintage car fraternity. One evening I struck up a conversation with the press officer of BEN – the Motor & Cycle Trades Benevolent Fund. Paul Finn, disabled with rheumatoid arthritis, was organising a concours at the charity's headquarters, Lynwood, in Sunningdale. He was hoping to attract an interesting entry for the event and I accepted his invitation to bring the Morgan. Paul's determination impressed me. The rheumatoid arthritis had taken its toll on this young man, who had been involved in the motor trade in Liverpool before undergoing surgery some four years previously. To convalesce Paul had been sent to Lynwood where he learnt typing and other office skills. He stayed on, later being recruited to the staff. We had a lot in common. His first car had also been a Morris Minor and we exchanged stories of our exploits. Unfortunately, the disability had left him unable to drive, at that stage, and I noticed him gaze longingly at some of the vintage cars.

The charity was originally set up in 1905 to provide financial assistance to people who had been involved in the bicycle trade; then in 1908 the motor trade was included. It wasn't until 1948 that Lynwood, a rather grand residence, was purchased and converted into a rest home. The charity also owned a small nursing home in Ealing but sold that and built the nursing wing at Lynwood, opened in 1965 by the Queen Mother.

On the day of the garden party a number of interesting cars lined up in the beautiful grounds of Lynwood. The guest was Kaye Don, the famous racing driver from the twenties and thirties. I'd never met anyone before who had competed successfully at Brooklands, the banked racing circuit that I had read so much about. Kaye Don's motor racing career had started on motorbikes and in the twenties he drove the Wolseley Viper at Brooklands. In 1928, he set a number of class and lap records in the three works Sunbeams, known as the Tiger, Tigress and Cub. The current owner of the Cub had brought it along to Lynwood to be reunited with the driver who brought it to its original fame. It was hard to believe that Kaye Don had been in his prime over forty years before. He just didn't look old enough. In fact, he informed us that his racing career had ended in 1934, quite tragically. On the Isle of Man he was involved in a road accident that killed his mechanic and resulted in a six-month prison sentence for manslaughter.

Tony Brooks, Formula 1 driver of the fifties, was also at Lynwood that day. His exploits in Ferraris were more familiar to me as I had been at Reims when he won the French Grand Prix in 1959. Lynwood was great fun and we became regular attendees at the charity's events there for some years to come. The cars were judged on their appearance and the Morgan once again returned home with a silver trophy.

Hearing so much about Brooklands, we decided to join the Brooklands Society, formed in 1967 to save the track from development. Brooklands, as well as being the first motor race circuit in the world, was also the place where Britain's first aeroplanes were designed, built and flown. An aerodrome was built within the 1907 track. Famous aeronautical names such as Sopwith, Hawker and Vickers were based at Brooklands in the decades between 1910 and 1970, and during the Second World War it was a major centre for aeronautical research and design. Barnes Wallis conducted many of his progressive experiments there. More recently, a large proportion of Concorde's airframe was manufactured by the British Aircraft Corporation at Brooklands. The disused circuit was just ten miles from where we lived and I had driven past many times, managing just a glimpse of part of the banking.

An evening film show provided the first taste of what motor racing at this famous track was really like during the twenties and thirties. Dudley Gahagan had spent most of his life collecting motorsport films, particularly of races at Brooklands.

To see and to hear the big chargers racing and breaking world records on the steep banking of the outer circuit was, for me, so much more exciting than a modern race. Then, the men and women drivers were daring heroes, and many became household names, even in countries as far away as Australia. What impressed me most that evening was that some of the drivers were actually there, watching the films at the Hand & Spear public house, just near Brooklands, which most of the drivers had used all those years back as their watering hole after gruelling race meetings. It was not difficult to recognise the elderly man wearing a beret and heartily smoking a pipe. Sammy Davis, well known as a journalist, author and artist, was more distinguished in my view as one of 'the Bentley Boys' and winner, despite a major accident, of the Le Mans, 24-hour sports car race in 1927. The much younger lady with him, smoking a curved pipe, was Susan, his wife. I'd never seen a lady smoking a pipe before and admired the confidence with which she did this in such a male-dominated audience.

Within a couple of months the annual Brooklands Society Reunion was scheduled to take place at the track. Many of the famous cars and drivers would be there. As the restoration of the 8C Alfa Romeo was not quite finished, my father decided to take the Morgan. Brooklands had still been in use as the most prestigious racing venue when our 1933 Morgan was manufactured.

It was difficult now, in the seventies, to gain access to look at the old track as the British Aircraft Corporation employed strict security procedures. As we drove through the gates on the morning of the reunion I felt a sense of wonderment that I was in the very place where circuit motor racing in Britain was born. When I saw the banked sections and attempted (unsuccessfully) to walk up the sides it was hard to imagine that cars, more than sixty years before, had competed at speeds of well over 100mph. Why they did not fall off the 100ft wide track, with parts of the banked section nearly 30ft high in places, and almost vertical, was hard to comprehend. If I'd not seen films of this, I'd never have believed it.

We heard so many stories that day, from the drivers who had achieved these extraordinary feats. Captain George Eyston was only too happy to recount the finer details of his land speed records at Pendine Sands and Bonneville, and the records taken at Brooklands. He drove many makes of cars and was particularly known for his association with MG. When my father showed him photographs of a Panhard et Levassor he'd just brought over from Australia, Eyston told us about his exploits in the single-seater Panhard, powered by a whopping sleeved valve, 8-litre engine. In 1932 Eyston was awarded his 130mph badge, driving the Panhard at Brooklands.

The achievements of Raymond Mays – founder of English Racing Automobiles (ERA) and British Racing Motors (BRM) – were more familiar to me. When I was a kid I'd seen Stirling Moss driving a BRM at Reims. That had left quite an impression on me, although very few successes were ever achieved by the marque, which failed after a short time. Mays did better in the works ERAs and was sitting in one when I first saw him at Brooklands that day, surrounded by on-lookers.

I also struck up a conversation with Sammy Davis and his wife. We seemed to hit it off straight away and I was invited to visit them at their home.

I learned that 'a track clearers' section of the Brooklands Society existed. The organiser John Wall insisted that I join. The idea was to meet on Sundays, pull weeds out and generally clear the track to prepare for the annual reunion. I sensed a feeling of optimism from John that one day the track would be restored to its original glory and become the motor racing centre of the world.

He demonstrated such enthusiasm that I couldn't refuse the invitation. The task did seem rather monumental though. During the Second World War, when Brooklands served as an aviation centre, parts of the banking had been demolished and trees were planted in the track to act as camouflage. With the area now surrounded by suburbia it seemed unlikely that the track would ever become fully operational, but I was glad to be included in the project. Brooklands, on occasional Sundays, was to provide a welcome escape from study and work; also it offered a chance to meet a band of dedicated, interesting people. John seemed to live Brooklands – its events, personalities, in fact anything that was connected with the historic track – and his engaging personality attracted people to the cause.

I spent many a late afternoon and evening wandering about the banked sections of the track with other enthusiasts, maybe hoping for a meeting with some ghosts. Many people, even now, are convinced that the ghosts of several drivers killed while participating on the circuit still have a presence at Brooklands.

The annual re-union was a cherished opportunity to talk with drivers who had survived racing at Brooklands. I met Whitney Straight, Kenneth Neve and others, but Bob Dicker, a mechanic involved with the first transatlantic flight, was one of the most amusing. He gained fame with his motorcycle exploits at Brooklands, not least the 600-mile record achieved in 1922, in partnership with Dick Mather, riding a Rudge, and numerous sidecar records on a Bradbury. Bob had a vast repertoire of risqué jokes. As he was a member of the track clearers club, we met many times over the following years and not once did I hear a repeat – there was always laughter when he was about.

One day a chap with a fairly new powerful motorcycle decided to take Bob for a pillion ride up the runway at Brooklands. Thinking the old man would only want to travel at a slow speed he was surprised when the passenger tapped him on the shoulder and yelled, 'what are you pissing about for?' The rider, not hearing the comment properly, thought he was being asked to pull up but when he stopped, Bob insisted he take control of the bike, with the owner as pillion. This old man certainly had not lost any of his taste for acceleration and reached speeds of well over the ton. When he finally stopped, the owner of the bike was seen to rush into the bushes and reappeared looking a very pale shade of grey.

Leo Villa, another entertaining chap, told me many a tale of the charismatic Campbell family. He started working as a mechanic for Malcolm Campbell during his Brooklands days, then was involved with the world speed record attempts and continued with son Donald Campbell's record attempts, right up to the ill-fated trial at Lake Windermere. Leo could talk for hours about the exploits of these two speed kings and eventually recorded his story in a book (*The Record Breakers*/1968).

After the team had cleaned the weeds from the Test Hill, runs up this famous section of track became part of the reunion. I drove the Morgan up the Test Hill at several of the events. It was a truly amazing experience, with thousands of spectators lining both sides of the track, some of them the original competitors. Although it was over thirty years since the track was closed, as a participant you could sense the excitement and atmosphere of those glory days. I am thankful that at least I have had some involvement with Brooklands when some of the original stars were present.

I took up Sammy Davis's invitation to visit him and Susie at their Guildford flat and became a regular visitor, sometimes on my way home from work. I was entertained for hours hearing about the colourful characters involved. It was obvious that Sammy was not very comfortable financially, in spite of his fame as winner of the 1927 Le Mans 24-hour race and other successes in the sport, as well as in his professional career when he was Sports Editor of *Autocar*. He was managing to eke out a meagre living doing oil paintings of cars. He asked if I knew anyone who might like to commission a painting, and over the next few years my father and I managed to introduce a number of new customers. One of the most asked-for subjects was the big accident at Le Mans in 1927 which Sammy depicted as he saw the calamity unfold in front of him. Some of the commissions were of particular cars that people owned and Sammy was familiar with.

One day Sammy phoned me in great excitement.

'Joy, my dear, I need your advice on a matter. Could you possibly call in when you are passing, as soon as possible?'

I couldn't imagine why Sammy, with his distinguished career and wisdom, would want my advice on anything at all.

'Come upstairs,' he instructed, leading the way up the narrow staircase into his study and sitting-room. The easel was in its usual place in the corner, but totally covered up with a cloth.

'I want your advice on this painting.'

He removed the cloth. I couldn't believe my eyes: there depicted was me, driving the Morgan along a tree-lined road. He'd painted this as a thank-you for all the commissions. I felt overwhelmed. The painting still hangs proudly in my study and reminds me of the many happy hours I spent in Sammy's company.

The Open University academic year was different from that of conventional universities. Our year started in February, and finished November, just like in Australia. As I had been away from Australia for four years, I started hankering to spend Christmas there after my first year of university studies. I thought I needed a reward and some sunshine. Working just part-time now, I had no excess income and agonised about spending my savings on a holiday. Then a brilliant idea came to mind! I would purchase a second-hand E-type, use this for one year in England, ship it to Australia and then sell it. That would definitely finance the trip, and perhaps give me a little extra.

Every Thursday morning I eagerly collected *Exchange & Mart* from the newsagent and scoured the Jaguar 'for sale' ads. The prices were in the region of £1,600 to £1,700 but unfortunately I only had £1,400. There was no point travelling great distances to view any without sufficient funds, but I still kept buying magazines in the hope one would appear at the price I could afford.

I couldn't believe my eyes one day. A 1970 FHC E-type was advertised with a price tag of £1,399, and not too far from West Horsley. I telephoned but there was no reply. All day I kept dialling the number until at last at 6pm a young lady answered. The car belonged to her boyfriend. He was away on business but I could come and view it, and she would take me for a test drive.

Although night had fallen before I arrived, I could tell that the owner had not treated his E as I felt it should be. For a start, the body and the engine compartment were filthy but the panels looked straight without ripples. As far as I could determine it had not been involved in an accident. The rear axle whined on overrun as we drove around the streets, and the clatter at the front of the engine, I guessed, might be a loose timing chain, a characteristic to which Jaguars were prone.

The price suited me and, as far as I knew, the problems could be fixed without major expense. But as a 'mere' female, I needed my father to inspect the car before a decision was made. I suggested that we would return the following evening. However, back at the lady's house to view the owner manual and service records, I heard the phone ringing non-stop. After five calls from potential buyers, I knew a decision had to be made, otherwise someone else might get there first.

I agreed to buy the E-type and arranged to pick it up the following evening. A restless night followed as I wondered if I'd got myself a clapped-out heap. My mechanic friend drove the E home to Wix Hill, and confirmed my original assessment of its condition, to my great relief. I was now the owner of a regency red 1970 E-type 4.2-litre, fixed-head coupé, with sunroof.

The next few weekends and evenings were spent stripping out every bit of upholstery and coating the inside of all the panels and sills with waxoyl, an anti-rust substance. New brake pads were fitted and I decided to clean the SU carburettors and carry out a good service with the aid of the Jaguar E-type workshop manual, while my father made up the pedal extensions. I wouldn't accept any help. I wanted to achieve all the maintenance myself. After two weeks I took the E-type out for its first run. It was wonderful to experience such power again and hear the soft purr of the 4.2-litre engine. Walking up the street I stopped and looked behind at the E, parked. What perfection! My love of this marque had not diminished one bit in ten years. For a while it was difficult to concentrate on studies: all I wanted to do was drive the E-type about. The novelty would not wear off, but the desire to pass examinations was also strong. If I failed then I would not deserve a holiday in Australia.

After eight months of proud ownership and every mile a sheer pleasure to drive, the time was nigh to phone around for quotes to freight the Jaguar to Australia. I'd studied hard and, with exams not far away, needed to motivate myself to work even harder. The thought of a six-week holiday in sunny Australia to escape part of the British winter provided considerable inspiration.

I'd checked on prices that E-types were realising in Melbourne and, assuming my car sold easily, then I should indeed return to England with money as well as a suntan. The prospect seemed attractive. But somehow I just couldn't force myself to make that phone-call to a freight-forwarding agency to enquire about shipping costs to Australia. It was as plain as day, I did not want to sell my E-type. My justification? E-types were not manufactured anymore. When my financial situation improved after these student days were over, where could I find such a good E-type again? Of course that would be impossible. It was therefore necessary to forego the trip and keep the car. I passed the exams and did not feel deprived. My reward was ownership of the E. I rejoiced in the aesthetics of that magnificent piece of engineering. Thirty years on, I still do. And anyway, suntans soon fade.

After the OU exams, and when the language school closed for Christmas, I decided to drive to Italy in the E-type, to visit Signora Luccarelli and friends in Perugia. My father had just about finished the restoration of the 8C Alfa and asked me to buy a Pocher model kit of a Monza Alfa at the Alfa factory in Milan. Luigi Fusi, the Alfa Romeo historian, was still involved at the factory and had told Dad I could purchase a model kit with a staff discount. But above all, Dad wanted me to give Fusi some photos of his near-completed Alfa.

I had no desire to stay in France; in fact, my determination was so strong that I found a night ferry crossing that landed in Dieppe at 7am. My plan was simple: to drive towards Paris until I met the AutoRoute, head south, turn left on sight of the Mediterranean, then find accommodation after crossing the border into Italy.

The schedule was rather ambitious. Leaving Dieppe precisely at 7am, I'd reached the outskirts of Paris at rush hour, along with half the city's driving public. Traffic was at a standstill for some time. I could see myself still in Paris by nightfall.

Eventually, the AutoRoute was in sight and the E and I were heading south. With no speed restrictions, I found the car comfortable at a cruising speed between 100 to 120mph. It was amazing just how quickly the miles were devoured at that speed, through several diverse weather conditions. Over the mountain ranges snow began to fall. I thought that had put paid to my ambitions of reaching Italy by early evening, but the weather soon improved and so did my speed.

Lethargy started to affect me after about an hour and a half of driving with such high concentration. Every time I felt too sluggish to use the indicators, I knew the time had arrived to stop the car and briskly exercise for a few minutes before resuming the fast drive. Eventually, near 8pm, I drove into San Remo, on the Italian Riviera, mission accomplished. Getting a second wind, I went to visit the Benassi family and next morning headed off to Perugia. As I pulled up in front of Numero 24, via delle Clarisse, Signora Luccarelli, my former Italian landlady, came running out – more excited to look at the E-type than speak to me.

'Che belissima, che macchina belissima,' she kept uttering.

Five days in Perugia flashed by. Then I headed for Milan where I spent a day at the Alfa Romeo factory and came away with the last remaining Pocher Alfa Romeo 8C model. On the way back through France, the effect of the fuel crisis, which started two days before I left England, was evident. Speed restrictions were now in force on the AutoStrada and AutoRoute – and were strictly imposed. I didn't dare extend the E-type's legs so the journey home passed in a much more sedate manner.

Chapter 8

ALFA MALE – AND FEMALE

Hill climb records and chilled champagne

With the 8C Alfa now finished and well sorted, Dad started competing at Prescott, Silverstone and other race venues. To my family, part of the pleasure of motorsport is driving the participating car to the events. That way the driver becomes familiar with the car's characteristics before competing. Most of the meetings were over 100 miles from where we lived in Surrey and the distance provided plenty of opportunity to test the car and learn to react instantaneously to the Alfa's unique foibles, in various traffic and road conditions. The E-type became the follow-up car, bringing most of the tools and spares. The two loped along nicely together despite their thirty-three year age gap.

Competition was fierce between the Alfa Monzas in the same class as my father. It was just like old times, with him racing and me in a support role, the difference now being that I was well and truly old enough to compete, should I so wish. But as my main focus was to study hard and gain a degree, I did not appear to be cultivating any great desire to take up motorsport actively.

That is, until I read the Jaguar Drivers' Club magazine one day and saw mention of a Jaguar class to be held at the Shelsley Walsh meeting in August. I had heard much about Shelsley Walsh – opened in 1905, the oldest motor race venue in the world still operating on its original course, and today reckoned to be the 'Blue Riband' of speed hill climbing. But none of my family had ever been there. Mum and Dad were in Australia at the time and, although I had absolutely no intention of competing, for some strange reason I requested the entry form and regulations. Who was I trying to delude? Perhaps myself. After agonising for some time, I filled in the entry form and sent it away.

Hill climbing is about one competitor at a time driving over a given tarmac road, from a standing start to a flying finish in the shortest possible time. Timing is calculated to a hundredth of a second and great precision in driving is essential. There is absolutely no margin for error. Courses are smooth and well surfaced, usually quite narrow – quite like a country lane with a steep gradient – and may include tricky corners, some sharp, some sweeping, with short straights or long straights.

My reason for even thinking about competing at this meeting was that no-one knew me at Shelsley and if I made a fool of myself then I could skulk off home, without comment. The family driving reputation would not be put at risk.

I was half expecting my entry not to be accepted and when the tickets and entry list arrived with my name included, it was too late to back out. On race day I left from Surrey quite early in the morning, arriving at Shelsley Walsh just before lunch. The other Jaguars in the class were parked in front of the barn in the paddock area, a sight I had seen in many photographs in motoring magazines, and I slotted the E into its allocated space. None of the other drivers were about at the time and when they returned and saw another Jaguar they started chatting to my passenger, a male friend, assuming that he was the driver. This did not contribute to my confidence.

The E sailed through scrutineering without any hitches, leaving plenty of time for practice. The first practice run had to be taken before 4pm. I watched the other competitors in my class practising, the main contender being a lightweight racing E-type shared by two drivers. The rest of the class was filled with other road-going E-types. Soon it would be my turn. The minutes were ticking by so quickly and I felt fearful that I would not be able to handle the E-type at all, would make an utter fool of myself and perhaps damage the car. The 1,000-yard hill had an average gradient of 1:9, I later learned, and there was no room for the driver to make any errors. I could not force myself to practise and kept wishing that I'd never put myself into such a stressful situation.

Then, not many minutes before 4pm, I came to the conclusion that I'd never been a shirker before and, like it or not, I had to go onto the track. So what if I emerged a complete idiot! Waiting in a queue to drive to the start-line felt like for ever and I wasn't sure if I was feeling sick or not. Then it was my turn, on to the start line and wait for the lights to change from red to green.

Green: and away with just the right amount of wheel spin, into second gear round the first corner, Kennel, up the short straight, into third gear, as fast as possible through Crossing, brake, down into second gear, left into Lower Ess, right round Top Ess and power down as soon as possible, into third gear with foot flat on the throttle until the finish line appeared, before braking hard. The six-cylinder Jaguar engine was purring nicely at 6,000rpm. After all that effort and then arriving at the top holding paddock before parking, I was shaking like a leaf but, oddly enough, the experience felt somewhat enjoyable.

As I gazed over the Worcestershire hills and Teme Valley from the top of the hill, I started to marvel at this wondrous place, steeped in so much motoring history. It was becoming clear now why so many famous racing drivers had such a fascination for Shelsley. Its addiction had started to work on me.

Returning down the hill to the paddock area, I felt anxiety rear its head again as I was convinced that my time would be slow and last in class. But it wasn't. I was placed somewhere in the middle. My confidence shot up to where it should have been in the first place and I did not hesitate to line up for my second practice run. And thankfully the time improved to boost my confidence even more. At the end of practice I felt like a different person. I felt joyful anticipation for the real competition next day.

The sun was shining brightly the following morning as I arrived at Shelsley, full of excitement and pleased that my entry had been accepted. After the first official run I was in third position, the quickest road-going E-type in the class. Perhaps it was beginner's luck I started to convince myself.

Lining up at the start it was now or never. The whole run felt quite reasonable. I was surprised that the time had improved: I ended up third outright and first on handicap in class. From feeling a failure one day to elation the next was rather emotional. I phoned my father in Australia that night.

'I drove my E-type at Shelsley Walsh today,' I began.

He was rather surprised and asked how I got on. When I told him, he said rather dryly, 'Well, that's not bad to begin with.'

The event at Shelsley Walsh was quite a significant episode in my life. Deep down I'd been harbouring feelings that perhaps I was not capable of handling a car in competition and I guess that was one of the main reasons why I had avoided entering any events up to this point.

The transformation was rather sudden, from no desire to compete, to wanting to do it regularly. But, with exams quite close, my first priority was study and it was not until the following year that the E was entered for its next event. Prescott and Shelsley Walsh became my favourite venues as I competed the E in the GT and Modified Sports Car over 1,600cc Class. But this Jaguar was a road-going car without modifications to enhance its performance for competition and in the class she was pitted against much-modified Porches, V8 Morgans and other marques, and was not particularly competitive. I was keen to keep the E as a normal road car and yet I also wanted to start trying for class honours, rather than just trying to improve my own time. So I was faced with a dilemma.

My father surprised me one day when he suggested that I compete at one of the Vintage Sports Car Club's Shelsley Walsh meetings in the Alfa Romeo 8C. As the E had not committed any misdemeanours at any venue with me in the cockpit, he must have felt confident enough to let me loose in his pride and joy. Although most likely a fluke, my time ended up 0.9sec quicker than Dad's at the meeting. I did feel rather privileged that he encouraged me to get behind the wheel of that magnificent machine, considering the number of years he had spent in total dedication to its restoration.

It came as no surprise to my father that I had yearnings for a competition car of my own. He managed to locate a very sorry-looking rolling chassis languishing in a barn not far from Silverstone. It was once an Alfa Romeo 6C saloon. Dad decided to purchase the pile of bits and build me a special so I could compete at vintage hill climbs.

'Just a basic special,' he said. 'Should only take a short time.' But once Dad had started he became more intrigued by the mechanics of this 6C Alfa: this had the makings of a new labour of love.

At last I was earning an income. As soon as the degree course was successfully completed, I started a language centre in Guildford, an ambitious project at the time, and one I needed to escape from on occasional weekends – or that was my reasoning anyway. And what better way to release oneself from the hectic traumas of business life than to participate in the friendly motorsport category of speed hill climbing?

I was now convinced that the E-type, my every day transport, should be retired from competition. The marque had not been manufactured for some years and I wanted this one to remain in my ownership for ever. To keep competing at modern car meetings I needed to buy a car for that purpose. After this monumental decision was reached, the search started for another sports car, as I wanted to stay in the same class but be faster.

A racing Lotus Elan was the first car to be given serious thought. Considerable work and money would be needed to restore it, however, and I just couldn't convince myself that this was the ideal choice. Then I heard about a Brabham for sale in the Midlands. I wasn't sure I wanted a single-seater racing car but went to inspect it anyway. It was in a totally dismantled state and hard to judge whether the right components were included in the boxes of parts and I didn't feel inclined to undertake a major rebuilding exercise so that was another thumbs down.

After agonising for some time about what type of competition car I really desired, an advertisement appeared in *Autosport* for a Dastle Clubmans car, fitted with a 1,600cc Lotus Vegatune twin-cam engine. As the car was in Surrey, not far away, I went to have a look. The price seemed right and I ended up surprising myself by buying it without much contemplation. The car had not achieved any great successes in its racing career, but that didn't bother me: at least there was no measuring stick on which my own performance could be judged.

When the car arrived at home my father showed some enthusiasm but, as an engineer, was rather keen to undertake considerable modifications before the first event, some months later. One of the first modifications, to alter the seating and controls to suit my short stature – usually fairly simple on a road car – proved complicated. Rather than move my seating position forward to reach the steering wheel, he decided to bring the steering back to my position to avoid upsetting the balance of the car. A longer steering column was made, and a new seat to suit my shape was moulded from aluminium, similar to one fitted to my go-kart years before.

Once the seating position was perfected, the time had arrived for the serious engineering stuff. In fact you couldn't hold my father back. But as he dismantled and delved he quickly came to the conclusion that, because of all the Dastle's faults, it would have been better to start with a clean sheet of paper and design and build the competition car from scratch. To undertake such a monumental project was not practical, however, and I was keen to start competing my new acquisition. We decided that I should use the car in its original state until I became accustomed to its

Not the quickest way to corner at Loton Park Hill Climb. The Murrain sports racing car, fitted with Cosworth FVC engine.

A letter I received from Raymond Mays, well-known for his glorious victories at Shelsley Walsh, after I first broke the Outright Ladies Record at Shelsley Walsh in 1979.

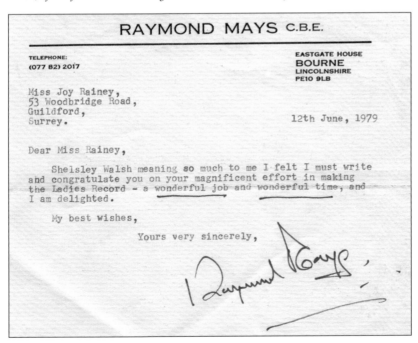

RAYMOND MAYS C.B.E.

TELEPHONE:
(077 82) 2017

EASTGATE HOUSE
BOURNE
LINCOLNSHIRE
PE10 9LB

Miss Joy Rainey,
53 Woodbridge Road,
Guildford,
Surrey.

12th June, 1979

Dear Miss Rainey,

    Shelsley Walsh meaning so much to me I felt I must write and congratulate you on your magnificent effort in making the Ladies Record - a wonderful job and wonderful time, and I am delighted.

    My best wishes,

               Yours very sincerely,

                     Raymond Mays

ABOVE *Kay Petre, holder of the Shelsley Ladies Record during the thirties, at Lynwood, headquarters of BEN, the Motor & Cycle Trades Benevolent Fund, in 1979. Kay was intrigued by the width of the rear tyres on the Murrain.*

RIGHT *Alan Jones, 1980 Formula 1 World Champion, and I reminisce about our karting days in Melbourne, when Alan drove a Rainey Kart.*

BELOW *The Murrain at Shelsley Walsh in 1979. The Outright Ladies Record was broken by the Murrain at every Shelsley meeting during 1979, with me in the driver's seat.*

My first competitive drive in Dad's newly restored 1937 Alfa Romeo 8C, at Shelsley Walsh in 1976.

The two Alfas, in the paddock at Brooklands just after Dad had finished rebuilding the 1936 6C for me to compete with.

The Alfa 6C, with roll-over bar fitted, competing at Shelsley Walsh.

Competitors in the first Disabled Drivers Sprint Championship in 1991. From left, Marc Haynes, Shaun Newcomb, me as the championship co-ordinator, Roger Duffield-Harding, Steve Weatherley, winner of the first and second championship, and Vincent Ross.

My Pilbeam MP 53 at Shelsley Walsh in 1987.

Paul Finn, press officer of BEN, just after supervising the signwriting on the Pilbeam.

An enjoyable first drive in my father's Cooper Mk 9 Norton at Prescott, 1988. (Derek Hibbert)

Family friend Ron Tauranac, designer of the Brabham and RALT racing cars, giving us some advice on setting up the suspension of the Pilbeam racing car, before my motorsport comeback in 2001. (Jerry Sturman)

My comeback drive at Shelsley Walsh in August 2001.

I felt so dejected when the Haynes Motor Museum 1900 Clement veteran car broke down during my first drive in the London to Brighton Veteran Car Run in 2001. (Trevor Hulks)

Competing the Pilbeam at Curborough Sprint Course, near Lichfield.

Trying out the Pilbeam cockpit after an absence of eight years. (Trevor Hulks)

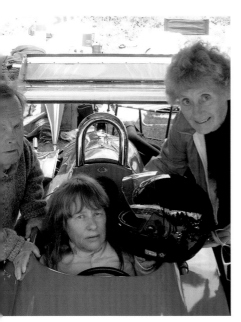

ABOVE LEFT *My father, me in the Pilbeam and my mother at Shelsley Walsh – August 2001.* (Trevor Hulks)

ABOVE RIGHT *That's me trying to fit the nosecone to the Pilbeam.* (Trevor Hulks)

BELOW *At last the A-series engine is installed in the Morris Minor just months before the start of the London to Sydney Marathon 2004. Trevor checks the carburettor while I insert the spark plugs.* (John Colley)

LEFT *Trevor looks pleased that the Minor is finished at last and I'm looking forward to the first test drive.* (John Colley)

BELOW *The Minor is flagged away at the start of the London to Sydney Marathon, 5 June 2004.* (Michael Johnson)

RIGHT *Loading the Minor into the Antonov aircraft for the airlift from Ankara, Turkey, to Cochin, India.* (Michael Johnson)

BELOW RIGHT *Lapping up all the attention from Indian enthusiasts in front of the Maharajah's Palace, Mysore.* (Michael Johnson)

Enjoying an isolated gravel road in outback southern Queensland. (Michael Johnson)

We made it! The Minor and two very happy rallyists, with Sydney Opera House in the background. (Jim Carr)

handling characteristics and only then consider making any major changes.

Every nut and bolt had to be checked as many were loose or their threads stripped. Our confidence was rather dented at the state of the rest of the car after examining the steering mechanism. Both tie-rods had been adjusted the wrong way, stripping the threads, and one was not connected at all. But once Dad was satisfied that the car was in a relatively fit and safe condition it was time for the new driver to show her stuff.

Finding a suitable location to test drive a competition car always proved difficult. Hill climb slick tyres are manufactured to an extremely soft compound. To lap continuously round a proper race circuit would quickly overheat the tyres, causing them to disintegrate. One day the local policeman, a car enthusiast, called in to check on the progress of the Dastle. He knew the owner of a grand house nearby which had a long drive. After a phone-call, permission was granted to test the car there. Not wanting to appear like an amateur, I felt rather nervous when the whole family of the grand household, the policeman and my own parents came out to watch my maiden drive in the new car.

As I climbed into the cockpit and pressed the starter, the 1,600cc twin-cam engine fired up on all four and I began to feel excited. This was my first real competition car and I hoped our future together would bring some success and not just failure and disappointment.

With such a high power-to-weight ratio, the power surge was an experience I'd not encountered before, as I let out the clutch and took off in first gear. The seating position, pedal and all controls were comfortable and, with about six runs up and down the half-mile drive, I began to acclimatise to the new mount. The time had arrived to send off the first entry form for the April 1977 Prescott meeting.

Prescott hill climb course is demanding, with many slow and tricky corners. I knew my first year with the Dastle would be a steep learning curve but fortunately I'd driven at Prescott in the

E-type and was familiar with the track. At least that was one less element to worry about. The weather forecast for the weekend provided some anxiety – rain was forecast. To drive a racing car for the first time in slippery conditions was something I had hoped to avoid.

When we arrived at Prescott early in the morning, the weather was dull but dry and the rain kept away all day, although there were two minor flurries of snow. Other competitors were keen to give me advice, mostly saying, 'Take it easy until you get the hang of it.'

Manoeuvring up to the start-line for the first practice run, although apprehensive, I was determined not to stray from the particularly unforgiving track, which meant driving fairly slowly. I approached every corner with caution, allowing at least double the braking distance necessary. Crossing the finishing line after the steady ascent I did feel quite relieved, but no longer frightened. The second practice run was slightly quicker and that gave me a gratifying sense of progress.

After lunch, when the real competition began, my aim was to improve the time as much as possible without taking any risks. With just under a minute in the cockpit per competitive run, it was quite obvious that at least a season of fairly regular competition was required before I became so familiar with every aspect of the new mount that there was no hesitation with gear-changing, braking and so on. I had driven the E-type many thousands of miles on the road and knew what to expect of it whilst competing, but to step into a new competition car without even turning a corner beforehand felt somewhat challenging.

My two runs were quite unspectacular: the times 58.87sec and 58.48sec. These might not exactly set the hill climbing scene on fire, but each run was an improvement. The class was won by Stephen Madge in his Mallock, with a time of 50.98sec; second was Bruce Ogilvie, 54.84sec; and third was Bob Soames, 56.31sec. At the end of the meeting I did not feel disappointed with the result for my first drive, I might have been last in class, but the 'Clubmans and Sports Cars up to 1,600cc' category was renowned for its extremely quick drivers. At the next Prescott meeting four weeks later, my time improved to 54.38sec and I was not last. But Norrie Galbraith from Scotland set a pace of 49.13sec to win the class. If I were to offer any challenge in the future then my times would need to improve dramatically.

Over the next few months I competed at Gurston Down, Loton Park and Wiscombe Park for the first time, as well as Shelsley Walsh and Prescott. I needed to learn about the new car and new tracks. My results usually ended up at the lower end or middle of the class but the improvements had started to level out and big chunks were not coming off the times any more. I did want to keep improving but just couldn't see how. At Shelsley one day Norrie asked what revs I took the twin cam up to. When I told him it was about 6,500rpm he replied in his broad Scottish lilt, 'take her up to 7,000rpm, lassie.'

For the next run I tried his advice but just before the Esses there was a mechanical clunking sound and the engine stopped. Back in our pit, as we removed the head from the engine, many of the competitors came to give a helping hand, offering encouraging words and hoping the damage was minor so I could get my second run. That was not to be. All but two of the valves were bent, but at least the head was not damaged.

Motor racing is an expensive sport. I was fortunate that my father's expertise was in engine building and as yet he had not touched the engine after I'd bought the Dastle.

Dad was rather disappointed and with hindsight felt we should have stripped the engine before I started using it. But there was no point in agonising and he dismantled the engine the next day and starting ordering the relevant bits.

While I was at work the following Thursday he telephoned me.

'I don't think it's much use spending a lot of money on that twin-cam engine,' he said. 'There's a Cosworth FVC engine advertised today. It's made specifically for competition. You'd be much better off with a competition engine, so how about buying it – that is, if you think you can afford it?'

I thought about the proposition for a few minutes, checked my finances and decided to go ahead. The vendor, in Kent, told us the FVC had recently been re-built by a professional engine-builder.

'It's ready to put straight into a chassis and race,' he assured me.

It was nerve-wracking, making the decision to purchase a competition engine without hearing it run, and I wavered for some time. Then I decided to buy it, despite feeling rather nervous that it might be a load of rubbish. I knew it was against my father's principles to run a competition engine without totally rebuilding it to his standards, but I had put him under pressure by wanting to compete in more hill climbs that season, particularly at the August Shelsley Walsh and September Prescott meetings.

The mountings needed to be modified to fit a different engine in the Dastle, but it was soon ready to start for the first time. It took quite a bit of turning over before it fired up and I was holding my breath. It sounded different from the twin-cam engine as though there were more, and not very pleasant, mechanical sounds.

Shelsley, the following weekend, now looked like a possibility. The 1,790cc bigger capacity of the FVC engine meant that I would be competing in a different class, the Sports Racing Car Class over 1,600cc. At the event, during practice I drove in a rather sedate manner and wasn't really impressed with the new engine. It did not appear to pull or run very well. Then, during the meeting, the engine came to an abrupt stop. I felt devastated. All my savings had gone on this. After checking everything we discovered that the timing had slipped.

Back home, on further investigation it was found that the front timing spindle normally had fine tolerances and at one stage in the past had come loose. It was not assembled correctly, just cobbled together. Other mechanical faults were discovered when the engine was completely dismantled. Fortunately Dad had contacts at Cosworth and after the engine was inspected they wrote a letter detailing all the faults.

The previous owner didn't agree that the engine was faulty, but unfortunately for him a solicitor I had consulted backed my claim. The legal assessment and Cosworth's own analysis convinced him that he should refund some of the money I had paid. I decided to forego the remaining hill climbs of that season rather than try to rebuild the FVC engine in haste.

My first season in the new car turned out to be more difficult than I had anticipated and I knew there was still much to be learned. I was still on the bottom rung of the ladder but definitely not daunted by the mechanical mishaps. There were seven months before the start of the 1978 competitive season. The workshop was about to become a hive of activity with every component of the Dastle totally transformed.

To be successful in hill climbing, the characteristics of the competing cars need to be different from race-circuit cars to suit the diverse venues and shorter running times. If you make a driving error, even a small one, you can't make up the lost time as you might when driving continuous laps on a race circuit.

Most engines, purpose-built for racing, concentrate on top end speed. A useful ingredient for many hill climb venues is to have low down torque to minimise the number of gearchanges. The time taken for an extra gearchange can add vital tenths of a second to a competitive run and ultimately affect the results. Some of the modifications that Dad made to the FVC engine to give a wider torque range from low revs were re-profiled camshafts with higher lift. The compression ratio was raised to 14:1. The fuel injection system was overhauled to convert it from petrol to methanol use. He also got busy with machining down the disc brakes to just 0.25in thickness, to shed weight from the car. In circuit racing, discs so thin would normally overheat quickly but with such short runs he thought they would be satisfactory.

Ron Tauranac came over to inspect the car. As designer and manufacturer of all of the Brabham Formula 1 cars until he sold out to Bernie Ecclestone and started building RALT racing cars, he was probably horrified when he saw the Dastle for the first time. This was no state-of-the-art modern racing car, paving the way ahead using modern technology, as Ron was accustomed to, but merely a space frame, amateur-built construction. He was most helpful with advice on changing and setting up the suspension and provided RALT parts and shock absorbers for the rear, as used in his Formula 3 cars. The shock absorbers we fitted to the front looked unusual as they were extremely small and were originally developed for the Tyrrell Formula 1 six-wheeler. Jack Knight Racing made new drive shafts to withstand the extra power and the new wider rear wheels and tyres. Also from Jack Knight came a special steering rack with a column designed to collapse on any impact, in case of an accident.

Ron wasn't impressed with the car's lack of aerodynamic design. Side pods and skirts were created and added, at his insistence, using some RALT materials. The whole car was now taking on an entirely different appearance. It was then that the decision was taken to change the name to Murrain.

We were fortunate to be living in Surrey, just one mile from the Tyrrell Racing stables and a few more miles from the RALT factory: it seemed that any obscure parts required to transform the Dastle could be obtained with a touch of friendly persuasion.

Just weeks before the first event of the season, the car was ready to be tested. We had gained permission to test on a disused airfield nearby. The engine had been fired up in the garage and sounded perfect but I was still nervous about driving the car, particularly after so much effort and man-hours had gone into it. Normally my father would test the cars, but this one was adapted especially for me and no-one else could fit into the driver's seat.

It was now my responsibility to set-up the competition car without any previous experience of driving modern racing cars. A challenging feat!

There was quite a marked improvement in the feel of the car and the engine was producing much more power than before. It felt very responsive and would idle at low revs, then without hesitation rev smoothly to high revs. My lack of set-up experience soon became obvious. The car felt fantastic to me, quite neutral and didn't require any changes. I kept insisting that I needed to get the hang of its characteristics first. The engineers expressed a different view.

A wet and slippery track greeted us at the first Prescott meeting on 2 April 1978. Not the sort of conditions to try to achieve fantastic results in my 'new' mount. During practice the rain would not stop and the following morning, although dry, the track remained muddy and very slippery. My quickest time was 57.20sec; the class won by Richard Brown with a time of 52.31sec in his new Mallock, fitted with a Hart 420R engine. Richard, I was to learn over the following years, is one of those rare, highly talented drivers who can get into a new car and win, first time out, regardless of the track conditions. Witnessing such skills tended to dent my confidence. I was disappointed in my own results, mainly because of the slippery track. I wasn't prepared to risk the car in such conditions and try to demonstrate any driving ability apart from staying on the track.

The next meeting provided more excitement than anticipated. Blackbushe, an airfield in Surrey, was the venue for a sprint meeting. As well as winning the class, I also achieved Best Time of the Day (BTD). What a boost! But I was a realist, aware that the top drivers were not competing. Even so, I must admit I went home feeling in a better frame of mind as I placed the trophies on the mantelpiece than if I'd returned empty handed.

Wet weather dogged most of the Prescott meetings that year, either in practice or the event. I was looking forward to a complete meeting with perfect track conditions for both days. Despite my dislike of a slippery track, at the July Members Meeting I did manage a second in class with 53.72sec, behind Richard Fry in his Mallock Hart with 51.60sec. When the final round at Prescott arrived, in September, so had the perfect weather – hot and sunny. The long-standing class record was broken by Ray Mallock, with a time of 45.57sec, but my effort was disappointing at 51.21sec. There was certainly a lot of time to make up before I could be competitive.

Elsewhere my results were mixed that year. It was not all doom and gloom though. I had another BTD at Blackbushe on 30 July – and that plus Dad winning his class in the 8C Alfa Romeo provided one weekly motoring magazine with a headline 'Definitely a Rainey day'.

Improvements were made to the Murrain throughout the season. Ground-effects became a popular area to experiment with. The Murrain sported a variety of side pods with venturis and, finally, sliding skirts that could be adjusted to road level. It was debatable, however, whether some of the aerodynamic features were operative until cars were travelling at over 50mph, which would render them useless at many hill climb venues such as Prescott with its slow corners and short straights.

On more than one occasion I had gear-change problems. Sometimes the gearing was not suited to the venue. The driver had to decide whether to change up to a higher gear for a short time or remain in a lower gear, mindful that every gearchange might add vital tenths of a second, but that staying in a gear could also slow performance. It was difficult to judge.

There were no competition gearboxes available for front-engined cars in which the gear ratios could be changed without considerable effort. Dad decided that having the ability to change ratios for every venue would be advantageous. We purchased a Hewland FT200 gearbox used in single-seater, rear-engined competition cars and with major adaptations – by turning the gear-box round – it was mounted in the front-engined Murrain ready for the 1979 season.

Ladies Records started to be a talking point with spectators and competitors. At times I felt slightly ambivalent towards Ladies Records. On the one hand I knew the Shelsley Walsh and Prescott

Outright Ladies Records were highly coveted, on the other hand, I thought that regardless of gender, all competitors are controlling a mechanical object and its success is not dependent on superior strength, but on driving ability. Occasionally I thought that the presentation of separate awards suggested that women could not drive as well as men. In fact, I've never been able to reconcile myself with the predicament.

Agnes Mickle had last broken Prescott's Ladies Record in 1972, with 48.76sec, driving a Brabham BT35. Despite a number of visits to Prescott, by 1979 my own time had not dipped below 50sec, so it was not likely to improve suddenly, although I was ever hopeful. The weather conditions had not helped. Most events that season, except the Classic Meeting when I drove the Alfa Romeo 6C, were held in damp conditions, so I started to believe that, given ideal track conditions, there was a remote possibility that I could achieve a time near the 48.76sec record in the Murrain. Patsy Burt, driving a McLaren, held the record at Shelsley Walsh at 31.87sec from August 1967, until Maggie Blankstone shaved 2/100sec off to leave it at 31.85sec driving a Mallock at the June 1978 meeting.

Shelsley was, and is, my favourite venue. This may partly be because it was the first hill climb course that I had driven at, back in 1974, in my Jaguar E-type. But it was also the atmosphere, the tradition and knowing that so many famous racing drivers had competed there in the past. The list is endless – Raymond Mays, Rudolf Caracciola, Basil Davenport, Ken Wharton and Stirling Moss, to name a few. Murray Walker began his long distinguished career in motorsport commentary at Shelsley in 1948.

To be a competitor at Shelsley can invoke powerful and sometimes strange emotions. I remember chatting to a rather agitated fellow competitor. Many of the facilities were to be upgraded, including a new toilet block to be constructed in the paddock area.

'I abhor the idea of a new toilet block,' I was astonished to hear. 'I derive such pleasure standing here, peeing in these toilets as they are now, knowing that so many famous racing drivers have peed in this very same place, and now that tradition will be taken away.'

I'm not sure I shared the sentiment but I could understand the depth of his passion. I couldn't know if I might ever be mentioned in the history books, amongst the famous lady racing drivers who had been holders of the Shelsley Walsh Outright Ladies Record, but I was sure of one thing: I was going to give it all my effort.

My team had now increased in number. Nick Herd had been Dad's mechanic on the rebuild of the 6C Alfa and assisted with the FVC engine and mechanics of the Murrain. He wasn't keen to travel to many hill climbs but Mick Pierce, an affable panel-beater and body-builder who constructed most of the body-panels for the Murrain in his spare time, rather liked weekends away at the 'hills', acting as a team member.

There seemed to be a competition within the hill climb fraternity about which competitor would turn up at the start of the season with the biggest and newest motorhome. Winnebagos of every shape and size filled the paddock area. My financial state wouldn't allow me to compete but I managed to find a Transit van fitted with a Luton body and windows, powered by a 6-cylinder engine. Equipped with former airline seats, it became the tow vehicle, driven by Mick, and hospitality unit at all the venues. I called it my 'WinneDago'.

The 1979 season started with damp meetings, much to my dislike. Wiscombe Park, on 1 April, proved very slippery, as did Prescott the following weekend, but I managed second in class behind Richard Fry, our times rather slow, 57.65sec and 58.57sec respectively. At Loton Park I also netted a second in class, but it wasn't until the 6 May Prescott meeting that the weather began to be kind: it was dry all weekend, if a little cool.

Despite this, the team was rather disappointed at my results and so was I. With all the work and effort that had gone into the car I thought we should be quicker. Richard Brown won the class with a 47.94sec time and was the only driver to score a sub-50sec result. My 53.37sec seemed slow by comparison.

At the June Shelsley Walsh meeting, expectations were high, the Murrain was running perfectly, but my practice times, in the 33sec range, did not seem to be an indicator of record-breaking stuff. The take-off for the first official run was reasonable and I managed to complete the course without mucking up on gear-changes, as I was sometimes prone to. When I crossed the finishing line I thought my climb was fairly quick but definitely not one for the record books. As I parked the car in the holding paddock, several fellow competitors came rushing over to tell me my time.

'I don't believe it,' was all I could utter when I heard 30.85 seconds. A whole second off the Ladies Record! It took me a minute or two to comprehend that I was now the holder of the outright Ladies Record at Shelsley Walsh.

I have never had so many kisses and hand shakes in such a short time!

When the batch had finished we returned in convoy to the paddock area. As the Murrain coasted down the hill the level of cheering and clapping from the officials and spectators was overwhelming. For a minute I thought the applause couldn't be for me and had to look behind me to check who was following.

Mick had rushed up to the front of the twelfth century church, which is on the return route for competitors, and launched himself onto the back of the Murrain to coast into the paddock. My mother and father were delighted with their daughter's achievement.

I wanted the second run to be still quicker but it wasn't. Perhaps I was a little too cautious. The time, 31.20sec, was inside the previous record. Richard Brown, the winner of the class, also put himself into the record books with a new class record of 29.13sec.

At the end of the meeting John Cozens, chairman of the Midland Automobile Club, presented me with an expensive bottle of champagne at the prize-giving. That weekend we returned home reasonably satisfied.

Two weeks later, at Gurston Down, we had another second in class, behind the two-litre Hart-engined Mallock of Richard Fry. I was beginning to like Gurston Down. The course, set out on a Wiltshire farm, is quite a high speed hill, starting with an unusual downhill run, where some cars reach well over 100mph, before a couple of slow corners. It was quite demanding but seemed to lack the atmosphere of Prescott and Shelsley.

My friend Paul Finn had asked me to exhibit the Murrain at the Motor & Cycle Trades Benevolent Fund annual fete at Lynwood, Sunningdale. I was happy to oblige, as there was time after the festivities to travel to Prescott for the one-day meeting on 1 July.

The VIP guests were Kay Petre, Jack Warner (star of the TV programme *Dixon of Dock Green*) and myself. Since I was a child I'd read about Kay Petre, the petite lady racing driver of the thirties, renowned for thundering round Brooklands in the enormous Delage and other cars, as well as breaking records at Shelsley Walsh in a Riley. After an enormous accident at Brooklands in 1937 she stopped competing, but on this day at Lynwood she was intrigued with my Murrain, particularly with the wide tyres and the fourteen seconds difference between her record at Shelsley Walsh in the 1930s and my new 1979 record.

I was engrossed with stories of her racing exploits, when Jack Warner interrupted our conversation. Obviously a Kay Petre fan, he said, 'I remember watching you in the twenties driving an MG round Brooklands.' The accolades continued for some time and I was surprised at Kay's comments, which I thought were rather off-handed to this old fan. As soon as he was out of earshot she said impatiently, 'I never drove in the twenties or ever in an MG. You'd think he'd get his facts straight!' Sixty years later the detail was still important.

At Prescott, the next day, I was keen to improve on my previous results. The track was dry and my confidence was high, particularly with one Ladies Record chalked up. My first official run of 49.54sec was the quickest I'd ever been but not close enough to the leader Richard Fry at 47.76sec. The second run improved to 48.98sec which got me second in class once again. The officials became rather excited at my time but when it was checked they discovered I was still 0.22 seconds outside Agnes Mickle's Outright Ladies Record.

My expectations were high the following weekend at Shelsley Walsh. So many spectators were asking if I was going to break the Ladies Record again that I started to feel a bit pressured. After my first run of 31.08sec, a time slower than my new record, I felt under even more pressure. But then the second run of 30.61sec broke the Ladies Record again and achieved another second in class behind Norman Hutchins in his Phoenix, which was powered by a similar FVC Cosworth engine as the Murrain.

I was beginning to enjoy being presented with a bottle of champagne.

New records seemed unlikely at the August Shelsley Walsh. Rain meant that the track was slightly damp in the Esses for the first runs and a further heavy shower just after lunch seemed to put paid to every driver's ambition. But, with a bit of a breeze and sunshine, the track soon dried out. Richard Brown and Richard Fry battled for class honours on both runs, with Richard Brown the eventual winner and a new class record of 29.04sec. All eyes were on me now. Throughout the weekend so many people kept asking the same question, 'Another record today Joy?' But once the green light appears on the startline and the competing car is away, those pressures are forgotten. To get to the finish line intact and as quickly as possible is of course always the objective.

By the time I had parked the car in the holding paddock after my last run some of the other drivers were applauding so I assumed a record had been broken, this time 30.08sec. I kept asking myself, why couldn't it have been 29.99sec? But there was always next year. At the presentation, however, John Cozens whispered in my ear, 'The champagne's chilled. We knew you'd break the record again.' He was such a charming man and I was enjoying the rare flattering remarks.

Shelsley Walsh, unlike other venues, felt like a stage. Once your performance had finished you coasted down the hill, in convoy, to the paddock area while the spectators rewarded you with accolades, should you be fortunate enough to break a record. It was an experience I will never forget and it happened at every Shelsley event in 1979.

Prescott, on the other hand, had a return road. After crossing the finish line it took some minutes, as you coasted back to your numbered parking area, before you knew what time you had achieved – and then, only if a team member bothered to hang about to tell you.

After my last run at the final Prescott meeting of the year, I agonized on the slow trip down the return road and when none of my team was in my numbered space in the paddock, I knew my results could not have been impressive. Third in class was not enough to compensate for the time of 49.34sec. It definitely wasn't a good weekend, but a class win at the Weston-super-Mare Speed Trials plus a win in the Alfa Romeo at a Greenham Common Sprint both contributed to my best year in motorsport so far.

Dad had more plans for improving the Murrain over the winter months. Skirts at road level were to be banned from the end of the 1979 season so the aerodynamic design of the side-pods needed to be looked at. Quite often I experienced difficulty changing gear and, although Dad had already modified the gate on the Hewland gearbox, he was keen for a radical change. As every hundredths of a second is crucial in hill climbing, he thought that valuable time could be saved if the driver did not have to take the right foot off the accelerator to brake but instead could brake with the left foot. That would enable me to keep the revs up while changing down and simultaneously braking.

Over the winter months he designed a system that featured a narrow clutch pedal, mounted well to the left and used only for take-offs. After leaving the start line the driver would then only use the left foot for braking. The gear lever was moved as normal but it incorporated a movement-sensitive switch that fired pressurised CO_2 that in turn activated a servo unit to release the clutch. The clutch re-engaged instantly the gear lever was used. All this action in just a split second!

By the start of the 1980 season the new design had been fitted to the Murrain. The design was years ahead of its time, before left foot braking and automatic gear-changing became the norm in Formula 1. I felt some trepidation before the first test, as a completely new driving technique had to be mastered. After years of right foot braking and using the left foot exclusively for activating the clutch, I now had to learn to brake differently. My imagination started to run amok with various scenarios – pressing the brake pedal by mistake with my left foot because I thought it was the clutch, or driving hard into a corner then being indecisive as to which foot to use. There was no time for dithering. It was essential that the left foot action became second nature or the consequence could be disastrous.

After running the car up and down the airfield runway and cornering on the mini circuit we had marked out, I continuously practised the new style of driving until it was automatic. And every night before I went to sleep, I went over the procedure a hundred more times in my mind. It must have worked. At the first meeting of that season, at Loton Park, I drove in fairly cautiously just in case I erred, but after pressing all the correct pedals with the correct feet under competition conditions then I was confident that the technique had been mastered.

'Are you going to break the Ladies Record here?' was the question I kept hearing at Prescott when we arrived for practice.

'Well, I'd really like to, but we'll have to wait and see,' was the only reply I could think of.

The first practice run didn't offer much hope for a record. The gear-changing problem started to dog. I just couldn't manage to change down. At Pardon, a very tight left-hander, I tried several times to change down into first gear but it just wouldn't go in. After the Esses, the same baulking problem occurred. As I went down the return road I wanted to go home. Dad was not able to make any further changes, but needed to modify the Hewland gearbox, which meant a workshop job.

'See if you can manage to get into gear on the next practice run using brute force,' he advised.

As I went to the startline I decided to try something different. I knew the FVC had real low-down torque and was very flexible, so I took off in second gear and remained in the same gear for the whole run. By the time I arrived back at the paddock, after the long, slow trek down the return road, I had made the decision to go home and be a non-starter for the event the next day. I couldn't understand why everyone was smiling as I removed my crash hat.

'You must have managed to get the gears into the right slots,' said my father.

'Why?'

'Well, you're over two-tenths of a second inside the Ladies Record.'

As people started to appear to pat me on the back I took my father aside. 'You'll never believe this,' I whispered, 'but I went the whole way in one gear. I'm not going to tell anyone.'

During a mostly sleepless night I agonised over whether to attempt to change gears during the official runs or drive in one gear. I chose the latter. Even if I didn't break the record this time, I was convinced that once the gearbox was functioning well, the car and driver were capable.

Maggie Blankstone, in her 2-litre Mallock, stopped the clock on her first run at 48.56sec. This was two-tenths of a second quicker than Agnes Mickle's 1972 Outright Ladies Record. The crowds were excited. At last after eight years the record had been broken. Then it was my turn: my hopes were not high.

My first run, the time was 47.12sec. It was a new Ladies Record by well over a second and taken using just one gear! To say I was astonished was an understatement, but what a delightful surprise. The second run, slower at 47.86sec, was still a second inside Agnes Mickle's previous record. My team were ecstatic.

John Cozens came to offer his congratulations, as did officials from the Bugatti Owners' Club, which was promoting the event. John said, 'They didn't have any champagne for you, but I think I've shamed them into it.' This was not to be, much to his disgust. However, two days later, at work, there was a knock on my office door and the biggest, most beautiful bouquet of yellow and blue flowers I have ever seen arrived from the Bugatti Owners' Club: yellow and blue were their theme colours. It took my breath away.

As 1980 was the 75th anniversary of BEN, the Murrain was painted in the fund's livery to promote the cause. Paul Finn – now mobile with his own transport and a holder of the Advanced Driving Test – came to several hill climbs to make sure the driver was performing well. I didn't want to disappoint.

At the 4 May Prescott meeting, both of my runs broke the Ladies Record again, at 46.44 and 46.24sec. The rains came down at the June Shelsley and, although by the afternoon the track had dried, no record was broken. That was disappointing. I'd grown used to going home with a bottle of champagne. The August Shelsley, the 75th anniversary meeting, provided a track in excellent condition and perfect weather. It was an exciting day. My time ended up at 29.75sec. I was the first woman competitor under the 30-second barrier. And, yes, another bottle of champagne was presented, chilled to perfection. This time it was opened and shared around. The course record was also broken that day, by Martyn Griffiths in his Pilbeam MP40G at 26.60sec.

The following weekend at Loton Park, Maggie Blankstone and I exchanged ladies records on every run. Maggie set the pace and a new record at 55.92sec. Then it was my turn at 55.77sec. Maggie again lowered the time to another new record at 55.33sec. The crowds were excited. On my last run I just managed to break the record once again to leave it at 55.17sec.

A battle at Prescott, two weeks later, managed to keep the crowds on their toes and me on mine as well. Maggie's first run of 45.04sec broke my record by over one second. I knew I had to perform well to beat that. The first run was going well, then as I tried to change down at Pardon I could not get the gear to engage no matter what I did. I ended up stalling the engine. The marshals turned me around and I coasted back down the hill in front of the crowd of spectators, feeling embarrassed.

Dad was sorely disappointed and tried to adjust the clutch engagement mechanism. It seemed to be operating when we tried it again with the car in a stationary state. But I could not drive the car for a proper test, as there is nowhere to test a competition car during a hill climb event.

Buoyed by her success Maggie smashed the record yet again to 44.24sec on her second run. My previous quickest was exactly two seconds slower, set at the meeting before. The adrenaline was pumping even harder than normal as I drove to the start-line for the last run of the year at Prescott.

The run felt reasonable and there were no missed gearchanges this time. Coasting down the return road felt like for ever and by the time I was near my numbered space I was convinced that the time would not be record breaking, but I was praying very, very hard, otherwise I would have to wait until the following year for another attempt. When I saw the smiles and clapping of everyone I began to suspect that I was wrong. And I was. I'd achieved 43.92 seconds, everyone kept telling me. Another record and lowered by a total of 4.84 seconds over the year! I also received the Ladies Award for the 1980 Midland Hill Climb Championship.

It was a fantastic way to end the year at Prescott.

At the last meeting of the year at Gurston Down, Richard Fry, now with a 2.3-litre Hart engine, beat me into first class position by just over a second. I was trying too hard to win on my last run and managed to overstretch myself by leaving the braking too late at the bottom of the hill and failing. But never mind, it was a good year.

Feeling more confident now, I decided to try to find some sponsorship to assist with the running costs for 1981. Every year Paul Finn and I would meet up for Press Day at the Motor Show. As we were walking past the Aston Martin stand I noticed Victor Gauntlett talking to several people. Victor was later to become chairman of Aston Martin but at this stage he was managing director of Pace Petroleum, the oil company he'd set up with over 400 outlets in Southern England. I'd known Victor for a number of years. Sometimes we competed at vintage hill climbs in the same class, he in his Bentley and me in the Alfa.

I wanted to ask Victor if he would consider offering some sponsorship for the following year but discovered I was a bit too shy. It almost felt like begging. However Paul insisted that this was too good an opportunity to miss, so I took a deep breath and walked towards where Victor was standing, by now with champagne glass in hand and two glamorous models hanging onto his every word.

'Excuse me Victor,' I interrupted. 'I know this is not the right time or the right place to ask, but would you consider sponsoring me next year?'

'You're right Joy,' he said. 'This is definitely not the right time or place, but here's my card. Give me ring on Monday and we'll discuss it.'

When I phoned on Monday morning, he told me to list all the running expenses I was likely to incur over the coming year and Pace Petroleum would cover them. He was a man of his word. For two years Pace Petroleum sponsored me.

I achieved no ladies records at Prescott during 1981. There were no big chunks being knocked off my times anymore, in fact, I did not equal my quickest time, much to the disappointment of my team. The weather conditions at some of the events did not favour record breaking driving either.

It wasn't until the May meeting at Gurston Down, when I netted a class win and qualified for the Hill Climb Championship Top Ten Run-Off, that the team's spirits were lifted. How I was longing for another bottle of champagne at Shelsley Walsh! Despite fine drizzle at the July meeting, fortunately not when I was due to compete, I broke the ladies record on both of my runs, at 29.38sec, followed by 29.36sec. I felt very privileged to experience applause from the spectators twice.

The biggest surprise came at the end of the class runs. The Murrain had qualified in tenth position for the Top Ten Run-Off. It was the first time a lady had qualified at Shelsley for more than ten years, I was told. Two more opportunities to break the ladies record, I kept thinking. Twenty-eight seconds flashed into my mind. Surely with the track in such fine condition I could achieve it!

As I sat in the Murrain, ready to strap myself in and put on my crash helmet, full of anticipation of what might be, my dreams were shattered. The heavens opened with something akin to a tropical downpour. The meeting was delayed as we changed our wheels to the treaded wets. Still the rain did not abate as I drove to the start-line, the first one away for the run-off to act as the benchmark for the other competitors. I drove steadily, recording a time of 41.79sec. My second run improved to 37.70sec and I claimed ninth for the day. Overall a good event, but I often think about what might have been, had the rains not come.

Record-breaking was addictive. Shelsley's record had been lowered and at the August Loton Park meeting the Murrain smashed the record again to leave it at 54.61 seconds. At the September Prescott, the last for the year, I really did want to lower the ladies record again.

The weather conditions were perfect, but my first time of 44.84sec was still just under a second slower than my previous record. I would have to try every trick in my book to end up quicker. The start of the second run seemed almost perfect. I braked later for Ettores and Pardon, power on earlier – everything was going so well – the Esses felt quicker. Then Semi-Circle, the last corner before the finishing line, a stab on the brakes and then as quick as a flash the Murrain veered to the right and came to an abrupt stop hard against the bank. I sat there – gutted. The offside front wheel was pointing in a peculiar angle and the suspension was damaged.

That was it for the season. Several spectators told me afterwards that they were convinced that run would have been my quickest ever, by far. To use a fisherman's analogy, 'it was the big one that got away.'

The 1982 season was a time of experimentation on the car, and not always enjoyable.

My father was continuously developing the Murrain. He was keen on forced-induction and decided to turbo the FVC engine, well aware of the lag problems that usually occur with turbo engines when accelerating. He devised an after-burner, with two spark plugs and a set of ignition in the exhaust manifold which ignited, fuelled by kerosene, and kept the turbo going.

The first time we tested the car on the runway I was moving steadily through the gears in a straight line when suddenly, without warning, the Murrain lurched violently into a monumental spin that seemed to last for ages. The turbo power came in too suddenly. From then on, I treated the Murrain in turbo form with some caution.

At a Prescott meeting the engine popped and banged and I couldn't keep it running smoothly. In testing, when Dad fitted a larger turbo the problem vanished.

When driving the Murrain, as soon as I lifted the accelerator pedal another coil came in and squirted kerosene in through a vaporising jet upstream. The idea worked well, the turbo kept going, but the driver had difficulty in controlling this power. It wasn't docile in any way at all. I found competing rather daunting, particularly on the narrow hill climb tracks lined with trees and steep banks.

At Shelsley, yearning for that bottle of fizz once again, I was determined to improve. As well as its turbo engine, the Murrain was sporting a bigger rear wing to provide more downforce. On my first run the takeoff seemed quick and I as started to go round Kennel, the first corner, I experienced understeer, a handling characteristic I'd not felt before in this car. I was unable to bring the front round and although I'm not aware of which wheel hit the bank and sleepers first, the Murrain appeared to be thrown up onto the bank and then ended up back on the track facing the right direction, but quite damaged. The accident probably didn't last long but it felt like slow motion. The meeting was brought to a halt until the efficient marshals retrieved the car and driver. I was not hurt physically but my pride was bruised. When people came to visit me in the Medical Centre and asked, 'Are you all right Joy?' I burst into tears. After an hour, however, the shock symptoms began to wear off and I could reply in a more controlled manner.

The Murrain was repaired in a short time, the damage more superficial than first thought. I finished the year with the FVC engine minus its turbo, but my times did not equal my previous best results. I have no doubts that if the turbo engine had been developed and improved further, it would have been very quick indeed. With a very busy work-life during the week I was unable to take time away from work to test every change made, much to the frustration of my father. At the end of the season we discovered that the Murrain chassis had begun to twist quite dramatically, due to the extra power output.

Driving to work one morning, several weeks after the last meeting, I suddenly thought I might have a year's sabbatical from driving. Next day the same thought was still lurking. Perhaps then for the 1984 season I would feel invigorated and ready for a new challenge?

With the chassis of the Murrain needing major surgery it was obvious that the financial input required would be considerable and I needed a year to save up.

During the year I met Trevor Hulks. He was competing in a Cooper Mk5. The class was very competitive and Trevor was one of the top drivers. At a party that one of the competitors organised Trevor and I started talking. Over the next year we found we got on fairly well – he didn't mind that I had a racing car and preferred competing to other more mundane activities. Gradually we started going everywhere together and a relationship started that continues to this day (even surviving the rigours of the 2004 London to Sydney Marathon).

By the time the first entry forms had arrived for the 1983 season, however, I just had to enter in something. Staying home every weekend, after competing at least twenty times per season over the past few years, was not an attractive alternative and I didn't feel inclined to find another absorbing hobby.

The Alfa Romeo 6C provided the answer and was entered for the Classic Car Class at Shelsley and Prescott. I felt very lucky to have such an opportunity. Not many drivers competed in two disciplines of the sport – with modern sports racing cars and at vintage meetings – and I enjoyed every second.

After the monumental rebuild of the 8C, my mother and I never thought my father would start so soon on another major project. I couldn't do it justice, writing about the rebuild of the 6C, and have chosen instead to borrow some excerpts from my father's book *Alfa Romeo Ferrari*, where he writes about the difficulties of this epic undertaking.

THE ALFA ROMEO 6C 2.3

A year or so after my 8C was finished, an advert appeared in *Motor Sport*, selling a 6C rolling chassis 1,750 Alfa Romeo for £800. I had a friend in Australia who wanted exactly this. I rang about the ad and was given all the details including how to get to where it was, near Milton Keynes. I said I would be up the next day, Sunday.

The weather was freezing but I took the trailer along in case and when we arrived I was directed into a large courtyard in a semi-derelict farm and in the middle stood the Alfa chassis. I didn't get out of the car. I could see it wasn't a 1,750 but a 6C 2,300, identifiable by the trailing arm suspension. The valley between the cam boxes had ice in it and I could see that the spark plugs were not in their holes.

I thanked the gentleman for showing it to me and bade him goodbye.

He said, 'Hang on a bit – give me an offer'.

I said, 'I don't want it'.

He said, 'It must be worth something'.

I pondered for a while, as I knew the suspension, brakes etc. were the same as the ones on my 8C, but I really didn't want to bother.

I said, 'I don't want to insult you with an offer'.

He said, 'Try me'.

I said, '£100'.

He said, 'It's yours'.

We loaded it up and trailered it home to Surrey. By the time we had arrived home the ice had melted on top but I thought I would like to get rid of the water in the cylinders so I hooked up a battery and pressed the starter button and a geyser of water shot into the air.

After quite a bit of this treatment I poured some oil down the plug holes and turned it over slowly. Some time later I borrowed a fibre optic probe light and looked down the bores and it seemed as though the water had not been in the cylinders all that long as there was only a brown ring mark on the walls. We put some plugs in and fiddled with ignition points and the carburettors and started her up.

I had a rough 328 BMW body, painted red, in a shed and I decided I would put this body on the chassis by wiring it on with fencing wire and selling it off for what I could get. Then the pressure from the milling throng started to build up. Why not do the BMW body up properly and make the grille like an Alfa and use it for a while. Why not this? Why not that? Hang on, hang on, I've already spent over two years building up an Alfa – I have already climbed Everest and I'm not going up again. Joy, my daughter, said she could finance part of it and drive it in the Vintage Hill Climbs.

Ah, well, I'll just have a look inside the engine and then make up my own mind. Hmmm, quite interesting, the engine has been rebuilt, rebored, crank ground, but not run to any extent. Oh God, here we go again. I was already on the lower slopes of Everest.

I decided to dismantle the engine completely and reassemble and just run it. The big end bearings were not quite up to scratch so I thought I would take a short cut and fit Vanwall thin wall big end shells. I ploughed through the Vanwall catalogue and found that the only big end bearing shells the size I required were listed under 'Pobeda'.

I rang Vanwalls to ask if and where I could get these. I think the chap on the other end of the line was a bit aghast but he said he would ring me back. Oh well, I suppose you can't get hurt for trying. Believe it or not he actually did ring me back and asked how many bearings I needed and I told him enough for one engine.

He asked, 'Where are you ringing from?'

I replied, 'West Horsley'.

He said, 'Right, I'll drop them in tonight as I go past your place'.

When he arrived, he produced a box about a foot and a half long in which there must have been a gross, at least.

I said, 'Give me the bearings and I'll pay you'.

He said, 'You've got the bearings – and there is no charge'.

He went on to tell me that they were made up for an order for 'Pobeda' in East Germany and they welshed on the deal and there were piles of them. He continued to say that if I wanted anymore to just yell.

I replied, 'Well, I've got enough here for the next million miles'.

What I did was melt the old white metal out and then carefully tin the backs off the brass shell with 50–50 solder and did likewise to the inside of the conrods big end.

I then put some bolts on and tightened them up somewhat and then played the blowtorch on to them until the solder just melted. While in this state I tightened the bolts, firmly removing them when cool and the joins cleaned up.

I then put new fine threaded, later Alfa, high tensile bolts in, tightened them to the correct tension and Guildford Autos bored the brass shells to the desired size of 55.001mm and filing the location nicks out, fitted in the shells and placed them on the crankshaft. Excellent.

At this stage, the outside pressure began to build up – an Alfa is not an Alfa unless it's supercharged. I asked Mark Ransome from George Godfreys if they had a second-hand cabin blower at the works. A few days later he came over and said, 'No, nothing – only one half the size required'.

That was that. But during the night I had an idea – I just wonder if they had two of these small blowers. I might be able to mount them on the side of the engine *à la* 2.9. I rang Mark to see if they possibly had two blowers. A couple of days later he rang me back to say no, they didn't have two. I cursed. He went on to say they had six, 'take the lot or none'.

Fortunately, three of them had the mounting casting still attached – they were cabin blowers off a Vampire. The mounting castings came in very handy as I was going to join the two superchargers together 'nose to nose', or driving gears to driving gears. I cut these castings to the width desired and milled them accurately and set the locating recess up on a turned spigot on the lathe and machined another male spigot at the join and the other casting had a female recess to take this. I made a tight fitting jig, bolted it together and had it argon welded.

The rotor shafts were hollow and were splined at the gear end. I had a long shaft made with a long spline end to fit across to both superchargers to drive them. I then made patterns for castings to mount the two blowers on the side of the block and another casting for the extended nose of the drive shaft to extend to the front of the engine to take the drive from the old drive pulley. The patterns and castings up to the inlet ports were much more complicated, as I wanted them to look just like the Alfa finned ones.

I now needed two updraft carburettors to suit. This became a major problem. I was friendly with Leonard Reece and had fitted one of his Reece-Fish carburettors to my Vauxhall Victor. On studying this, I realised that it wouldn't make any difference to the functioning of the carburettor if the air went upwards or downwards. Len told me that the carburettor was designed in 1938 and no basic alterations had been made since then. He added that the original housing was made from brass. I asked if his patterns could be used to cast in brass and the answer was, 'why not?'

That was carried out with the jet holes on the butterfly shaft reversed and a flange silver soldered on the top.

The next problem was that the engine would stand too high in the chassis with a wet sump, so I looked at the drawings of the Mille Miglia 6C 2,300 to see how it was dry sumped. I found that I could cut 4 inches out of the sump by cutting off the top flange and argon welding it to where the fins started on the wet sump.

The difficulty now was where to mount a scavenge pump, the only place available, on the end of the dynamo. I obtained a pump, redirected the main oil pipes and galleries and fitted a full flow oil filter but then found that the pump would not cope with the oil accumulating in the sump.

The reason is that the 6C 2,300 engine had the oil pump incorporated in the front main bearing and thus the gears were of gigantic proportion for an oil pump. This meant that it displaced large quantities of oil and probably 90% went straight back into the sump via the pressure relief valve. All of the oil had to be collected and returned to the remote oil tank, so a much bigger scavenge pump had to be fitted. I found one, which I believe came from a Dakota aeroplane engine.

The rest of the engine went together with the same care as to the 8C previously, then, mounted into the chassis.

Fred and Alex from Robert Peel (the builders of the 8C body) came out one evening for a visit and when they saw the 6C rolling chassis, one of them said, 'You're not planning to put that old BMW on this? You've still got the jigs and patterns used for the 8C and the tool for cutting the big louvres. It will be so much easier to make a complete body'.

What could I do – I had to go the whole distance. I suppose it was the right, logical thing to do and so it all came to pass.

To finish it we made a new radiator, exhaust and silencer, seats, petrol and radiator type caps, obtained instruments and folding windscreens, spray painted and it all functioned and ran very well.

The first outing for the 6C was a driving test day at Brooklands. I drove the 8C and Joy drove the 6C.

We had some teething trouble as the lubrication for the two superchargers was just a simple small tube, coming down to the blowers from the cam cavity housing but somehow the exhaust smoked badly and the spark plugs became oiled up. I made up small jets to restrict the flow of oil until virtually no oil was coming through; but still the problem persisted.

On the way to Prescott, after coming down the long steep hill into Aylesbury and going along the High Street, I was afraid someone would call out the Fire Brigade, there was so much smoke. I started to have thoughts about what I had done wrong inside – have the rings all seized up, etc?

At Prescott for the climb, I completely blocked off the oil supply to the supercharger and it went up quite cleanly, smokewise. For the rest of the meeting I ran the engine with the oil feed connected and just before each climb, blocked it off again. That seemed to prove it was something to do with the supercharger lubrication.

There have been quite lengthy debates in the bar at such places as the Phoenix Inn about which way the lips on the oil seals should face, especially on cabin blowers. It was argued that on an aircraft it has only to blow whereas on an engine it has to overcome the vacuum pressure on over-run so the oil seals must be reversed. I chose to ignore this advice and I had fitted up the oil seals with the lips facing inwards towards the rotors. Possibly, this is where I slipped up.

There was only one way to know: strip them all down again and reverse the seals, then decide. After completely dismantling the superchargers, cleaning and laying everything out, I was baffled – and then it happened! On closely examining the oil seals I discovered the whole eight of them were faulty. The neoprene lip seal section had not vulcanised to the outer steel ring housing, thus allowing the oil into the rotors with hardly any restriction.

I had fitted these brand-new.

The oil seals were manufactured by a well-known company. When I rang to tell them about the problem, they denied their product could be faulty and offered excuses. 'You have overheated the supercharger ... you haven't fitted them properly ... however, send them back and we will have a look'.

After denials that the seals were faulty, the company replaced the oil seals.

There was a lengthy discussion but they always denied that the seals were faulty even though I had some samples where I could put my fingernail under the neoprene and easily separate the bonding on to the steel outer.

Anyway, the new seals they supplied worked very well. I left them as before with the lips pointing inwards.

By now the 6C seemed to be going really well and even though it was only 2.3-litres it seemed to have as much steam as the 8C and felt as though the power came in much earlier. Probably this was due to two small blowers instead of one.

The next problem was the single plate clutch. Off the line at Shelsley it just sat there with the clutch slipping. I took it apart and fitted much stronger clutch springs – so strong I almost had to lie on the floor to press the clutch pedal. It didn't work. To pieces again and fit an AP twin plate copper sintered clutch. Did this make it work? And how!

After the next meeting at Shelsley, on the way home to Surrey, there was quite a bit of vibration at around 70. Upon examination the next day I found the propeller shaft had twisted 180-degrees and a much thicker and heavy gauge T45 one had to be made.

My ego started to become dented because frequently Joy was beating me at Shelsley and Prescott and she was in the 6C and only 2.3-litres while I was driving the 8C 2.6-litres. Was this a sign of the onset of senility? But no, not quite, as we shared the 6C at Prescott and I just pipped her.

On one occasion coming home from Prescott we both arrived at the Witney by-pass together and, as there was no traffic about, Joy took off and so did I. We went flat-out for a mile or so, but I couldn't make any impression on her lead of about 20 yards or so. I suppose we were doing about 120mph – and then it happened! I looked in the rear vision mirror and there just behind was a gentleman, with crash hat on, riding a BMW of familiar colour scheme. Joy saw him at about the same time so we both – er – decided it was time to, er, lift off somewhat pronto and slow down to 70 or so. The gentleman on the motorcycle passed me and gave me a real barrack salute. He then went on and as he passed Joy he repeated the gesture and away he rode.

In 1983 I drove the 6C at Gurston Down Hill Climb. Brian Chant in his 4.3-litre Alvis was in the same class. On my first run I could not better his time. On his second run he couldn't better his first run so for my second run I was determined to get my record back. I started perfectly and went down into Hollow faster than I had done before, through Hollow in a four-wheel drift that would have made Nuvolari envious, through Carousal absolutely on the limit, up to Ash Corner and around it – God knows how – then flat-out up towards the finish, then out rushes a marshal with a red flag near the finish.

'What the hell?'

'The car in front hadn't crossed the line when you appeared. We were frightened you would catch him up before the line. Don't worry, you'll get another run.'

I sulked and went home.

At some meetings where I was competing the Murrain, my father entered the 6C if there was an appropriate class. The rivalry with Brian Chant in his Alvis continued for several years at Gurston Down. At the last meeting of the year in 1980 they were staging a battle for class honours but Dad pulled something special out of the bag and emerged the class winner as well as breaking the class record by nearly three seconds.

Back to 1983! After three meetings at Prescott and Shelsley in the Midland Hill Climb Championship rounds, we were leading on points. That provided a perfect incentive to continue competing for the year and the 1936 Alfa Romeo, with me in the driver's seat, ended up the winner of the Midland Hill Climb Championship's Classic Car Class.

Chapter 9

STRUGGLES WITH A PILBEAM

Bumpy times, both on and off the track

For several years I'd been feeling dissatisfied at work. My job, as principal of The Language Centre of Guildford, was demanding. Our speciality was running small classes, continuously. I was responsible for everything from planning specific courses, selling our expertise to companies and foreign embassies, and sorting out teacher/student problems, to instructing people on cultural differences and, when the cleaners didn't turn up, tidying the place up. A holiday in Australia, to escape part of the dreary British winter and recharge my batteries, didn't oblige with a miraculous cure to restore enthusiasm and I knew I had run out of zeal. The school needed new blood and new ideas – not mine any more. Nine years after founding it I was ready to move on.

I knew that selling an obscure business like this might take time. Motorsport, in such a period of uncertainty and change, had to take a back seat. My sabbatical from driving a modern racing car was extended and, instead, during 1984 I campaigned the 1936 Alfa once again at some hill climbs.

Eventually, in 1985, I sold the school and moved to Worcestershire. Trevor lived there, so did some friends. Another draw was that houses were cheaper than in Surrey. Also, hill climb venues Prescott and Shelsley were just a short distance away.

It was fun driving the Alfa again, although the yearning for a modern competition car was always lurking in the back of my mind. I was in the Alfa at Shelsley Walsh the day Gillian

Fortescue-Thomas clipped half a second off my record, driving Alan Payne's V8 powered Anson single-seater. I'm not sure whether Gillian's new record, or Trevor's casual suggestion that I should buy a single-seater racing car rather than a road-going sports car, had any influence on my decision but it wasn't long before I was scouring the 'for sale' ads for a single-seater.

After looking at a number of these over a period of months, I finally settled for the 1984-built Pilbeam MP53H/01 (without engine) of Max Harvey and Martyn Griffiths. The engine I favoured most was the 2.5-litre Hart but none came available during my search and I purchased a 2.3-litre version instead. Just as I was about to take delivery of the Pilbeam, Max and Martyn had a mishap while competing their current car and stripped the front suspension from their old car to use immediately. 'My' car was then sent to the Pilbeam factory for a new front suspension to be fitted and set up.

When the car finally arrived, we had to make quite major adaptations to enable me to drive – and I was hoping to compete at several meetings before the end of the season. Trevor set to work, moving the pedal box, the scuttle and dashboard closer to my driving position, fitting a new seat and altering the bodywork to suit. The Hart engine had already been rebuilt by my father, fitting camshafts with the same profile used in the Cosworth FVC. Once the air-operated clutch had been fitted and perfected the Pilbeam was ready for its first test on Long Marston drag strip.

Apart from a minor fuel leak, there appeared to be no mechanical difficulties. I managed a few miles up and down the strip in a steady manner to bed in the mechanical bits and familiarise myself with piloting a rear-engined competition car for the first time. It seemed odd, changing gear with my right hand. The left foot braking came as second nature and soon I felt quite comfortable driving. We placed some markers in strategic positions to simulate corners. With the rough surface it was difficult to judge whether the car's handling characteristics were acceptable but at least I felt ready for our maiden competition together – the August Loton Park meeting. I was quite excited.

During the first practice run I had taken off in a spirited manner, took Hall, the first corner – then, along the short straight through Loggerheads, without warning the Pilbeam suddenly darted slightly off the track onto the grass. I continued, mindful of the advice given by several people beforehand to get the feel of the car with the engine in the 'wrong place', as it would handle quite differently from a front-engined car.

I backed off a little, not wanting to bend the Pilbeam. But at the top of the hill, waiting for the convoy to return to the paddock, I started to feel concerned that I'd had no sensation that it might be about to dart off until this actually happened. Later I told everyone that I would probably take a while to get the hang of this thoroughbred. The way I thought about it, if I had a problem with the handling, this must be a failing of my own technique so I should try to adapt rather than blame the machinery.

Two events later, I happened to mention that the handling wasn't getting any easier and I had started to believe that perhaps it wouldn't. As I wasn't able to enlighten my team about what the problem actually might be, I kept saying that it would take me a while to get used to the car. When Dad decided to check all the suspension he found that the wheel alignment, both camber and toe-in, was out by a great margin and needed resetting. As the manufacturer had carried out the suspension set-up we assumed it would be spot-on.

Over the winter months other areas were examined. The chassis was found to flex, which wouldn't contribute to stable handling. To help stiffen the chassis Trevor made a stay out of thick aluminium to connect to the roll-over bar and rear of the engine and added two more struts to the roll-over bar. The additions appeared to stiffen the chassis quite considerably.

My first Prescott event for the 1986 season started with some embarrassment. On both official runs I failed, leaving the braking too late at Ettores and not managing to get round. On the second run I just could not change down at Pardon and ended up stopping.

Despite damp and slippery conditions, at the next two Prescott meetings I was beginning to feel slightly more confident. With the handling more stable, and no involuntary excursions off the track, it was time to deliver. I felt quite daunted competing in the 'big boys' class, particularly as my Pilbeam's engine was much smaller than the rest. At National Championship meetings my objective became not to win the class but simply not to be last!

Wet weather followed us to many events. My ideal situation would be a dry track for both practice and official runs at all meetings for a whole year, but that was never to be. The August Shelsley Walsh meeting was dry for the first runs. My practice times were not particularly competitive but at least each run improved. Gillian, driving Alan Payne's V8 powered Anson single-seater, was looking to break the Outright Ladies Record again. I had similar aspirations but thought the chances less likely as my previous quickest time in the Pilbeam was in the 29 seconds bracket.

There was considerable speculation all weekend about two ladies competing in the same class driving single-seater racing cars.

'Which one of you will break the ladies record?'

'Are you going to get your record back again, Joy?'

I kept hearing this sort of thing. The pressures were increasing. And then it was time for my first run.

As I manoeuvred and parked the Pilbeam in the holding paddock at the top of the hill at the end of my first official run, instead of leaping out of the cockpit to rush to the timing hut as usual, I slowly clambered out, I was so convinced that the run was definitely not record breaking. It felt smooth, with no apparent mistakes, but not particularly quick. When one of the marshals came rushing over to shake my hand, I just could not believe the time he told me: 28.32 seconds kept ringing in my ear. I had to rush to the timing hut myself just to confirm that this was correct. It was – and over half a second off the previous record.

As I coasted down the hill in convoy, I was so overwhelmed by the cheering spectators that by the time I had reached the paddock area I was just about blubbering like a four-year-old. My confidence shot right up now and I couldn't wait for the second runs. I wanted to knock a further chunk off the time. But during the afternoon the heavens opened and that put paid to my aspirations. Once again, champagne was presented. I also received the HSA Driver of the Day award.

Improvements to the aerodynamics and suspension were made to the Pilbeam over the winter months. The financial burden of managing a competition car was eased by having sponsorship for the 1987 season. Sponsorship occasionally comes in an odd way. At the Midland Automobile Club annual dinner dance and presentation, after listening to the speeches I needed to go to the lavatory. As I pushed my chair away from the table to get out, a gentleman at the table behind did the same thing and we collided. We started talking, continuing late into the night. He was Richard Allan, chairman of a group of companies, one being Queen Anne Silverware. He left the dinner that night as sponsor of my Pilbeam for 1987.

Whether he regretted this decision I'll never know but we travelled far and wide that year, including north to Doune in Stirlingshire. I had always wanted to compete there, after meeting so many entertaining Scottish drivers over the years. I was also looking forward to sampling the water. My curiosity about Scottish water had started earlier in the year at Shelsley when I noticed a very grey-faced and ill-looking Scottish driver called Tom McMillan on a Sunday morning. When I commented sarcastically that he must have had a good night, he replied in a broad accent, 'It's the English water. It's so impure. I had to put some whisky in to make it drinkable.' There was no shortage of pure water at Doune on my first trip: very heavy rain disrupted the meeting, making the track look like an ice rink.

Prescott had started experimenting with track variations for every meeting. The original short course was used for one meeting, then in 1989 the new cross-over course was introduced and, including the long course, gave three different combinations. With such a limited time on the track at any event it added to the challenge having to familiarise yourself with new terrain each time – I found this quite difficult.

My quickest time on the Prescott long course in the Pilbeam barely equalled my time in the Murrain seven years earlier. This was getting frustrating.

At Shelsley Walsh, keen to smash the Ladies Record again, I may have been trying too hard. At Kennel, I couldn't manage to get the Pilbeam to come out of the corner but ended up perched on the bank through the hedge. As I tried to regain my senses I recall a spectator calling out in a concerned way, 'Are you all right, Joy?' When the marshals came to rescue me and the car, all I could utter was, 'That's it. It's time to retire, I don't get on with this car.' In the Medical Centre, with time to reflect after the shock had worn off, I realised that I really didn't want to retire: all I wanted was to have as much confidence in the Pilbeam as I'd had in the Murrain, and to do reasonably well.

In spite of the disappointments and mishaps, over the next year the trophy cabinet in my lounge steadily filled up with class wins and placings from sprints and hill climbs, but I was not able to break my Shelsley Walsh Ladies Record.

At many of the venues the historic Formula 3 cars had started making a comeback and the class was closely contested, providing excitement for the spectators. My father started to hanker for his old Cooper, but the current owner, since Dad sold it in 1961 in Australia, would not part with his pride and joy. At the Beaulieu Autojumble, where we had taken a lot of bits and pieces to dispose of, Trevor came back from one of his forays round the other stalls and told Dad he had seen a Manx Norton engine on sale.

As Manx Nortons were hard to come by, my father replied, 'Yeah, pull the other one.'

'No, seriously, I really did see one.'

Dad took off like a rocket to find the stall. About half an hour later he returned with his new acquisition.

'What are you going to do with that?' I asked.

'I'm going to find a Cooper to put it in,' was the crisp reply.

A couple of months later Dad purchased a Mk9 Cooper. He had already rebuilt the engine to similar specifications to his engine in the 1950s and, at the age of seventy, once again started to compete in a Cooper Manx Norton.

I was too young to drive when Dad's original Cooper was sold – although I had spent many happy hours sitting behind the steering wheel dreaming – but I never thought I would ever actually compete one propelled by a Manx Norton. My chance came at the Prescott Classic Meeting and what fun it turned out to be. Some days before the event I had a few goes up the runway at Long Marston to get familiar with the positive stop, sequential gear-change procedure, a technique I had not experienced before. And I wasn't too displeased with my performance at Prescott, ending up somewhere in the middle of the large entry class.

Whilst holidaying in Australia at the beginning of 1989, one morning as I clambered out of bed to go for an early morning swim, my shoulder felt quite stiff and I was unable to lift my arm very far. After returning to England the following week there was no improvement, in fact it felt worse. It was sixteen months before the shoulder was back to normal and my competitive driving was severely disrupted.

During the non-driving period I got more involved with the organisational side of motorsport, becoming competitions secretary of the Hill Climb & Sprint Association (HSA), organising three events a year. I wasn't a newcomer to organising. As a competitions committee member of the Bugatti Owners' Club for four years I'd done my stint as secretary of the meeting at one Prescott event. It was very educational. I was impressed and entertained with some of my fellow competitors' ingenuity in attempting to get an entry after the closing date.

Some of the excuses I'd heard before – perhaps I'd even used them myself in the past – but I learned some new ones too. None worked, of course.

As I was out of action for most of 1989 it was a good time to review where I was going with motorsport. Paul Gething, a fellow competitor driving Alan Payne's Anson, mentioned to me that he had developed some software to analyse suspension behaviour. Both Alan and Paul had watched my Pilbeam competing at Shelsley. They were not impressed and asked if they could analyse its characteristics. The time was right. I knew I wasn't progressing but, as usual, had blamed the driver not the car.

The current geometry of the Pilbeam's suspension didn't rate very highly on the tests set up by Paul and Alan. The roll centre was too high and the swing axle length far too short, which would create rather unstable cornering characteristics. The spring rates and front roll bars were also contributing to the unbalanced state of the car. Oddly enough, having these faults identified gave me hope. Perhaps the lack of performance wasn't entirely my fault.

By the time my shoulder had almost healed the Pilbeam was ready with its new suspension set-up. I'd missed being a competitor and looked forward to regular driving again. At Shelsley Walsh, on my way to the start line, I'd just done one false start to warm up the tyres when there was a loud mechanical bang and the engine stopped. Oil was pouring out and when we removed the engine cover there, staring us in the face, was a hole in the side of the block. Not only was it the end of my Shelsley meeting but the demise of my 2,260cc Hart engine.

After recovering from the shock there was only one thing to do: buy another engine. The 2.5-litre Hart engine I preferred was hard to find but I eventually bought a 2-litre version, which would put me into a different category – the 1,600 to 2,000cc single-seater racing car class.

It was a very competitive class and I entered as many meetings as possible in 1992. We achieved regular class placings and some wins. At the Shenstone & District Car Club's Curborough June sprint meeting, as well as winning the class I had FTD (fastest time of the day) and set a new Outright Ladies Record. Things were beginning to look up, at last. It was harder work, however – the 2-litre engine required more gear-changes than its predecessor, much to my regret.

My record at Shelsley remained elusive. I couldn't get near it. Class wins elsewhere provided some compensation but I couldn't get rid of my addiction for a Shelsley record.

One day at Shelsley Walsh a pleasant chap who was a wheelchair user started asking questions about the Pilbeam. He told me he'd also like to compete. When I asked what was stopping him his reply was disturbing. 'The RAC Motor Sports Association won't give drivers a competition licence if they need hand-controls on their car.'

I thought the information must be wrong, but when I contacted the RAC the following week, this was confirmed. That to my mind was unfair, particularly in the sport of hill climbing and sprinting when the competitor is racing against the clock. It's a great opportunity for beginners as you are not in danger from other cars spinning off – and why shouldn't drivers with hand-controls take part, particularly when they are licensed to drive on the roads, so deemed able to cope with hazards like traffic and pedestrians? In my official capacity as competitions secretary of the HSA, I began negotiations with the RAC MSA, resulting in a Speed Championship for Disabled Drivers in hand-controlled vehicles. I became the Championship Coordinator.

The drivers only had permission to compete in their own class of road-going saloons with hand-controls fitted, not in any other class. But it was a beginning. The Championship lasted for three years, with close competition at every meeting. And it was an important breakthrough because following this – presumably having proved themselves as safe as anyone else – disabled drivers were allowed to compete in any class or car without restrictions. Two of the original competitors, Steve Weatherley and Marc Haynes (son of John Haynes, chairman of Haynes Publishing) became successful race circuit drivers.

Not everything went so happily. I'd been involved in an automotive business venture since 1990 with a man I had known since childhood. This involved me in rather a lot of 15-hour working days but during 1991 the rewards had started rolling in. When my father became concerned that I had no contract, in my innocence I assured him that my colleague and I had a gentleman's agreement, so there was no cause for worry. I trusted my friend. As soon as the venture became very lucrative, however, that agreement seemed to evaporate and I was disposed of. Despite some gruelling legal challenges I found myself left with nothing. By the end of 1992 my income had plummeted from generous to zero. It was a humiliating shock.

Motorsport had to be shelved – no money – and I found that such a wrench after a lifetime involvement. It was especially galling because, having weathered all those handling and mechanical upsets, I was just starting to come to terms with the Pilbeam and really wanted to continue. How could I begin to earn an income again, one that would support this passion? I agonised for a while, feeling quite bitter towards certain members of the human race, but finally decided it was time to move on. There had to be new territory to explore, one with decent, moral individuals.

It was then that my other great interest started to blossom. Back in 1975 when studying for my OU degree, I was asked, during a lecture, about relations between European Australians and the indigenous people of Australia. The question was difficult. I'd only met one Aboriginal person in my whole life and that was Lionel Rose, who had won the World featherweight boxing title and returned to Australia from Japan a hero. I'd never seen any other Aborigines. Not being able to answer the question was embarrassing. I felt confused.

My secondary education in Australia took place at a well-respected girls grammar school in our hometown of Geelong.

History had been one of my favourite subjects, particularly Australian history. I was taught about the heroic exploits of the courageous explorers. I remember feeling proud that my country was colonised without conflict or civil war: a uniquely peaceful place run on egalitarian principles where a 'fair go' existed for everyone.

But clearly my education had passed over the shameful facts about colonisation. I could recall a mention in one of my books that Captain Cook had some contact with Australia's indigenous people and I remember the shock of hearing from one of our teachers that the Aboriginal race would eventually die out. Now I needed to know more.

On a trip back to Australia I found newly published books about the relations between Europeans and Aboriginal Australians. I read about massacres, bloody conflicts, deliberate poisoning of Aboriginal water sources. The more I read, the more horrified I became. It was almost too painful to grasp. I hadn't known that Aboriginal people were confined to missions and reserves, akin to prisons. Or that Aboriginal children were placed in institutions thousand of miles from home, never to meet their families again.

The more I read, the angrier I got. Was this the egalitarian country I was brought up in? If this barbarity was true then why weren't we taught about it at school? I realised I knew nothing about racism in my homeland. The effects of dispossession were frightening. If my family and I were turfed off our own land with nowhere to go, denied of our food sources and basic human rights, how could we possibly cope? And this would be without having any spiritual connection to our land, as do the Aboriginal people.

All this was so upsetting that it started me off on an obsessive personal journey of discovery that has lasted thirty years and taken me to many isolated parts of Australia. I have heard so many tales of sorrow and maltreatment, largely a result of the immigrants' ignorance and greed. I have witnessed the devastating impact that the white man had, and the poverty suffered by most Aborigines, even now. I felt ashamed.

On the positive side, nowadays attitudes are changing, forced along by public opinion and Government legislation. Australia's history is being re-written, and tolerance – even celebration – of racial difference is increasing. There is still a long way to go, of course. Not everyone can accept the new realism. But to deal with the present we need to understand and come to terms with our past. In the early 1990s a 'reconciliation' was started with the aim of relieving the social and financial disadvantage experienced by Aboriginal Australians. Central to the success of this was the acceptance by both cultures of their own and the other's past so that a framework for a shared future could be built. It was also important to establish partnerships between individuals from the different cultures.

On my previous trips to North Queensland I'd met a number of crafts people and artists selling their products and in 1993, I decided to set up an outlet in Worcestershire, retailing and wholesaling Aboriginal products. Didgeridoos, boomerangs, artefacts, paintings and other items were proudly displayed and sold. I visited every supplier, many of whom were based in co-operatives and businesses in remote areas of Australia, and met all the people creating the artefacts. I was impressed with their honesty and integrity and that continues to this day.

The shop, named Aboriginalia, was eventually a success, with a clientele of discerning British and foreign enthusiasts, but it took considerable effort to devise ways of promoting interest. For the first two years I worked there seven days a week. It wasn't easy being confined to one room in the middle of a shopping precinct, without natural light. During the summer I would be aware that it was Shelsley or Prescott or Loton Park that weekend and I couldn't be there. It took three years before the desire to compete had diminished to tolerable levels. I'm not sure, truly, if I ever became accustomed to a more 'conventional' life style, but the sheer weight of that workload distracted my thoughts.

In the late nineties, I competed in the Alfa Romeo a couple of times, just to taste the atmosphere at Shelsley Walsh again, but I was convinced that my days of driving a single-seater were over. However, at the end of 2000 I heard that, to celebrate its centenary, the Midland Automobile Club was to hold a three-day Shelsley Walsh extravaganza in August 2001. Many motorsport personalities of the past and present were to be invited to drive. It was possible that I would be included. The outright Ladies Course Record was, surprisingly, still mine after fifteen years. What a perfect event at which to make an appearance again, in the actual car that took the record in 1986.

After agonising through the winter and with a feeling of spring now in the air, I decided to drag the covers and years of dust off the Pilbeam MP53. Horror! The gleaming car that I had last seen in 1994 was pitiful. The casing of the magnesium gearbox looked as though a bonsai forest was growing all over it. The engine was covered in grunge, with strange fungus sprouting out.

I decided to push the car out of its dark corner to a more spacious part of the garage for a thorough examination, but it wouldn't move. Jammed solid. Removing the back casing of the gearbox, I discovered that the vegetable-based oil had solidified like gooey glue onto the gears, preventing any movement. Even the limited slip differential was stuck.

If the oil in the gearbox had changed its characteristics then it was likely that the engine would also be suffering. I had hoped that little more than a thorough cleaning would be required before competing again but soon realised that a complete dismantling and rebuilding of every component was necessary. The enormity of this was overwhelming. I decided to replace the dust covers and forget about motor racing. It was misery. I really did want to drive again at Shelsley. To console myself I came to the conclusion that I wouldn't be invited anyway.

Two days later, on 12 March, the invitation arrived. It really was extraordinary the effect that piece of paper had on me, with just a few words inviting me to drive the Pilbeam at Shelsley

Walsh on 19 August. Yes of course I'd be there, and in the Pilbeam! I immediately posted the acceptance, before there was time to reflect.

With just five months before the event, I was going to need help. I attempted to summon up some feminine charm in order to persuade Trevor that working on my single-seater racing car might broaden his horizons after concentrating on the restoration of vintage cars. I'm not sure how convincing my argument was but he did agree.

My father, with his unique engineering experience, had always built the engines for my competition cars in the past, but he was now nearly 84 years old and opting for a quieter life. It didn't take much to entice him out of the warm sitting-room, however, and into the chill of his workshop. Every spare minute over the next four months was spent there, firstly dismantling every component right down to the bare chassis, gearbox and engine.

My day job, in the shop, felt frustratingly slow. All I wanted to do was rush home to work on the Pilbeam. I was mainly involved with the cleaning and non-heavy jobs. Getting the heavily pitted aluminium chassis, the suspension and all the engine parts to pristine condition took plenty of effort before they were assembled by the experts. We were working on the car every evening and weekend.

To help finance the project I wrote a piece for the *Daily Telegraph* motoring section. I was rather astonished when the motoring editor, Peter Hall, telephoned to commission a 'racing diary' as a series running over seventeen weeks. With this new responsibility of a weekly deadline it was essential that work on the car had to progress to give me enough to write about and photograph. In fact the diary was a major element in driving the rebuild forward. I'd been so long out of motorsport and totally immersed in my work life that it would have been temptingly easy to shelve the project for another year or so.

Six weeks before the big event, the total rebuild of the Pilbeam was finished. It was time for the first test at Curborough. I felt slightly nervous, particularly about remembering the left foot braking technique, but after a couple of laps this felt like second nature. The main problem was adapting to the speed. When I was a regular competitor it used to take me five meetings at the start of every season before I could equal my fastest times from the previous season.

I intended to enter five minor events before the Shelsley Centenary so that I felt completely in tune with the car. However, after filling in the entry forms I never posted any of them, apart from a Shelsley Walsh meeting to be held two weeks before. This was odd. I wanted to become a regular competitor again so couldn't quite understand my reluctance.

'Mid-life crisis,' a friend joked.

I'm not sure about that, but during the rebuild of the Pilbeam I also put my business on the market and negotiations had started with a potential purchaser. Perhaps I was ready to change my life dramatically again?

I wrote *Daily Telegraph* articles immediately after both Shelsley Walsh meetings and these (reproduced with the newspaper's kind permission) give some insight into the way I was feeling.

WEEK FIFTEEN
JOY RAINEY'S RACING DIARY

When I heard that the postponed May meeting at Shelsley Walsh Hill Climb was rescheduled for the first weekend in August, I decided that if the re-build of the Pilbeam was finished and the driver was satisfied with the car, then I would enter. And that's just what happened. But then nagging thoughts kept flashing into my mind that I needed more testing to become completely familiar with the car, before actually competing.

One's normal work seems to get in the way of hobbies and there was just no time available to test, so in the end, I compromised. The 5th August meeting at Shelsley would be a test day in preparation for the invitation 100th year event on 19th August. It would be an opportunity to drive on my favourite hill climb course again, particularly on the parts that had been resurfaced a few months back, after the heavy winter and spring rainfall had caused a landslide.

Just as I was becoming accustomed to the hot weather, the rain arrived towards the end of the week. The dry weather had lulled me into a sense of false security but I knew I could not take the risk of competing without any wet weather tyres. Although there was no spare time for the trek to Birmingham, fortunately I managed to combine a business trip. The business trip could have waited but the tyre requirement could not. So now the Pilbeam is prepared for all weather conditions, but I'm still hoping that the wet weather tyres will not be used at all.

After heavy rain on Saturday it was such a relief that Sunday was a rather glorious day.

Looking at the entry list for the two-litre racing car class, it could have been compiled fifteen years ago. There was Bill Morris, Chris Drewett and me. So nothing much has changed over the years, or anyway, at this particular event. Just proves how addictive this sport of hill climbing is. It felt like a reunion to me, but my fellow competitors have hardly missed a meeting for years.

Waiting in the queue for my first practice run, I started questioning my sanity. 'What the hell am I doing here sitting in this very quick racing car after eight years of sedentary living,' I kept asking myself. But after a couple of tyre warming dummy starts I'd arrived at the start line. Too late now to chicken out!

The light turned green, into first gear, rev to 6000rpm, let the clutch out and away. Change into second gear, then the first corner, Kennel, arrived rather quickly. Too slow round Kennel, but at least I was still facing the right direction. Plant the right foot flat-out, up into next gear, but then I lifted off the throttle slightly, or probably a lot, over Crossing and lifted off far too early for bottom Esse, down a gear, out of top Esse, hard on throttle, up into next gear, flat-out into top gear and eventually arriving at the finish line.

A digital readout is now placed in the braking area so I knew my time immediately. Slow, six seconds slower than my record here. But worst of all, everything appeared to happen so quickly, but then to console myself, I thought back to my regular competing days. At the start of each season after just five or six months away from competing, I needed about five events before achieving similar times to the end of the previous season. So after eight years away, perhaps I need a bit more time, or that's my excuse for now.

Next practice run, the car appeared much more stable and I realised that, well, perhaps the driver was starting to get the feel of the car and the time was over a second quicker. First competitive run, another second quicker, but more importantly I was beginning to feel much more familiar with the car and the corners didn't feel as though they were arriving too quickly.

Last run, well ... driver problem. Missed a gear. Felt rather annoyed and a bit of a prat. But I was fortunate, just managed to scrape into the top twelve run-off, which meant another run, and another second quicker. So yes, it's coming. Apart from the missed gear run, every climb was quicker. But of course, I would have felt happier if I'd been a bit quicker overall, but then, that's what keeps competitors keep competing ... next time will be much faster.

The winner of the day was Bill Morris in his Pilbeam MP84, the first time he'd achieved Fastest Time of Day at Shelsley Walsh. That was quite an achievement after so many years of hill climbing.

Most of the talk at Shelsley Walsh on Sunday was about the Midland Automobile Club's 100th anniversary three-day celebrations next week. The line-up of former British Hill Climb Champions, former course record holders and other motoring personalities is quite impressive as well as the cars representing every era of Shelsley's exciting history. With a big screen placed in the paddock area, similar to major sporting events and pop concerts, spectators and competitors alike, at the bottom of the hill, will not miss out on any of the action on any part of the course. My support team will be watching my every move with a critical eye. There'll be no opportunity for me to make excuses for any lack of performance or driver error.

Jaguar Cars are supporting the event and bringing an array of delectable machinery including a 1905 Daimler, C-type, D-type, XJ13 and the XK180 Concept car. It should be exciting to see if the Daimler, manufactured the same year as the first Shelsley event, can improve next week on the original best time of 77.6 seconds, set at the first ever event. The current outright Shelsley record holder, Graeme Wight Junior, and leader of the 2001 British Hill Climb Championship, will be looking to improve on his sensational time of 25.28 seconds (over 52 seconds quicker than the first course record), driving the latest Gould racing car. I'm looking forward to see how Martin Stretton, in the six-wheel Tyrrell Formula One car, manages to corner at the Esses. Will the four front wheels be an advantage on this narrow, demanding course? That should be really spectacular to see. In fact, it's an event not to be missed.

Week seventeen
Joy Rainey's racing diary

What a wonderful atmosphere greeted us as we drove through the entrance gates of Shelsley Walsh Hill Climb. Over three hundred competing cars were gathering over a vast area. And I couldn't think of a better way to spend a

Friday than driving a racing car up my favourite hill climb course, practising for the Midland Automobile Club's 100th anniversary celebration event.

I'd become an avid watcher of the five-day weather forecast over the week, and each day had predicted a not-too-glorious weekend. Although weather forecasts have become rather reliable in recent years, I was hoping this time they were wrong.

Well, Friday stayed sunny all day. After the Pilbeam racing car passed through scrutineering, I booked my two practice runs as early as possible to avoid the predicted afternoon heavy rain showers. My first practice run time was 32.50 seconds. Not as quick as I would have liked, but then, they never are. Just after the lunch break my second run ended up 31.25 seconds. Well, I was rather disappointed, would've preferred a low 30 seconds. Then later on I met Martyn Griffiths, five times British Hill Climb Champion in 1979, 86, 87, 90 and 91. He'd been away from the sport for ten years and when he told me his times, driving the Pilbeam MP57, 2.5-litre Hart, were practically identical to mine, my mood was suddenly uplifted. So I started to believe that ... well ... perhaps ... I was doing alright under the circumstances, but really needing much more track time.

After I'd practised my father then took his turn in the 1936 Alfa Romeo 6C. But the left hand brake had started to lock, driving to Shelsley in the morning and its condition didn't improve during the practice runs, so Dad, at 84 years old, decided just to enjoy himself and not risk a problem.

As we neared Shelsley on Saturday morning, the rain started. Not heavy rain, but light rain which continued all day. Despite the damp conditions and the slippery track the one-day event passed off without any major incidents. This event was mainly vintage, with a variety of delectable machinery, and some modern and classic cars owned by members of the promoting club. Some of the most spectacular to watch were the GNs, twin cylinder chain-driven racing specials of the 1920s that for many years challenged sophisticated purpose-built racers from major manufacturers, particularly at Shelsley. The big screen, situated in the paddock area, was a huge success as all of the action could be viewed from many viewpoints. I watched every section of my father's run. With the adverse track conditions and the locking brake of the Alfa, he leisurely motored up the hill. Fastest time of the day was achieved by Ken Simms in a Metro 6R4 and significantly, the fastest pre-war car, on 41.79 seconds, was David Leigh in the GN Spyder, the car was the previous winner of no less than seven Fastest Times of the Day during the 20s, driven by Basil Davenport.

The big day arrived dull and gloomy. As we drove through the gates of Shelsley at 8am the heavens opened, not light rain but like a tropical downpour. And it continued for some time, which meant wet tyres. Competitors had the opportunity of one practice run in the morning, which was necessary for this competitor as I'd not driven in wet conditions for about ten years. My support team was so efficient, changing all the four wheels in quite a respectable time. By the time my practice run arrived, the track had started to dry in parts, but it's difficult to know just what the conditions are like until actually on the track. The start line was slippery and I was slow getting away – too much wheel spin.

But after Kennel (the first corner) the track had started to dry and I pressed on quite well, changing down a gear at the approach to First Esse. Then, as I was just almost around, the back-end stepped out quite dramatically in the damp conditions and I lost control, the Pilbeam ending up travelling along the steep banking for quite some distance. When I managed to bring the car to a halt, the right wheels were just on the track with the left side wheels wedged up at an acute angle on the banking. I thought considerable damage was done to the car and my pride plummeted to such depths that when the marshals arrived and asked if I was alright, I could hardly speak, I felt so gutted.

But I was OK physically and when I walked to the front of the car, the damage looked superficial. It was hard to tell at this stage whether the suspension was damaged, but the front left hand aerofoil certainly was. But what impressed me was the delicate way the marshals extricated the car from the banking with the aim of not inflicting further damage to the car. This took some time, but when the car was back on the track, the four wheels seemed to be pointing in the right direction and I was eventually permitted to coast the car back down the hill.

Back in the paddock my pit crew worked like demons. Trevor removed the wing, replacing the locating bar with some panel beating to straighten the wing. Ron Tauranac and Allan England stepped in with some modifications to increase the incidence of the front wing to put more downforce on the front. And to the rear, Ron decided to reduce the roll stiffness of the rear suspension with the purpose of increasing the traction in the corners.

The modifications to my Pilbeam were just finished in time for the first competitive run. By then, the track had dried considerably and it was back to slick tyres. I drove with considerable caution, mindful of the excursion off the tarmac in the previous run, and my time was 35.39 seconds. A whole four seconds slower than my quickest practice run on Friday. I actually felt rather embarrassed, particularly as my crew had put in so much effort. In the class Sandra Tomlin and Maggie Blankstone-Schoiber ended up with identical times of 30.99 seconds, both driving Pilbeams MP58s powered by 2.8-litre Hart engines and, less than a second behind, Lynne Whitehead in the smaller-engined Pilbeam.

Some hours had passed before the second competitive runs and I was mentally fired up to improve my time. And then, the rain came! I couldn't believe what was happening. The rain didn't last long, just long enough to dampen the track, and my confidence. To end the story, my time didn't improve and I felt considerably disappointed, particularly as my team had put in such effort, and I would have liked to end this historic day with the whole team feeling happy with their driver.

The event was a huge success, so many hill climb champions and motoring personalities and such super efficient organisation by the Midland Automobile Club. Best Time of the Day was achieved by the outright Shelsley record holder and current British Hill Climb Championship leader, Graeme Wight Jnr. on 25.97 seconds in his Gould single-seater. The fastest pre-war time was 35.65 seconds by David Morris in the ERA R11B.

As you are aware, to achieve the objective of competing at Shelsley Walsh last weekend involved the help and support of so many people. I'm so grateful to my father Murray, my mother Norma, and Trevor for their endless support, and my pit crew Les and Maureen Stone, Ron Tauranac and Allan England.

This is my last weekly diary, which makes me feel so sad. I wish to express my gratitude to the many *Telegraph* readers who journeyed to Shelsley last weekend. You overwhelmed me with your kind words and generosity of spirit, and I hope your first experience of the hill climbing scene was enjoyable and won't be your last.

As for me, well, I wasn't too pleased with my end result. I guess the only consolation is that my own outright Ladies Hill Climb Record is still intact at 28.32 seconds. But looks like I'll have to enter for the next Shelsley Walsh meeting in four weeks time. This sport sure is addictive.

And I did enter the September Shelsley Walsh meeting. The times were coming down again to the 31 seconds bracket, but I started to experience gear-changing difficulties and the water pump stopped functioning after the first run, causing me to cancel the final run.

As I left my favourite hill climb at the end of the day, I wasn't sure that I would be campaigning the Pilbeam at every meeting during 2002. To be competitive, the driver needs to commit entirely to the sport. I looked in the rear vision mirror, saw the Pilbeam on the trailer as we drove away from Shelsley and didn't seem to be feeling the same passion as I had all those years back.

One of the disadvantages of needing special adaptations to a motorcar means that you are excluded from test-driving any other vehicle unless you purchase it first. Occasionally, I was offered a drive in other cars but had to turn this down. It's quite a major task making up new pedal extensions, raising the seat and carrying out any other modification, but when Marc Haynes, managing director of the Haynes Motor Museum, offered me a drive in the museum's 1900 Clement, I went to investigate the possibility.

On the drive down to the museum – part of the Haynes Publishing Group at Sparkford, in the heart of Somerset – I convinced myself that the modifications would be so major that it would be foolish to even contemplate a run up the road, let alone an entry in a veteran car event. I was so delighted, therefore, when I clambered onto the high seat of the Clement, to find that the steering wheel and controls were reachable. Also, the pedals were not far away from my feet and required just short extensions, which Trevor made, and that's how we became entrants in the 2001 London to Brighton Run.

Starting at 7.30am on 4 November, 366 pre-1905 cars of all shapes and sizes were flagged off at Hyde Park. I felt apprehensive at first but soon adapted to the style of driving, with the left hand operating the manual ignition control to regulate the engine speed and the right hand changing from high to low gear. I was trying to keep modern cars at a distance because their brakes were much more efficient than those on our 101-year-old vehicle. To avoid having to stop and start at traffic lights, I tried to maintain a steady speed to save using the clutch too much and spare the one-cylinder engine from the strains of building up to speed again from a standing start.

Crossing Westminster Bridge we were really into our stride, overtaking more of the slower vehicles. The first hill we came to I expected the little de Dion engine to struggle but she climbed steadily in low gear and, much to the relief of my passenger Trevor, his assistance was not required for pushing.

The Clement's performance was really starting to impress me. She was behaving magnificently. Then, as we were climbing Norbury Hill, the 2¼ hp engine started to lose power and came to an abrupt stop. Andy Bracher, the museum's chief mechanic, had brought spares and tools for every conceivable mechanical problem, but when we saw the crankcase had a big split running right across, we knew that this was beyond any roadside repair. I was really disappointed that we would not experience the pleasure of arriving at Madeira Drive and parking the Clement next to the other successful veteran cars, but my appetite was whetted – from now on I wanted to compete in as many types of motoring event as possible.

When a brochure announcing a London to Sydney classic car rally arrived in the post, I couldn't stop thinking about it. The business was sold and I felt ready for a big new challenge.

Chapter 10

HOW IT WAS DONE

Preparing the Minor for the London to Sydney Marathon

As with every crazy idea that enters my mind, it's better to put it on hold and if the strong urge to pursue the particular activity is still there weeks later, then further deliberation may be in order. And weeks later, the London to Sydney Marathon was still nagging at me.

I was consumed with the excitement of traversing so many countries and continents in just one month. The route was to take the competitors over demanding roads, through rural France, over the Alps into Italy, along part of the famous Mille Miglia route, across the Adriatic to Greece and Turkey before an airlift to Cochin in India. Then there were six days of driving in the hill country and tea and coffee plantations before another airlift to Alice Springs. After a spectacular drive through the Australian outback to the Pacific coast, north of Brisbane, the rally finally was to arrive at the Sydney Opera House.

Almost 10,000 miles in just thirty days! And ending up in the land of my birth!

This sort of adventure is probably not on everyone's 'must do' list but I soon decided that my participation was essential. Trevor, my co-driver, and I weighed up the pros and cons of all the classic car makes in an affordable price bracket that we considered might be robust enough to undertake such a journey. And our choice was a Morris Minor.

It's a relatively simple car, we decided, easy to maintain and, with an upgraded engine, gearbox and suspension, should be capable of sustaining acceptable average speeds. Buying the

Morris Minor would be the cheapest part, of course. It was the thorough ground-up restoration and preparation to international rally standards required to enable the Minor to endure such rough and perhaps tortuous roads, that would soak up the funds.

To gauge reaction about both the rally and the choice of car, I mentioned our plan to a non-motoring friend. He looked at me with disbelief, then fell about in such a paroxysm of laughter that I thought he must know something I didn't. But then he had never been involved with motorsport. To him a car was for getting from A to B, filling up with fuel and replacing when worn out. I couldn't expect him to share my passion.

Or ... perhaps my friend was right, it was a silly idea? But I just couldn't seem to join in his mirth. The laughter abruptly stopped when I told him the estimated cost of the entry fee – £23,000 – plus restoration and preparation of a smallish classic car, which would be a further £30,000. That was outside the parameters of this man's experience. He left, muttering something about cuckoo land.

The only conceivable way I could participate in the proposed rally was to obtain hefty sponsorship so I decided that the next months would be spent pursuing this. If there were no likely prospects I would give up, albeit reluctantly, and perhaps take up knitting, as my chauvinist friend suggested.

I intended to start my search for a Morris Minor during the spring. I knew we would have to travel far and wide throughout the country to find a car that had not been repaired over and over again with welded implants, as happens so often just to get a vehicle through the MoT as cheaply as possible. The timing for this search, I thought, would be perfect after the dreary winter months and by then I might have found a sponsor.

Normally I rarely read the *Evesham Journal*, the local weekly newspaper, but in October 2002 I flicked through and my eyes leapt on a small block advertisement for a 1970 Morris Minor. The wording sounded perfect, although it has to be said that most ads for used cars suggest that they are practically fault free. And anyway I wasn't really ready to start looking just then – in fact, not for another five or six months. After agonising for a few days I thought that if the local Morris Minor was still available then a quick look might be useful, just to gain some insight into how a car with over thirty years of constant road use had fared.

Trevor was keen and went ahead to check it over.

'It's in reasonable condition,' he said. 'Hasn't been welded very much underneath. Some of the Minors I've seen in the past look like a patch-work quilt and that provides much more work undoing the mess.'

I felt that we weren't quite ready to buy a car, which was a pity.

'But then again, if after the winter we have to travel for miles looking at every Morris Minor advertised, we may spend a considerable amount of money on petrol … and there's the time needed. Oh all right! Let's go and have a proper look and if we think that this is ideal for our project, then it will probably save a considerable amount of time if we buy it now.'

We did a thorough check, crawling underneath and examining every panel, and decided that this Morris had been fairly well cared for. The front mudguards had been recently replaced but were lacking in a final coat of paint. The sills at some point in the past had been renewed but the undertray, at least, hadn't been welded in small sections. Rust was developing on areas of the bodywork but the car was indeed just ready for a major rebuild before it deteriorated any further.

The owner, John Clark, himself a vintage car enthusiast, had pieced together the history of the Morris from its first keeper, a Miss Rigby, who had owned it for almost eighteen years. During that period the Minor had covered only 20,000 miles, just double the distance I was intending to drive in four weeks. All its annual MoT certificates were kept and John had prepared a graph of the annual mileage. For the last four years of Miss Rigby's ownership the Minor was driven for just seventy-two miles. But Miss Rigby, by then, was in her nineties.

The next owner purchased the car for his daughter, then it became the shopping car of John Clark's wife.

Rather than rush into a decision (I had already made up my mind) that might be regretted we decided to wait for a few days. It wasn't until the following weekend that I became the owner of a 1970 Morris Minor, for the price of £500. I wasn't really sure whether to tell John about the plan to drive his Minor to Sydney but when he asked me I had to confess. At least he didn't appear to suggest that I'd taken leave of my senses – in fact, he was pleased it was to be involved in such an exciting project.

When I saw the Minor parked at home for the first time, it took me right back to my teenage days in Australia. Dad had purchased a nine-year-old Morris Minor when I was old enough to take the driving test. The car was immaculate, just as if it had emerged from the showroom. Its elderly owner had never driven his pride and joy in the wet, and averaged only 1,000 sedate miles a year. The only driving experience of its new young owner was racing go-karts and blasting a Holden FC flat-out round a makeshift racetrack at the family farm.

I always think fondly of that first car – it hardly ever let me down in spite of all the harsh treatment – but I never guessed that I might become the owner of another Minor in later life, particularly in association with such an adventurous event as the London to Sydney Marathon. At least this time the driver was experienced.

Finding sponsorship, I knew, wouldn't be my forte. It almost felt like begging – asking a company to fork out a large sum of money so that I could participate in an event for my own enjoyment. And then, when the expected rejection arrived, to try not to feel personally humiliated.

One friend in particular bolstered my resolve. 'How do you think the Formula 1 teams would survive without sponsorship,' he asked, 'and anyway, you're not asking for something for nothing. Aren't you going to work hard to generate considerable media coverage for your sponsor?'

He was right. I needed to make my approach positive. I'd heard discouraging stories about people sending out hundreds or even thousands of letters asking for sponsorship and receiving no acknowledgement at all, then phoning and being thwarted by the efficient receptionist before they could explain their proposal.

I was beginning to admit defeat before I had even started. But I really did want to participate in this event, so to give up at the first hurdle would mean that I would never get to the start-line in London, let alone pull up in front of the Sydney Opera House in my Morris Minor.

I spent hours designing and perfecting a proposal pack and thought it looked rather professional. This went out, then after several weeks I phoned some of the potential 'targets' and to my surprise was, in the majority of cases, put through. However the rejections came thick and fast. Some companies offered products, but first I needed funds to cover that entry fee, otherwise I could not take advantage of any goodies that might be on offer, let alone tackle the event.

Just as I was beginning to despair, luck came my way. I was put in touch with Guy Ainsley, the marketing director of Inchcape plc and he seemed interested in discussing a sponsorship arrangement.

After several months and committee meetings, Inchcape – parent company of Autobytel, the one-stop shopping service via which the public can buy, sell, lease, finance and insure a car – offered to cover the entry fee. Some minutes passed before I could grasp what this meant. Such joy! I could now post off the entry form. When I pushed the envelope, addressed to Trans World Events, through the post box, I felt overcome with emotion – so many months had passed that I'd almost given up hope of reaching this point.

It was difficult springing into action and dismantling the Minor. There was no room in the garage. First, all the components for other future projects had to be sorted out and put on shelves to give enough space. That took about a month. Then the big day arrived. The Minor was parked in the garage and the dismantling began.

Although the Minor is a relatively small car, I did start to feel daunted at the enormity of the job when we were attempting to remove the first mudguard. Most of the bolts were rusted and the grinder had to be used in virtually impossible positions.

Thankfully this car had been maintained by an enthusiast and under-sealed in all of the accessible areas, but even so, once the front and rear wings were removed, a different picture started to emerge. There were a few welded implants but many of the crucial brackets and seams were completely rusted away. As each section of the body-shell was dismantled, rusted out sections were evident in the engine bay and under the sills, nearside and offside. Parts of the rear door frames and rear wheel arches had disappeared completely. More discouragement. Trevor wasn't uttering encouraging noises either.

He wasn't looking forward to cutting out and welding in new pieces of metal where the rusted out holes and brackets were, but was particularly worried that once the welding was completed, the body shell might end up distorted. He started to imagine the dramas that might happen if the wings and doors didn't fit properly.

My enthusiasm at this stage started to wane dramatically.

One of the advantages of restoring a fairly common car, however, is that there are a number of specialists supplying all of the replacement body panels and other components required. I knew from the advertisements that there were considerable price variations on similar parts so I contacted every business listed to find the best deal. One dealer just happened to mention that he had a brand-new original BMC body shell in stock. It had been in storage for about 35 years but he didn't seem too keen to sell it. Perhaps that was his selling ploy? When we eventually went to view the body shell he changed his mind and I became the new owner for the princely sum of £2,200.

The thought of assembling everything onto a new body shell seemed to make the project more desirable or so I convinced myself, with Trevor's help. Once the car was finished it would be a practically brand-new Morris Minor. I started to feel more confident about spending a considerable amount on buying new suspension and mechanical parts.

Much of the shell was covered in surface rust and old paint and needed shot-blasting before final painting, but first a number of modifications were required so that the suspension could be up-rated and strengthened.

We chose telescopic shock absorbers, rather than the standard push pull lever type, to help the Minor withstand the rough road conditions expected. We had to make the mountings for the shock absorbers, which required several designs before Trevor was satisfied. On the rear it was necessary to provide a secure fixing under the floor but, without reinforcement, this was not rigid enough. Finally Trevor made a bridge that went across the boot floor and was then securely bolted into new bushes that had been welded into the box section.

The front needed some experimentation before the designer was satisfied that the mountings were strong enough, due to the limited space available and the need to incorporate mountings for an anti-roll bar.

The engine mountings required strengthening and the spring hangers were modified so that if we happened to run over an obstruction, rather than catching the vulnerable lower parts, the Minor should glide on intact. As road clearance was an important element, the new sump guard had to be positioned as close to the sump as possible. Trevor designed and built the guard out of heavy steel, with streamlined lines.

Morris Minors are renowned for brake fade when under intense use. As much of the marathon route would take us over twisty and demanding mountainous roads we wanted to be confident that the car would have superior stopping power whenever required. Discs on the front offered a likely solution and an early seventies Marina provided the parts, with only one modification required, to alter the spacing of the wheel studs to match the Minor wheels.

In case the fuel became contaminated, a second tank (ex Mini Traveller), with its own separate fuel pump, was mounted in the boot area above the original tank. The two fuel pumps, equipped with an independent fuel filter, were all situated in the rear boot area; the idea was to help guard against fuel vaporisation while travelling in hot climates.

I started to feel anxious as I ticked the weeks off the calendar one by one. The months were passing by so rapidly and the body-shell was still not painted. All the modifications needed to be finished, fitted, approved and then dismantled again before they were sent off to be shot-blasted.

Seven months before the start of the marathon my anxiety accelerated. Were we making fast enough progress? Would we finish in time? Work was advancing on restoring and rebuilding every little component, from door catches and hinges to the boot lid, and on making new fittings for every area of the car imaginable, but it was difficult to measure the actual result. Once the new bits were made they were removed from the body-shell and put on the shelves waiting for the final assembly. When I walked into the garage nothing looked any different. Here was just an unused, 35-year-old body-shell covered in surface rust and old paint. One of my non-motoring acquaintances visited and I knew what he meant when he said, 'gosh, I thought the car would be finished by now. It doesn't look any different from the last time I called in six months ago!'

I realised that after the body-shell was painted the components would be assembled for the final time and then it would be easier to measure progress, but it seemed to be taking forever to get to that stage, and already we were approaching the year end.

When most of the modifications were finished and the time had arrived to book the body-shell in for its protective electro-coating, there were even more delays. The company offering the undercoating process was not accustomed to one-off bookings, their usual business being production-line new cars. The Minor had to wait for an available slot, when a run of new cars was to be changed. We needed notice as the body-shell had to be taken first for shot-blasting, together with the doors, mudguards, bonnet and boot lid. If it was left for too long after shot-blasting then surface rust would appear, so the two appointments had to be coordinated. Not easy.

I was almost convinced that we would have to devise an alternative plan and forego the electro-coating, then finally, after more than a month of waiting, the all clear was given and we swung into action. Once the shot-blasting was finished we brought the Minor back to its workshop again to vacuum the grit from the box sections where it had collected, otherwise the paint in the dipping tank would become contaminated. At least half a bucket of grit had accumulated. Then, with great haste, we delivered the body-shell ready for its dip.

After the electro-coating, some unevenness showed up in the roof section and extra work was required to resolve the problem before the primer and final coating of paint could be applied. The complete process took much longer than anticipated.

While the body-shell was away, it was a chance to get on with the mechanical side. To enable us to maintain reasonable average speeds we decided to install a 1,275cc A Series engine. When we were first considering entering the marathon we'd found a good example in a local breaker's yard for £50. It was originally from a Marina van and, when dismantled, revealed very little wear. The engine rebuild turned out to be routine, fitting new bearings, pistons and bigger valves. We opted for a lower compression ration of 8:1 just in case we encountered lower octane petrol. Valve seats and bigger valves were fitted to enable the engine to run on unleaded fuel. The new camshaft was profiled to give slightly more power but one that would not require the engine to be revved a lot. A smaller flywheel was fitted and the Minor backplate was used and modified to suit the cylinder block of the bigger engine. Instead of using a single row timing chain, a duplex version was chosen which should not wear out so quickly and upset the valve timing.

The components were balanced and assembled and new water and oil pumps and an alternator fitted. After the single SU carburettor was completely rebuilt and fitted, the engine was placed on the shelf waiting for the rest of the car to be completed. The gearbox, originally from an MG Midget, with closer gear ratios than a Minor, was found to be in reasonably good condition, however the first gear ratio was showing signs of wear and we replaced it with a new gear, bearings, gaskets and plungers.

Trevor dismantled and cleaned the back axle, ready to be assembled with all new bits. He decided to check the casing in the lathe and was dismayed to find this was bent. To the naked eye it looked fine but we suspected, having seen it rotated between centres, that it must have been involved in an accident at sometime. Two more back axles that we acquired seemed to be suffering from the same problem. Some time was spent trying to locate more Morris Minor back axles. One of the specialists had a supply and after Trevor had dismantled three more axles, at last he discovered a casing that was not bent. This appeared just at the right time as we were beginning to think that all Morris Minor back axle casings must be bent.

As the 2004 new year approached, the Minor was finally back in the workshop, looking pristine, decked out in blue, ready to be assembled into a complete car for the final time.

In just a matter of days – with the back axle, front suspension and steering mechanism in place and the car sitting on its own wheels – my mood suddenly lifted.

Visible progress slowed down at times, particularly when new brackets and fixings had to be made to enable the specialist rally equipment to be installed. The assembly process would have been much easier if all the parts used had been standard.

Eventually, just seven weeks before the start of the event, the car was ready for its first road trip – to the local garage for an MoT. The mechanic was impressed with the standard of workmanship and commented, as he handed Trevor the important piece of paper, that he had never seen a Minor in such good condition.

Although there were many finishing-off jobs to do, we were keen to get some miles up to bed-in the mechanical parts and in case any unexpected problems arose. The first 500 miles were driven at a maximum speed of 40mph. It takes a long time to cover 500 miles at this pace. It was almost embarrassing at times as we caused long tailbacks on country roads. When some impatient drivers eventually overtook us their stares of disdain made me realise that the next time I am stuck behind a slower driver I should show more tolerance as they might have a valid reason … well, anyway I hope to be more charitable.

After two weeks of driving whenever possible, the Minor had only reached 400 miles. But with such limited time available, if we were out driving then the final jobs weren't being tackled. And I had still not experienced my first drive, as my pedal conversion was rather complicated and Trevor needed time to perfect his design.

Normally, when a car is converted for me to drive, I am the only driver, and after the conversion is completed it stays intact until the car is sold. But as Trevor and I were to share the driving of the Minor on the marathon, the conversion needed to incorporate a system that could be removed and replaced in a very short time.

The seats in the Minor had no height adjustment and I needed to be raised about 4 inches. Sitting on a cushion was not acceptable but a relative easy solution was found in an unlikely place – a lorry breaker's yard. Some older commercial vehicles had a spring counter-balanced height adjuster under the seats. Two were found and we were amazed that, when offered up, they matched the existing holes in the floor. It was just a matter of then connecting the seats to the adjusters with new brackets. The end result: both front seats now had a range of 6 inches height adjustment.

An added luxury made the conversion worthwhile. There were two springs, one tilted the front of the seat and the other tilted the rear – ideal if the co-driver felt like a nap. Trevor was so impressed with the new arrangement that he constructed a headrest and I fitted padding and a matching vinyl cover. I started to imagine the zizzing sound coming from my left as he tilted back into a relaxing position and dozed while I drove across some remote area.

Eventually, my pedal controls and footrest were mounted onto a new section attached to the front of the seat frame. They operated the existing pedals by push-rods which could be detached quickly – changeover of driver was possible in a matter of seconds without the use of tools.

Time now for me to get behind the wheel. The pedal controls worked perfectly and the seating position couldn't have been better but I'm not sure what I was expecting from the Morris Minor. All the other cars I had been involved with over a long period of restoration and preparation, when driven were extremely powerful. Although the Minor was prepared for reliability and durability and not outright speed, my subconscious must have been expecting an initial power surge when I planted my right foot.

But after driving the Minor up steep hills and testing up and down some Welsh mountains on several long treks, I have to admit that my attitude changed somewhat. I may have been 19 years of age when I last drove a standard Morris Minor, but I could tell that this 1970 model, with its feisty replacement engine, was definitely putting out more power than the standard version. I started to feel confident about its ability to endure the long and hazardous journey from here to the Sydney Opera House.

Just days before the start of the marathon the Minor was ready and packed. We had to be ruthless with the amount of luggage we took. With no back-up service crew it was necessary to carry any spare parts we thought might be needed, yet did not want to add too much weight to the car. The second fuel tank, mounted in the boot area, reduced the luggage space considerably. The rear seat was left out and a plywood base made to fit over the space. The space under the plywood was packed with spares, and above where the seat squab was usually placed, on one side we mounted a large plastic box containing foodstuffs and water containers. On the other side the plastic toolbox was mounted with a vast array of tools. Our clothing, stored in two small overnight bags, comprised just two sets of clothes for driving and one decent outfit for the after-event dinner. These were stowed in the small boot space. When the car was fully packed I was surprised that it didn't appear to be cluttered.

It would have been easy to continue finding jobs or alterations, which might or might not have been necessary, but we had to stop somewhere. And the team? A bit apprehensive, but excited too. We were about to start the most adventurous trip of our lives.

Chapter 11

THE GREATEST ADVENTURE OF ALL

Around the world in 30 days

The London to Sydney Marathon was to start at the Renaissance Hotel, Heathrow, on Saturday, 5 June 2004. Organised by Trans World Events, it was a blue riband event, run at two levels. The Rally was a speed competition for rally-prepared cars, which required the driver to have an international grade competition licence issued by his or her country's governing body of motorsport. We were entering the Clowes Cup, a regularity event. This required robust driving over the same very demanding route as the rally cars, but the idea was to get as close as possible to a preset (fairly low) average speed in the timed sections, rather than driving flat-out. Cars had to be equipped with a computerised digital odometer to measure the distance travelled accurately, to two decimal points of a kilometre. They also had to carry a first aid kit, fire extinguisher and warning triangle, but that was about it as far as technical preparations went – the rest was up to the team. The Clowes Cup, which could be entered on an ordinary driving licence, attracted twenty-seven cars. In our class, for classic cars, there were five entrants – the Minor being the smallest.

A couple of days before the marathon began, we were due in London for scrutineering and pre-event briefing. The cars were to be checked over to ensure that all safety equipment, lights and so on functioned. The briefing was to inform the competitors and service crews about road laws and driving conditions in the various countries and also to explain how the event would be run.

Midday was the time we had decided to leave our home, near Evesham in Worcestershire, as this would allow us to get to the

M25 before the commuter traffic built up. But the day before departure, both the BBC and ITV Midlands television units had asked to come and film us in the Morris Minor as we were leaving. I refused at first, not wanting anything to delay us, but when the TV people promised that the filming wouldn't take much time, I relented. It was also an opportunity for the charity we were supporting, St. Richard's Hospice in Worcester, to get some worthwhile publicity.

Nothing ever goes to plan. A serious accident outside Evesham, involving two lorries, caused traffic delays and both television units stopped to film the aftermath. Eventually, at 3pm, we waved home goodbye and set out on the adventure of our lives.

Two hours later we pulled up in the car park of the Renaissance Hotel. I began to feel a bit intimidated when I saw the other participating cars, such as Ford Falcons, Holdens and modern 4x4s. Our little hyacinth-blue Minor looked somewhat out of place beside those big brutes. Had we made the right decision about the choice of car for such a demanding event? Would it really get us to Sydney? These questions kept dogging me as I wandered around, looking at the opposition and hearing their racy engines.

But it was too late now: we had to go through with this.

A number of Morris Minor enthusiasts turned up to the start line to wave us off and they didn't seem to have any doubts at all so, right choice or not, I was about to give it all my effort for the next thirty days. When the union flag was dropped, I leapt into action with great enthusiasm.

The first competitive sections – gravel, off-road stages – were in the forests near Yateley, in Hampshire. I'd never experienced a rally stage before and the last time I drove on gravel I was a teenager in Australia. Although many people repeatedly told me that a regularity run was easy, I felt quite concerned that I would make a mess of the whole experience. But the competitive spirit came rushing back. It was Trevor's job, aided by the electronic odometer, to instruct me when to slow and when to floor the throttle in order to maintain the average speed that had been presented to us at the start of the stage. I was rather surprised when the instructions kept coming from Trevor that I was behind time and had to make up with more speed.

The Minor performed magnificently and I was enjoying every minute of the nearly sixteen kilometres of demanding gravel roads through the forest – that is, until I caught up with the competitor in front, even though he had started one minute ahead. That shouldn't have happened unless one of us was seriously misjudging the average speed. Trevor was convinced that we had performed well on both stages but when the results were posted that evening we were placed right down the list. My average speed was too fast and it was certain that we had to learn the correct techniques of regularity competition instead of the flat-out driving I was accustomed to. At the end of the first day I felt somewhat disappointed that our results were mediocre but at least there were 29 days left of competition. Fortunately the organisers planned the first day as practice.

The first overnight stop was on the ferry from Portsmouth to St. Malo. That provided a good opportunity to get to know the other competitors. When I woke in the morning, again I suffered serious doubts about the suitability of the car and also of my own ability to sustain such long driving stints with high levels of concentration on demanding roads every single day for more than a month. It was a lazy type of feeling – not wanting to exert any more effort than I was used to.

But once we were off the ferry and driving along on the open road, in glorious sunshine, I could hear the wonderful unique note of the Minor engine bouncing off hedges and cliffs. The car swept round corners as if it was on rails and suddenly those doubts vanished, never to return – this Morris Minor driver was determined to pull up at the Sydney Opera House on 4 July.

To add to my confidence, the first stages in France were run round closed roads that wove through farmyards and hamlets. It was good fun, and we finished up leading the classic car class.

It seemed natural at first, after the competitive action of the day was over, to stop for refreshments. As a hill climber, I was used to competitive stints that usually lasted less than a minute and then I was ready for a bite. The rally stages were considerably longer than a hill climb course and no less demanding, but on the second day when we stopped for a coffee it meant we arrived late for the next time control and received penalties. The competitive sections may have been over but there were still about 350 miles to go before that night's stop. A few days had passed before we really adapted to a marathon attitude, which meant driving continuously.

Usually night stops were at a hotel, where the rally took over most of the rooms. Breakfast was specially prepared and lots of us managed to make up a few sandwiches for lunch, to avoid the necessity for either stopping or starving.

The long driving stints were strenuous, especially in an elderly car with none of the driver aids such as power steering or air-conditioning. And without power-assisted brakes, considerable foot pressure was needed when slowing. I had placed a thermometer on the dashboard of the Minor and at times, particularly on the European leg, the cockpit temperature regularly reached 44 degrees Celsius and hardly ever dropped below 36 degrees during the day. We always carried about five litres of mineral water and usually drank most of it.

Although the seating position felt comfortable, my back ached badly in the afternoon stint and the pain took some time to wear off at night. I was rather surprised, as I had prepared myself over the past year by swimming at least three times a week for an hour at a time, as well as exercising. I started to wonder how I could manage more than a month of this, as the pain got worse each day. Then, quite suddenly, it disappeared after a week and I could happily drive all day without a twinge. Trevor started to take over the driving during the afternoon sections to share some of the long-distance stints.

On the second day in France I had a powerful desire to increase our lead in the competitive regularity stages but the situation changed dramatically. The day's stages included steep inclines with sharp curves and the Minor lost speed which I could not make up – first gear was too low and second too high, so I had to proceed steadily in first gear. John Tallis, driving a Volvo 120, took the lead that day.

From then on we kept dropping points, particularly on Day 4 when the driver and co-driver fell out during the first stage!

I'd heard many stories about previous rallies when driving partners, under extreme pressure, found their nerves somewhat frayed. The clerk of the course, John Trevethick, had told me that the relationship between a co-driver and driver is more intense than a marriage. And within a few days I had first-hand knowledge of the tension that two individuals can suffer, seated in a very confined space, both grappling with new techniques in a highly competitive environment and straining to the limit. Several cars were planted in hedges during the stages and that was all due to communication difficulties in the cab. The Minor did not come to grief – but the language inside was fairly ripe!

One of the most spectacular stages in France was also used on the Monte Carlo Rally, up and down mountain passes, through forests – it was magnificent. And then ... Trevor became carsick and we had to abandon the timed run. Five days into the marathon I came to the conclusion that to actually arrive at the destination was the most important aim. If we did well on some stages that would be a bonus, but I knew when the inclines were steep we could not compete with the bigger engined cars and it was better to not risk our Minor too much by driving on the limit – or, indeed, strain my relationship with Trevor. After all, we were meant to be enjoying ourselves.

The scenery through France, Italy, Greece and Turkey was spectacular, but this was a marathon – there was no time to linger over any of the breathtaking views or cultural pursuits of the area. After several days we had both adapted well and accepted that we were not able to deviate or stop, other than to refuel the car, if we were to reach the next time control on time. It was as if we were passing through each country via a passage and the scenery just whizzed by.

The driver followed instructions from the co-driver all day and he received his instructions from the tulip diagrams in the road book supplied by the organisers. We were given nine road books at the start of the marathon. These provided detailed diagrams and instructions on every turn and characteristic of the daily route. There could be no excuse for getting lost, if the road book was followed correctly.

In theory it wasn't necessary to look at a map but that was frustrating at times, particularly when we were passing some beautiful place or saw a village perched on a hill in the distance, as we did not know precisely where we were. But then once the mind had tuned into 'marathon mentality' that did not seem to matter: it was the final destination that became so compelling.

Driving long distances through Europe meant that we would experience several contrasts in one day – from rolling plains and open roads to hills, then up through steep, curvy mountain roads. The weather, hot at low altitudes, suddenly chilled as we rose above the snow line, particularly crossing the French Alps over the Col della Maddelena into Italy.

As we descended the mountain route into the first Italian town, I couldn't wait to fill the car up with petrol and, about thirty years since my last visit, practise my very rusty Italian. It was rusty, but I managed to get by.

There were just three days in Italy and each one was a long driving schedule, which left little time to talk to the locals. On the way to Ancona to catch the overnight ferry to Greece, I was surprised to see a road sign showing we were just 56kms from Perugia. Although I'd wanted to visit my youthful haunt again for some time, I wasn't tempted to deviate from the chosen route.

The more I drove the Morris Minor the more impressed I became with its handling characteristics and, on the open road, the way it pulled in third and top gear.

From the ferry at Igoumenitsa, in Greece, the road wound its way up the mountain. There were numerous lorries, all heavily laden, coming from the port. We were pacing David Miller's MGB for hours. But then, just as the Minor started to coast down the mountain descents, the engine began to cut out. When it was under load, however, things improved. Driving into Thessaloniki for the night's stop we found that the problem worsened. The engine would barely run and we could smell petrol – the SU carburettor was flooding. Once we arrived at the hotel, Trevor dismantled the carburettor. He could not find anything wrong, and decided to reassemble the unit with a new float. However the next morning the problem continued as we set off. Although some of the stages had been on dusty roads there was no trace of any dirt in the carburettor.

On further investigation Trevor found that at the lower end of the float's travel it was jamming against the side of the float chamber and causing the carburettor to flood. Although the parts were new, this modern copy of the original component was not entirely accurate. The dimensions of the second spare float looked the same but, fortunately, were just sufficiently different to clear. By the time the problem was sorted we had missed the competitive stages and pressed on with the long drive to the night stop at Alexandroupoli, in southern Greece.

We arrived in mid afternoon. It was the first time we'd had several hours of daylight to enjoy and, with the hotel right on the coast, we were able to soak up the Mediterranean air while checking the Minor over and hanging out the day's washing. Because we had room for so few clothes, daily washing was essential and if the clothes were not dry in the morning, the safety roll-over bar mounted in the Minor provided a handy clothes line.

Every evening, no matter how late we arrived at the hotel, Trevor checked the suspension and all nuts and bolts, to be ready for the next day's motoring.

One of our first stages in Turkey was on the peninsular of Gallipoli. On this particular day, the organisers had allowed time in the programme for us to visit the First World War memorial sites. It was emotional, wandering around the vast area and actually seeing the places where so many young men of so many nationalities had died, all in vain. I recognised Anzac Cove, from the many documentaries and films I had seen over the years, but it was poignant to actually stand at the place where I know some of my ancestors tried to land.

The more we drove east the more erratic the local driving became. In Turkey the bus drivers would barge aggressively onto any road and on several occasions I had to brake and swerve to avoid contact. Once I was following some slower traffic, waiting for an opportunity to overtake, when a bus started to overtake me. With oncoming traffic the bus needed my road space to avoid a head-on collision so the only alternative was for me to run off the road – so did the oncoming car. That evening, while recounting my 'near miss' to Mike Summerfield, deputy clerk of the course, I mentioned that at least driving in Turkey was preparing me for driving in India. 'Oh no,' he said, 'you ain't seen nothing yet!' He was right.

The marathon cars were airlifted from Ankara to India in two Antonovs. The drivers loaded their cars onto the giant aircraft and then boarded a chartered Malaysian Airways Airbus. When we arrived at Cochin, in the region of Kerala in southern India, the cars had already been unloaded and were waiting on the fringe of the airport to be driven away.

Trevor went to pick up the Minor while I waited outside the airport building. The sun had just set and darkness quickly descended. Thousands of people were waiting and, as soon as we walked out, camera flashes came from every direction. For the townsfolk the drivers were celebrities – we were interviewed for television and newspapers of every persuasion.

At the start of the first day's activities in Kerala we were promised a festival atmosphere, with girls dressed up in local traditional costumes. There were also to be drummers and elephants. I was looking forward to this.

Crowds lined the road as we came to the start area. As soon as the Minor halted we were engulfed by thousands of people. All I could see were male faces. At first it felt so frightening but I quickly realised that everyone was smiling and very interested in the car, asking many polite questions. With so many appearances on television, and photographs in the main newspapers, the Minor had become the star of the event in India. Eventually we made our way to the start but there were so many enthusiasts surrounding the car that I did not get to see the cultural display.

As the Minor was flagged off, people lined the route cheering and waving and wishing us all the luck in the world. We were overwhelmed by the generous spirit and enthusiasm of the locals.

The 150km drive to the first stages in the tea plantations of the mountain region of Munnar was an adventure in itself. The roads became flooded during a heavy monsoon downpour and it was difficult to follow our route. Most of the roads were rough, some with enormous potholes – and that was the ones we could actually see, before they filled up with tropical rain. Some of the potholes we bumped into brought tears to my eyes as the Minor's suspension bottomed.

As we passed through the busy towns and villages, the driver had to make sure her concentration powers were functioning 100 per cent. Pedestrians, cyclists, motorcyclists, dogs, cows, and all types of motorised and non-motorised devices charged on to any road, major or minor, on either side, without looking. I was always amazed at the risks people took. No-one checked for hazards like oncoming traffic – instead they expected to be warned by a blast on the horn.

My hand was poised at all times, ready to hit the horn.

Most drivers appeared to ignore every commonsense road rule consistent with safety. For example, approaching sharp, blind corners we might be confronted with an overtaking car, bus or truck approaching at speed on our side. Extreme avoidance tactics were necessary for survival. Then again, if you did not apply similar techniques but waited behind slower traffic for a sensible place to pass, the local driver would push you off the road. He has to get past immediately – it doesn't matter what is coming the other way. This might be why we saw so many gruesome accidents during our travels in India.

By the time we arrived at the time control before the start of the first stage three and half hours later, I felt exhausted. The stage itself turned out to be yet another adventure. Winding up the side of a mountain through the tea plantations, then down again, for 30km, we saw unique scenery, with layer after layer of well-tended tea plants – but the road was narrow and broken up and the Minor could not reach the average speed set by the organisers. These conditions and speed were more suited to the 4x4s, yet some of the drivers in that category were experiencing difficulty too.

After the stage, Peter Taylor, privateer entrant, driving a Toyota Corolla in the Group N showroom car class, told me, 'The conditions were so demanding because of the rocks and obstacles on apexes, broken tarmac, potholes and combined with rain, slush, fog and, the worst feature of all, the tea pickers appeared at any moment out of the plantation onto the road … that is the most treacherous rally stage I have ever competed on.'

That evening, when we reached our hotel, an old hill station formerly used by the British to escape the oppressive summer heat, I felt so relieved that the Minor and her crew had arrived intact. The next day's competitive sections were run on the same roads but in the opposite direction. It's hard to admit this, but we skived off and missed the stages. The Minor couldn't reach the required speed, thus receiving maximum penalties, and we didn't imagine that the conditions would improve just by going in the other direction. In any case, the car-breaking conditions were so severe I didn't want to risk the Minor. Instead we headed straight to the night stop at Coimbatore, a six-hour drive through a state forest with little traffic, then back to the usual manic driving conditions of the towns.

In every country visited, the competitive sections of the marathon were organised by local car clubs. Spitfire Motorsports of India arranged a variety of stages with contrasting conditions.

After we left Coimbatore, the gravel rally stages were run at a wind farm, round the wind turbines. Although parts were rough, I thought the sections were acceptable for classic cars. Queuing up for the start of the first stage, the Minor as usual attracted considerable attention from the spectators. This time I was surprised as a number of women came over to talk. They had seen the media coverage and came over to tell me that I was an inspiration to women, by driving a car in such a male-dominated event. I was very touched by their kind words and couldn't help feeling lucky that I lived in a country where equal opportunities exist if the individual is prepared to seek them out.

After Coimbatore we were relishing the thought of the next night at Mysore, in the Maharajah's Palace. Winding our way up the long drive, now a public road, we could see the impressive building perched on a hill. As I parked the Minor in front, crowds swarmed round, every individual wanting to communicate. I couldn't help noticing that they waited in turn to talk – no-one pushed or shoved or interrupted. And above all, every person asked permission to talk or take a photograph, despite the vast numbers. The crowd behaved in a very orderly, respectful manner.

The stage the following morning, near Mysore, was my favourite. It was a fairly fast hill climb with sweeping corners on tarmac – not too many potholes – and we did rather well, compared to the tea plantation stage.

The programme was shortened in India. The final stages and overnight stop in Ooty, another high altitude former British hill station, were cancelled. Some of us were extremely disappointed at missing out on the opportunity to visit Ooty but at the pre-start briefing in London, the marathon organiser Nick Brittan had already warned us about the change in the programme.

We all had to return to Cochin for an extra day to clean our cars to ensure that they passed the stringent quarantine conditions required for entering Australia. The cars and teams were originally flying into Alice Springs for one day of rest before the first stage of the Australian sector to Uluru (Ayers Rock). We were informed that although two Australian quarantine officials were to inspect the cars at Cochin before they were loaded onto the aircraft, if any car did not pass then it would have to remain in India. Because Alice Springs did not have any quarantine cleaning facilities, our destination was to be changed to Darwin, which had the technology to clean any failed cars. However, the cost, not to say hassle, of getting the cars and crews to Alice, the day after arriving in Darwin, over 900 miles to the south, was the responsibility of the teams. This caused much anger among the competitors.

Arriving back in Cochin at 4.30pm, exhausted after a hair-raising 8½-hour drive from Mysore, we immediately stripped everything out of the Minor and started to purge every speck of dust from the spare parts, tools, carpet and upholstery. The next day the process continued, even to the extent of getting the engine and underneath the mudguards and floorpan washed with a high-pressure hose. Two days of cleaning and we were ready for the official process to be carried out. Only one member of the crew was permitted to go to the airport for the inspection. Trevor took the car at 6.30am to queue, then stripped the car yet again for the official cleaning to take place before the quarantine officer began his examination.

Rumours kept filtering back all day to us bored crew members marooned at the hotel. Apparently very few cars were passing the test – and as the Antonovs had to be loaded by late afternoon, we wondered what the outcome would be. Trevor eventually arrived back at 3pm – the Minor was one of the few that had passed its test. Returning at 6pm to drive the car onto the Antonov he learned that 20 cars had not passed, not necessarily because they were dirty but as the inspectors had run out of time.

At Darwin the 'failed' cars were impounded. However Nick Brittan announced during our flight from Cochin that arrangements had been made for the cars to undergo the cleaning process throughout the night, ready for the inspection first thing in the morning. Participants could then set out on the long drive to Alice Springs or arrange for their cars to be transported. Unfortunately, the night cleaning did not take place and the final car was not cleared until 5pm the following day. Some of the 4x4 drivers piloted their cars throughout the night to Alice, then straight on to Uluru – a total of 1,300 miles – to arrive in time for the start of the Uluru to Coober Pedy section. Others transported their cars by road-train, but they then had to drive straight to Coober Pedy from Alice Springs, to catch up the rally.

I considered driving to Alice, but felt that 900 miles in one day in the Australian winter, when there were only about 11 hours of daylight, would be too much for both the Minor and us, so when the opportunity of transporting on a road-train became an option, we chose that.

With so many negative things happening, completely out of our control, a feeling of despair overtook most participants of the Clowes Cup. By necessity two days of our stages were cancelled, until we could be reunited, which finally happened at Coober Pedy. Three participants quit the rally. Sadly they missed some of the most exciting parts of outback Australia that not many people are privileged to witness.

When we picked up the Minor at Alice Springs, the steering was damaged, with the wheels out of alignment by 3/8in. This was probably because it had been bumped heavily when rolling off the loading ramp. A local garage had all the right equipment to set up the steering, but we had to wait until there was an available time slot to fit the Minor in. This was frustrating. I really wanted to arrive in Uluru, the most sacred site in Aboriginal Australia, to watch the sun set. At lunchtime the adjustments were finished and we headed off. We managed to cover the 350-mile trip in 4½ hours, just minutes before the sun went down. It was a wonderful sight and spiritually uplifting. Next day we went there to watch the sun rise before setting off on the 500-mile trek to Coober Pedy.

The outback of Australia might be isolated but the terrain I could never find boring. Sometimes there were areas of stunted trees, and the red colour of the soil in the Uluru area seemed to alter in intensity throughout the day because of the changing angles of the sunlight.

At sunset we arrived at Coober Pedy after managing a respectable average speed on the smooth bitumen roads with little traffic. It was too late to visit any of the underground buildings in this well-known opal mining area. Although Nick Brittan's brochure advertised the Australian sector as 'the sting in the tail' of the event, I must have been lulled into a relaxed feeling. Next came a rude awakening.

Just three miles out of Coober Pedy, at sunrise the following day, the instructions indicated that we were to turn left off the tarmac road. For the next two days, and 1,000 miles, the roads traversed some of the most desolate, harsh country that man can encounter. It was a run of 250 miles to our only stage of the day, near Marree. In 1884, before the railway came, this had been a major transport depot when camel trains were the main freight carriers in the outback.

At first the road was fine powdery dust and gravel, but there were dips and crests throughout. Three weeks before, several days of heavy rain had, unusually, soaked the desert area and caused bog holes on the gravel road – some had dried, leaving deep ruts, which were hard to see until it was too late. The Minor's suspension bottomed when I had no warning of the state of the road. I had to concentrate one hundred per cent, with no lapse.

The upside was that the rain had left this usually barren area gloriously fertile. Everywhere we looked the land was green, almost plush, and in places ablaze with yellow desert flowers. In the distance we could see that Lake Eyre, where Donald Campbell attempted the land speed record in 1964, rippled with water. Sometimes, when the road went straight for miles, the heat haze gave the impression of water. I had to stop at the lake just to check. It really was water – the first seen there for four years. Interestingly, the outside temperature was not very hot and the cockpit temperature in the Minor rarely rose above 25 degrees Celsius. It seemed odd to be in one of Australia's most inhospitable areas and not sweltering.

The first competitive stage, on a cattle station just out of Marree, had sandy sections, bog holes, gullies, creek crossings and rough areas but none of it too severe. Trevor had decided to change his technique of co-driving by using a set of average speed tables and stopwatches. After we finished the six-mile section he thought that our results should be better than previous ones. I'd heard that comment before but it wouldn't be until the night camp that we got confirmation. We set off north on the well-known Birdsville Track, originally used to drive cattle south from Queensland. Between 1884 and 1916 a string of artesian bores was dug at intervals of approximately 30 miles to provide watering holes for the animals.

The bores still exist and the first of our desert camps, 150 miles north of Marree, was sited at one of these. There were trees, a service station and roadhouse, outback-style (a shack with a bar and room for eating) – and, amazingly, the artesian bore spouted hot water so we could swim. Over 100 tents had been set up for the marathon competitors, service crews and officials. Catering – barbecue at night and a fry-up for breakfast – was provided by the family who ran the roadhouse.

A few hours after sunset, in the crisp clear atmosphere the temperature plummeted to below freezing. The following morning there were more than a few disgruntled faces, not happy with their chill sleeping conditions. Normally, I hardly eat breakfast but on such a cold day I relished the large plate of bacon and eggs.

When the results of the regularity had been posted the night before, Trevor was right: we did achieve an almost perfect score. It provided some excitement and I felt determined to continue the trend.

That morning the clerk of the course advised us to leave Mungarannie after the rally cars. The competition side had been cancelled due to flooding and he thought we might get pelted with flying stones if the rally cars had to overtake us on the stony road. The road book described the 500-mile journey to the next stop as 'an easy driving day' and I wasn't particularly worried about leaving near 9am.

The road was smooth in some places but deep ruts and big holes seem to appear suddenly, causing the Minor's sump guard to bottom. At one point I came up behind a slower car. To get out of his dust stream so that I could see ahead, I went to the right side of the road and decided to overtake. Just as I was level – it was David Miller's MGB – I noticed a massive bog hole right across the road. I was committed though and had to go right through the middle instead of perhaps braking and slowly driving at the side of the bog. The windscreen became completely covered with red mud. I couldn't see a thing. It was a frightening moment until the windscreen washers did their stuff.

What we didn't know at the time was that the MGB's suspension was about to collapse. David and his co-driver Bob Walters were stranded on the Birdsville Track until rescued by a truck and towed into Birdsville where they spent the night. The next day a local mechanic helped get the MGB on its way again and they caught us up three days later.

From Birdsville the road headed east but was in an even worse condition than the one running south. The gravel road, with enormous rocks and sharp razorlike edges, had been ploughed into high ridges by the previous traffic. The Minor's sump guard was continually pounded, with rocks jamming beneath. I needed to take extreme care not to allow the wheels to catch on one of the ridges, causing the car to snake and possibly roll over. There were a number of cattle grids and the gravel had worn away, causing quite big bumps. These were hard to see. The Minor bottomed many times before I learned to slow right down before going over. Both the Volvos in our class shredded tyres, the Ford

Escort rolled two and a half times and was lifted back on to its wheels and drove on slowly. It was the most frightening road I've ever driven on but I was surprised that the Minor experienced no problems. As the sun started to set, the changing light made shadows in the ruts and it became still more difficult to judge the conditions. We were a long way from the night camp but knew there was an asphalt road some way ahead. I was determined to reach that if possible before nightfall.

We got there just as the light faded. The road was only single track, and we still had 70 miles to go before the night stop, but at least the surface was smooth. An hour and a half later, in the distance we could see the lights of the camp at Windorah – they were visible for miles. It was such a relief to arrive unscathed. Many stories unfolded that evening about competitor mishaps.

The next day, as we progressed eastwards towards the Pacific coast, suddenly trees appeared and grass – also, sadly, dead kangaroos every hundred yards or so, the victims of road kill. We were back in civilisation, with road-trains, the occasional car and house. It meant adapting to traffic again. I'd started to like the isolation of the desert roads, a welcome respite after the crazy conditions in India, but I wasn't sorry to be driving on much smoother roads.

The roads for the rest of the marathon were in good condition but the competitive stages seemed to get tougher each day. The longest stage of the event – 30 miles, estimated to take over an hour – was held in the forests of southern Queensland, three days before the finish in Sydney. The roads and scenery to get to the stage were spectacular but, once driving on the stage, I felt my optimistic mood sink and I thought it ridiculous to put the Minor through such a severe ordeal, perhaps suited to 4x4 vehicles but not small classic cars. As the Minor banged and bottomed over gullies, rocks, sand, deep ruts, fords and creek beds, I started to feel angry. I couldn't see that such tortuous conditions were necessary to test the skill of the driver and co-driver. I'd expected rough roads, but not like this.

The classic cars were given the same average speed as the 4x4s. The Minor had no chance of reaching the set speed, let alone maintaining the average. On the way to the next time control, hearing that seven cars experienced difficulties on the first stage and one of the 4x4s had plunged 30ft down a cliff, I started to consider missing the next stage to protect our car.

Trevor told me to press on as we were late for the time control. Then, my mind crammed with so many experiences from the past month, I thought my eyes were playing tricks. In the distance there seemed to be a number of Morris Minors at the side of the road. This was no hallucination, however. Amazingly, parked up waiting for us were seven Australian Morris Minors, miles from anywhere, with balloons and streamers blowing in the breeze – they had travelled great distances to welcome our car. With such support we just had to stop for a photo shoot. We missed the competitive stage and received maximum penalties.

Suddenly it was the last day of the marathon and only 300 miles to Sydney! I'd been told about previous marathons when last-minute mechanical problems forced competitors to withdraw and never reach their destination. I kept hearing imaginary mechanical sounds, which seemed to get louder as we got closer to Sydney. At one point I thought the engine had cut out momentarily, but as it didn't happen again I put this down to an overactive imagination.

Just 20 miles north of Sydney, in the rear view mirror I noticed three Morris Minors – momentarily, again I thought it was my imagination, but a second look confirmed it all. They had been waiting to escort the LSM Minor into Sydney. Slowing down so that they could overtake and take photographs, I was moved all over again. Just as I was feeling emotional, something unbelievable happened. The engine cut out and I could not get it started. We were forced to stop on the side of the busy freeway, helped by members of various Australian Morris Minor clubs. Just 15 miles from the chequered flag, after completing 10,000 awesome miles so gallantly, this elderly Minor looked like she wasn't going to make it.

Trevor lifted the bonnet, found no visible problem, fiddled about with the fuses and suddenly she sprang into life again. The final 15 miles turned out to be the most tense run of all. I could hardly speak. I just hung on to the co-driver's instructions. Then suddenly, I recognised Sydney Harbour Bridge. And there was the Opera House. We had done it!

Talk about emotion. Crowds of Morris Minor enthusiasts greeted us, some had journeyed 500 miles for the occasion. Pat Anderson, the girl I travelled with in the seventies in a Morris Minor, had flown up from Melbourne. I felt deeply honoured.

After parking the car I stepped back to take in the view – the Morris Minor parked at Circular Quay with the Sydney Opera House in the background. I couldn't believe we had made it after two years of planning and preparing the car. I stood there just staring until well after the sun had set, but the scene did not seem realistic.

A wonderful camaraderie and sportsmanship existed between most competitors during the event. An example of this was when John Tallis ran off the road on the last stage of the event. The next competitor, Jose de Sousa in a Volvo 142S, stopped to help. John told him to continue, which would have given Jose first place, but he refused. John Tallis won the classic class, a well-deserved compensation for failing only 700 miles from the finish on the original 1968 event, in the same car. The Minor ended up fourth in class.

When I saw some of the battered cars that made it to the finish I did feel lucky that the Minor had arrived intact, no dents apart from the sump guard, and with such a minimal amount of mechanical trouble. At the finish I thanked Trevor for his excellent workmanship and success in preparing the car for such a demanding trip and he was embarrassed – but I am sure he must be proud.

The finish was brilliant. All the competitors went round congratulating each other on making it to Sydney. With first-hand knowledge of the tough conditions, we knew that anyone who had completed the marathon deserved special praise.

However the official celebration dinner in the evening, a fairly low-key affair where Nick Brittan presented plaques to the class winners, felt such an anti-climax. I couldn't understand why. Perhaps it was all catching up with me – the past year of considerable anxiety, relentless hard work in preparing the car, and then wondering whether it would actually make it to the chequered flag. I was still in a state of disbelief. But as we were leaving the celebrations at about midnight, Ron Jackson, UK manager of Trans World Events, said to me, 'We didn't think you would make it to Sydney.' Without hesitation, I replied, 'Well, we did – and without a dent on the car.' That's when Trevor and I acknowledged that we really had achieved something special.

The next day we took the Minor to the docks with the other marathon cars to be transported back to the UK. As I handed the keys over to the shipping agent I felt sad – I didn't want to leave her. Trevor and I had both become very attached to our little Minor. When two people wanted to buy her, the answer was a firm No!

My next challenge is to adapt back to normal life. It isn't easy. More hill climbs lie ahead. And long-distance rallying? I can't wait for the next one, wherever that might be.

ACKNOWLEDGEMENTS

Writing a book involves a number of people. I am grateful to John Haynes for giving me the opportunity, Mark Hughes for his support, and Flora Myer for her invaluable advice and skilful editing.

My thanks also to the photographers and to the people who supplied me with photographs over the years but whose names now escape me.

The *Daily Telegraph* kindly gave me permission to reproduce two of my articles and I am most grateful.

I am also indebted to the sponsors who contributed to our participation in the London to Sydney Marathon 2004. They are, in alphabetical order: Autobytel; Avon Tyres; Earl's Performance Products UK Ltd; HMG Paints Ltd; Holden Vintage & Classic Ltd; Houseremovals.com; Lifeline Fire & Safety Systems Ltd; Peter May Engineering Ltd; Minor Mania; Morelli Ltd; Piper Cams; Sony UK Ltd; and Teng Tools. But most of all I want to thank my co-driver Trevor Hulks for providing a very reliable Morris Minor.

Thank you all for your valuable support.

INDEX

277